OS/2

OS/2™

FEATURES, FUNCTIONS, AND APPLICATIONS

STANDARD EDITION 1.0

Jeffrey I. Krantz
Ann M. Mizell
Robert L. Williams

JOHN WILEY & SONS, INC.
New York / Chichester / Brisbane / Toronto / Singapore

Publisher: Stephen Kippur
Editor: Therese A. Zak
Managing Editor: Ruth Greif
Editing, Design & Production: G&H SOHO, Ltd.

Library of Congress Cataloging-in-Publication Data

Krantz, Jeffrey I.
  OS/2: features, functions, and applications / Jeffrey I. Krantz, Ann
M. Mizell, Robert L. Williams.
    p.   cm.
  ISBN 0-471-60709-6
  1. MS OS/2 (Computer operating system) I. Mizell, Ann M.
II. Williams, Robert L. III. Title.
QA76.76.063K74 1988
005.4'469—dc19   87-34469
                                                CIP

Printed in the United States of America
88 89 10 9 8 7 6 5 4 3 2 1

This book is dedicated to those individuals whose insight and creativity will fundamentally impact the role of intelligent workstations in the world of information processing.

Trademarks

IBM is a registered trademark of the International Business Machines Corporation.

Microsoft is a registered trademark of Microsoft Corporation.

Intel is a registered trademark of Intel Corporation.

Operating System/2 and OS/2 are trademarks of the International Business Machines Corporation.

PC XT is a trademark of the International Business Machines Corporation.

Personal System/2 and PS/2 are trademarks of the International Business Machines Corporation.

Personal Computer AT and AT are registered trademarks of the International Business Machines Corporation.

Presentation Manager is a trademark of the International Business Machines Corporation.

Personal Computer XT Model 286 is a trademark of the International Business Machines Corporation.

Micro Channel is a trademark of the International Business Machines Corporation.

Acknowledgments

WE WOULD LIKE TO THANK Jim Archer, Jay Martinson, Bill Gates, Steve Ballmer, and the IBM and Microsoft management teams, planners, designers, developers, and testers whose individual and team efforts have made OS/2 Version 1.0 and future versions of OS/2 a reality.

Contents

Preface	**xix**
How to Read This Book	xx
Introduction: A Historical Perspective	**1**
The Early to Mid 70s	**1**
The Mid to Late 70s	**2**
The Late 70s to Mid 80s	**3**
The IBM Personal Computer and DOS	4
1. The OS/2 Perspective	**5**
Why OS/2?	**5**
Advancing Workstation Hardware Technologies and Capabilities	5
IBM Hardware Systems Supported by OS/2	7
New Systems Environments	8
Users Maturing in Their Use of Personal Computers	9
The Power of OS/2	**10**
The DOS Execution Environment and the OS/2 Execution Environment	10
Some DOS Application Restrictions and Considerations	12
Large Real Memory and Virtual Memory	13
Memory Overcommit	14
Multiple Applications	15
Multitasking	16

Interprocess Communications   17
Dynamic Linked Call/Return Interface. High Level Language Support.   17
File System Compatibility with DOS   20
Interrupt–Driven Device Management   20
Video, Keyboard, and Mouse Subsystems   21
National Language Support and Message Handling Facilities   21

Migration of Applications from DOS to OS/2   **23**
OS/2 Application Programming Interface Characteristics   **24**
80286 Microprocessor Overview   **24**
The Personal Computer System   25
    System Bus   *25*
    System Memory   *26*
    System Devices   *27*
    Direct Memory Access (DMA)   *27*
    Interrupts   *28*
    Numeric Coprocessor   *29*
    The Microprocessor   *29*
80286 State Description and Operation   30
80286 Addressing—Real Mode versus Protect Mode   32
    Physical Address Generation in Real Mode   *32*
    Physical Address Generation in Protect Mode   *34*
Protection and Privilege   37
Interrupt Handling   39
Summary   **41**

---

2. OS/2 Memory Capabilities   43

Major Benefits   **44**
Memory Overcommitment   **45**
Memory Protection   **46**
System Memory Characteristics   **46**
Segment Preload versus Load on Demand   **47**
User Settable Characteristics   **47**
Module Definition File Segment Characteristics   **48**
Performance and System Considerations   **48**
Memory Programming Interfaces   **49**
Capabilities of the Memory Programming Interfaces   49
Managing Memory Segments   50

Sharing Memory Segments   52
Name–Shared Segments   52
Managing Huge Memory Segments   53
Memory Suballocation Package   54

Device Related Memory Management Capabilities   **55**
Memory Mapped I/O Devices   55
DMA Devices   55

3. Multitasking and Multiple Applications   57

Multiple Applications   **59**
Multiple Sessions—A User's Perspective   60
Session Programming Interfaces   61

Processes and Threads   **62**
Process Programming Interfaces   65
Thread Programming Interfaces   67
Priority Programming Interfaces   68

Interprocess Communications   **70**
Pipes   70
Queues   71
Signals   74
Semaphores   75
System Semaphore Interfaces   *76*
Semaphore Ownership Interfaces   *77*
Semaphore Signalling Interfaces   *78*

Timer Services   **79**
Global and Local Infoseg   **81**

4. Illustrating Concepts in Programming Examples   83

C Programming Conventions and Syntax Review   **84**
Compiling   84
Linking   85
Compiling and Linking in One Step   86
Reading an OS/2 Program Written in C   87

I/O with Video and Keyboard   **89**
Describing the Sample Program   89
OS/2 Function Calls   91

VioWrtTTY   91
KbdStringIn   91
DosExit   92
Completing the Description of the Sample Program   92

Multitasking—One Process with Two Threads   **93**
OS/2 Function Calls   95
DosSemSet   95
DosSemClear   96
DosSemRequest   96
DosCreateThread   97
KbdCharIn   97
Description of the Multiple Threads Sample Program   98

Multitasking—Two Processes with Multiple Threads   **98**
OS/2 Function Calls   100
VioScrollUp   100
VioWrtCharStr and VioWrtCharStrAtt   102
VioSetCurPos   104
DosMakePipe   105
DosWrite   107
DosRead   110
DosExecPgm   110
DosSleep   112
Description of the Multiple Process Sample Program   112

Memory Overcommitment   **114**
OS/2 Function Calls   115
DosAllocSeg   115
Description of the Memory Overcommitment Sample Program   116

5. Application Input/Output Capabilities   **119**

File System I/O   **121**
File Devices   122
Character Devices   126
Standard Devices   129
Pipe Devices   130
Logical Disk/Diskette Devices   130
General-Purpose Interfaces   131
File-Based Interfaces   134

File Name-Based Interfaces	*135*
File Handle-Based Interfaces	*136*
Directory-Based Interfaces	137
File Device Interfaces	138
Character Device I/O Subsystems	**139**
VIO: Video I/O	139
VIO Character I/O	*141*
VIO Cursor Control	*142*
VIO Scroll Management	*142*
VIO Video Device Control	*143*
VIO Pop-up Management	*144*
VIO Logical Video Buffer Management	*145*
VIO Physical Video Buffer Management	*145*
VIO Function Replacement	*148*
KBD: Keyboard I/O	148
KBD Character I/O	*150*
KBD Device Control	*151*
KBD Logical Keyboard Management	*152*
KBD Function Replacement	*153*
MOU: Mouse I/O	153
MOU Data I/O	*156*
MOU Cursor Control	*156*
MOU Device Control	*157*
MOU Function Replacement	*159*
I/O Control (IOCtl) Capabilities	**159**
Use of Character Device Monitors	**161**
Direct I/O to Hardware	**164**
6. Interrupt-Driven Device Management	**167**
The Role of Device Drivers	**169**
Device Drivers and Application I/O	**171**
Block Device Commands	175
Character Device Commands	178
System Services for Device Drivers	**180**
Process Management	181
Semaphore Management	182
Request Queue Management	183

Character Queue Management   183
Memory Management   184
Interrupt Management   185
Timer Services   185
Character Monitor Management   186
Advanced BIOS Management   186

Device Driver Components and Their Contexts   **186**
The Strategy Routine   186
The Hardware Interrupt Handler   188
The Timer Handler   190
The Software Interrupt Handler   192

Bimodal Considerations   **194**
Operational Considerations   **195**
Memory Addressability   195
Synchronization   196
Nesting of Interrupts   198
System Performance   199

Initialization of OS/2 Device Drivers   **200**
Advanced BIOS and Interrupt Sharing   **201**
Advanced BIOS   201
Hardware Interrupt Sharing   205

Creating an OS/2 Device Driver   **207**
Standard Devices on OS/2   **211**
Clock   212
Disk/Diskette   212
Screen   212
Keyboard   213
Printer   213
Mouse   213
Pointer Draw   213
Asynchronous Communications   214
Virtual Disk   214
External Disk   214
ANSI   214
EGA   215

OS/2 Support of DOS Device Drivers   **215**

7. Advanced Programming Concepts   217

Linking an Application   217
  Preload Segments   219
  Load on Demand Segments   219
Dynamic Linking   220
  Load Time Dynamic Linking   220
  Run Time Dynamic Linking   221
  Building a Dynamic Link Library   222
    Import Librarian   224
Module Definition File Statements   226
Run Time Dynamic Linking Programming Example   228
  Allowing the User to Select the Library   229
    VioGetCurType and VioSetCurType   231
    DosBeep   232
    Description of SelectLibrary   233
  A New Process 2   233
    DosLoadModule   236
    DosGetProcAddr   238
    DosFreeModule   239
    Description of Process 2   239
  The Dynamic Link Library   240

8. Supporting the International Environment   245

OS/2 Language Support   245
Message Facilities   246
  Message Facility Summary   250
Configuring the System for Different Countries   251
  Country-Dependent Information   251
  Code Page Switching   252
  Double Byte Character Set (DBCS) Enabling   253
  OS/2 NLS Facilities   253
    CONFIG.SYS NLS Commands   254
    User NLS Commands   254
    Dynamic Link NLS API   254

9. Beyond System Defaults: A User's Perspective   257

Configuration Options   259
    Interactive Initialization   259
    File System Operations   260
    Device Support   261
    Country Support   261
    Protection Scope   262
    OS/2 Application Environment   262
    Multitasking   263
    Memory Management   265
    The DOS Environment   265
Automatic Execution   266
Program Selection   267
Batch Files and Batch Language   267

10. Where to Go from Here   269

The Presentation Manager   270
The Database Manager   270
The Communications Manager   271
The Stage Is Set   271

Index   273

Preface

THE DECISION TO WRITE this book was an easy one. Since we, the authors, are key members of the OS/2™ design team, we found ourselves with a tremendous amount of knowledge in the depth and breadth of the product. We felt that one way to put this knowledge to good use was to write a book. Unfortunately, that was easier said than done. The amount of information about the product that we have in our heads would fill many volumes. We wanted, however, to write a book that our audience could digest. Most people have real work to do but only a finite amount of time to do it in. The difficult question that we wrestled with was what kind of book we should write. *We wanted to maximize the usefulness of our detailed technical knowledge to best address your needs.* We accomplish this by selectively covering the large amount of information that is generally available on OS/2.

What you have in your hands is the result of our efforts. The book covers what we consider to be the most important aspects of *Operating System/2™: Standard Edition 1.0.* If you are a member of any of the following groups you will find this book very useful:

- Users of DOS on PCs.
- People curious about the applicability of OS/2 to their problems.
- Systems analysts.
- Systems designers.
- Systems planners.
- Application developers.

You do not need to be familiar with the details of IBM Personal Computer DOS (DOS) or Intel® 80286 microprocessors to benefit from this book. We cover background material so you can understand OS/2 and how its power can be applied. In addition, because OS/2 transcends the simple personal computer environment and provides sophisticated large system functions, we explain the operating system concepts used in this book.

This book explains why the capabilities of OS/2 are important to you. It also explains why the problems that OS/2 solves are important to you. We use the capabilities of DOS as a reference point where applicable.

HOW TO READ THIS BOOK

Because of the sheer mass of information and data available on OS/2, we have selectively chosen to describe in this book what we consider to be the most important features of the product. We have also reduced the mass of detail covering each feature to a digestible level. Once you have read this book on the capabilities of OS/2, using the detailed technical references available for the product will be a simple and productive task. We have structured the descriptions of the various OS/2 capabilities into three general levels of detail. These different levels allow you to be flexible in how you navigate through the book.

First, we describe many of the OS/2 capabilities in a generic sense so you can understand the concept, the usefulness of the function provided, and how it can be applied to real problems that you need to solve. We then take you a level deeper into the specifics of a given capability (such as memory management) by describing the corresponding application programming interfaces. At this level, we present the most important details of the interfaces so that you can see how OS/2 achieves the stated capability. This second level of detail is particularly important because it allows you to see how your specific application can be structured to utilize the capabilities of OS/2. We provide a third level of detail for those who want to see how to use the capabilities of OS/2 in actual code. We have included two chapters that demonstrate some of the key capabilities of OS/2 in actual programming examples that can be compiled and run.

By organizing the description of OS/2 into these different levels of detail, we enable you to choose your own path through this book. If you are not interested in programming examples, you can skip them entirely in Chapters 4 and 7. On the other hand, you may prefer to go directly to the memory overcommitment program example in Chapter 4 after reading the introductory discussion of the OS/2 memory capabilities in Chapter 2. After reviewing the programming example, you can then go back to Chapter 2 to read the descriptions of the OS/2 memory programming interfaces that interest you. Or, you may want to read this book from front to back to get the broadest description of OS/2 with the most detail. We have specifically structured this book to allow you to plot your own course through it, depending upon the amount of detail and the order of presentation you prefer.

Introduction:
A Historical Perspective

IN ORDER TO UNDERSTAND where OS/2 is taking personal computing, we feel that it is important to remember where we have been. What follows is the combined personal perspectives of the authors.

THE EARLY TO MID 70s

This period of our experience in the world of computing was essentially our first and occurred in an academic environment. It was characterized by the following:

- A "large" (physically!) centralized computing center.
- Keypunch machines.
- Batch jobstreams via operator intermediary.

Today, that early environment can be described, at best, as primitive from a usability and productivity viewpoint. All data entry and programming was done via keypunch machines. People stored their personal data and programs as large decks of cards. Productivity features of this environment were considered to be the keypunch drum or maybe a digital column counter on your keypunch machine (if you were lucky). It was always good practice to have sequence numbers punched in your card deck. Then, when the operator decided to drop your deck, or if the card reader decided that it was hungry, it was possible to recover. Personal disk space was considered a very expensive resource and was not usually available in enough quantity for the average user.

All the users' decks of cards were gathered together by the computer operator as a random function of time and were fed into the card reader. This procedure is known as batch processing, where user programs are submitted in bunches with no user interaction. Sometime later, usually half a day or more, you waited in line

1

for the opportunity to get a printout of the results of your program. If your program did not work properly, you had to start this long process all over again. Obviously, learning from your mistakes was tedious and slow. The price of a single mistake could easily be an entire elapsed day.

Also, the computing cost was enormous. Many items had to be accounted and charged for:

- Every hundredth or thousandth of a computer second.
- Every time the computer did input or output to a device.
- Every unit of mass storage that was used.
- Every action that the operator needed to take to make your program run.
- Every line or page of printed output that you received.

The amount of computer resource that a program used was also very limited. For example, in a fixed memory partition environment, a program requiring more than 256 KB of system memory usually needed the dispensation of the computer center manager.

In this academic environment, the biggest challenge of all was getting assistance when it was needed. The computer operator, as a rule, was the only person that users (students) saw on a regular basis. Generally, the computer operator was not a very useful source of technical assistance. You gave the operator your cards, and he or she gave you cards and printouts back. If you needed help, you had to consult with the systems programmer. The systems programmer was the expert. This person possessed the knowledge and experience to make things outside of your ordinary routine happen.

In looking back at our student days of programming, we can characterize this period of computing in the following way:

- Expensive.
- Long turnaround cycle.
- Users separated from computer system.
- Scarce computer resources.
- Slow and difficult learning process.
- Difficult to experiment.
- Hard to get assistance.

THE MID TO LATE 70s

In this period, we experienced some fundamental changes in the large centralized computer center. Interactive CRT (display) terminals were installed in very large quantities. It finally became possible for the end user to interact directly with the computer.

A user entered data through the terminal's keyboard and could proofread it directly on the screen. Then, a user could view the output of his or her programs on the screen before requesting a printout. When mistakes were made, this capability significantly speeded up the feedback process. User programs could be run either in batch mode or interactively, with real-time feedback on the CRT display. Of course, you quickly learned to run programs that needed more than a trivial amount of computer resource in batch mode.

Because the computer center resource was still very expensive, a large number of users needed to be able to use the computer at the same time. In some environments there was a temptation to overload the computer system in order to keep the cost per user down. If the system was heavily used, you might not be able to get on it because too many people were already using it. This overloading could also cause the time between requests of the system and the system responding to your screen to become unbearably slow.

In the beginning, the new CRT terminals were relatively expensive. People normally did not have personal CRT terminals on their desks. Between response time problems due to overloaded systems and finding an available terminal, the productivity gains that could have been achieved in an interactive computing environment were not maximized.

However, the mid to late 70s marked the beginning of the period of personal interaction between the user and the computer. Because this interaction appeared to be one on one, the time delay between experiences became significantly shorter, and the user became motivated to learn how to do more and more things with the system.

THE LATE 70s TO MID 80s

This period could best be characterized as "the time when the computer reached the average person" or "the advent of personal computing." The large computing environment also improved during this period as the large computing center resource became significantly more powerful, flexible, and cheaper. CRT terminals began to appear on everybody's desk, and terminal rooms began to disappear. But that was the natural evolution of the previous decade. The real story was the major revolution taking place in personal computing.

When an entire computer system could be purchased for only a small percentage of a person's annual salary and could fit in the corner of a person's desk, the characteristics of computing were significantly changed. These new computers were cheap enough that they did not need to be shared at the same time by many different people. They could be designed as single user systems. This development greatly reduced the complexity of the system software that was needed to manage the system resource. A person could have control over what his or her personal computer was asked to do. This level of control allows people to trade off the workload on the personal computer and the desired response time.

The number of people who had access to computers increased by orders of magnitude. Even preschoolers began to have access to personal computers. The computer literacy of our society literally exploded because of the following:

- The one-on-one relationship that was possible with personal computers.
- The simple nature of that relationship.
- The ability to receive immediate feedback on what you were doing.
- Easy access to personal computers.

These developments did not mean that the usefulness and need for large computer systems diminished. In fact, they increased. The new personal computers did not replace the function or need for the large computer systems. Instead, they created their own need driven by a whole new set of people and markets. The large computer systems became more powerful and created new opportunities as their price/performance continued to improve.

The IBM Personal Computer and DOS

With the introduction of the IBM Personal Computer and DOS in the early 80s, IBM created what was destined to become one of the most popular personal computing environments. Most people attribute the success of the IBM PC system not only to the hardware characteristics of the system, but also to the incredible amount of application software that was available for the machine from IBM and third party vendors in a very short period of time.

The application software and the environment in which it ran did more than solve real problems that a large number of people or businesses had. The usability of the software environment also made it accessible to large numbers of people. The characteristics of the application software of this period were driven by the operating system software environment (DOS) and, of course, the hardware environment of the IBM PC and PC XT™.

These are the characteristics of this environment:

- Single user.
- 640 KB of RAM for program and data.
- Single tasking (serialization of function).
- One application at a time.

This environment appears to have met an extraordinary market need and solved problems for a large number of businesses and people. So where do we go from here? And why do we want to go anywhere from here anyway?

1

The OS/2 Perspective

THE MAJOR BENEFITS of the first version of OS/2 can be categorized as follows:

- Breaks the 640 KB memory barrier.
- Provides multitasking support.
- Provides a dynamic linking call/return application programming interface.
- Provides a multiple applications environment.
- Executes a DOS application.
- Provides improved usability and a consistent user interface.

WHY OS/2?

What do these things mean to you? Why should you be interested in things like "multitasking" and a dynamic linking application programming interface (API)? Why is it possible that the current DOS environment may not meet your present and future needs? To begin to understand the answers, let's look at some of the user needs and user environments that are causing such benefits to be considered important:

- Advancing workstation hardware technologies and capabilities.
- New systems environments.
- Users maturing in their use of personal computers.

Advancing Workstation Hardware Technologies and Capabilities

Technology is improving by leaps and bounds. Ten years ago systems that had 48 kilobytes (KB) of Random Access Memory (see the section in this chapter titled 80286 Microprocessor Overview) and a 16 line by 64 column display were considered very useful and popular personal computers. The new Personal System/2™ com-

5

puters from IBM start with a megabyte of Random Access Memory (RAM) on the system board in the Model 50, while the Model 80 can have as much as 4 megabytes (MB) right on the system board (no additional slot usage required). This improvement in the price/performance of hardware technology has been considered business as usual in the computer industry for decades. *The DOS level of function is unable to fully exploit the new and expanded hardware capablities.*

The most obvious improvements in hardware are in the speed and capabilities of the **processor** itself (Intel 8088 to Intel 80286 to Intel 80386) and in the amount of physical RAM **memory** that these systems can have. In addition, the capabilities of the high end displays are comparable to those of dedicated graphics-oriented systems.

DOS provides a level of function that fully exploits the Intel 8088 microprocessor. The IBM Personal Computer AT® and IBM Personal System/2 Models 50 and 60 have an Intel 80286 microprocessor instead of an 8088. The IBM PS/2™ Model 80 has an Intel 80386 microprocessor. The 80286/80386 has a mode called **real mode** which is compatible to the 8088. This is the mode that DOS uses when the 80286 or 80386 is used on an IBM AT® or Personal System/2 Model 50 and above. This use of real mode does not allow the use of any of the new features of the 80286 in its full function mode, which is also known as **protect mode**. And yes, we do care about using those new features. For example, the 80286 provides the ability to protect the operating system code and data from application code and to protect different applications from each other. The 80286 also enables virtual memory support and support of real memory greater than 1 megabyte. The 8088 has no protection capability and supports real memory of only 1 megabyte. OS/2 itself exploits the features of the 80286 and also allows application programs to exploit those features. We can see how we need to migrate to OS/2 in order to take full advantage of the functionality and capabilities of the new microprocessor technologies.

As time marches on, the microprocessors and the systems in which they exist are getting faster and faster. In order to make full use of this system potential, the operating system needs to support the execution of more than one task at a time. What this means is that the operating system needs to allow multiple pieces of work or applications to appear as if they are going on "at the same time." For example, when one piece of work needs to wait for some data from an I/O device, the system can process another piece of work. As the systems become more and more powerful, this capability becomes more and more important. DOS does not provide a general mechanism for this but OS/2 does.

Because DOS supports only the 8088 or the real mode of the 80286, it can support only application usage of 640 KB of physical memory (RAM) in the IBM PC system. The address space between 640 KB and 1 MB is used by memory mapped input/output devices (and displays) as well as the BIOS ROM (Read Only Memory) code in the IBM PC systems. There is no way for DOS to allow application code to execute in memory above 640 KB. Applications cannot directly access their data if that data exists above the 640 KB barrier. Because of this, applications run in a DOS environment cannot optimize the usage of all the memory that is available in the new personal computer systems. OS/2, however, allows applications to run in the 80286 protect mode environment. These applications can then execute in more than 1 MB of memory and can access data directly in more than 1 MB of memory.

As applications become more sophisticated, they need more memory space in which their instructions can be executed. In addition, as the amount of data that needs to be processed at a given time increases, the additional memory space for application data becomes critical for adequate application responsiveness. As the applications begin to exploit the more sophisticated graphics displays with greater resolution and more colors, the amount of data space required by the applications also increases. We can see why we would want to take advantage of all these megabytes of memory in the new hardware systems.

It has been said that a picture is worth a thousand words. A graphics-based user interface is significantly more usable and can support more sophisticated applications environments than a text-based user interface. As a user manipulates more things at the same time, he or she needs to view them in the kind of **windowing environment** that a graphics-based user interface can provide. In a windowing environment, different applications can own different portions of the screen. The first version of the Standard Edition of OS/2 (version 1.0) provides a text-based full screen user interface. Version 1.1 of OS/2 will allow applications to fully exploit a graphics-based windowing user interface with the Presentation Manager™.

IBM Hardware Systems Supported by OS/2

OS/2 does not run on personal computer systems that have 8088 or 8086 microprocessors. This means that OS/2 does not run on systems like the IBM PC, PC XT, PS/2 Models 25 and 30, or the Convertible.

As of the writing of this book, OS/2 supports the following IBM hardware systems.

- □ IBM Personal Computer AT (5170) Models 068 with fixed disk (equivalent to Model 099), 099, 239, 319, and 339.
- □ IBM Personal Computer XT Model 286™ (5162).
- □ IBM PS/2 Models 50, 60, and 80.

The 80386 in the PS/2 Model 80 is supported as an 80286.

Not every adapter available for every model is supported by OS/2. OS/2 requires at least one high capacity diskette drive, a fixed disk, a keyboard, and a display adapter with its associated display. OS/2 requires at least 1.5 megabytes of RAM when it runs only the OS/2 execution environment. If the DOS execution environment is also used, OS/2 requires at least 2 megabytes of RAM. We describe the OS/2 execution environment and the DOS execution environment later in this chapter.

New Systems Environments

The introduction to this book discusses how up until now we have had two separate types of computing environments evolving: the personal computer environment and the large system environment. Personal computers are designed to be used and controlled right at the individual's desk. They allow people to tailor the processing of their data the way they want it. But the power of the personal computer is limited, and the amount and range of the data stored on the personal computer is limited. The large systems environment is used for applications that require large quantities of processing power and large amounts of data that is shared across many users. A large system could consist of many users spanning many different geographic locations using the computing power at one or many computer centers. The data that the users would be accessing could be centralized in one giant computer center or distributed across many computer centers. The large systems environment could also be limited to one physical location.

However, in reality, not all applications or systems solutions fit best in either of the above categories. For example, a financial analyst at a large corporation could never hope to store all the data necessary to do his or her job on a personal computer. However, the analyst would prefer to use a personal computer because with it he or she has a great deal of flexibility to process, analyze, and manipulate data. Some large systems tend to have less personal flexibility but can handle all the data that such people potentially need to do their jobs. Another example would be a systems application that requires very short response times at the user's terminal under certain conditions and under other conditions requires heavy processing at a large computer. The best systems design for both examples is the next logical step in the evolution of personal computers and large systems. It is called **cooperative processing**. In cooperative processing, the local workstation (personal computer) does the jobs that it is best suited for and the large computer system does the jobs best suited for it.

In a cooperative processing environment, the application software on personal computers needs more than a single tasking level of function. The systems software provided for the personal computer application software must be able to (1) support sophisticated real-time communications hardware, and (2) provide access to complex logical communications and network protocols in addition to data transfer architectures. This support requires an enormous amount of systems software, which would not adequately fit in 640 KB along with a high function application program. The systems environment must be able to support real-time interrupt driven hardware and multitasking. This level of function has already been provided by specialized programs in a DOS environment for specific systems environments or applications. In an OS/2 environment, however, the support can be provided in a general manner that gives a modular base for growth and an extendability for an entire spectrum of application programs or subsystems. The OS/2 dynamic link call/return API is a major factor in providing this important modular base.

The OS/2 environment allows very large cooperative processing applications or systems to be designed and developed in a general fashion without the designer having to understand all the ways in which the system might be used by additional application programs in the future. This presents an opportunity not only for independent software vendors who wish to provide subsystems, but also for corporations who wish to amortize their investment in sophisticated systems software extensions over the life of many uses of that systems environment. Because OS/2 supports multiple applications working concurrently in a well-defined way and because a consistent user interface is provided, the potential for exploitation of systems enhancements that are either supplied or separately developed is enormous. Applications can now be written for the systems environment and architecture in such a way that they will work even if additional applications are added to the system or if the subsystems beneath it change. Subsystems may change because the real external environment to the workstation changes or because the kind of physical hardware that is being supported changes. The user will be able to take advantage of these multiple applications because the system's user interface not only allows the separate applications to coexist but also allows the user to have them all running "at the same time."

Users Maturing in Their Use of Personal Computers

We live in an age of rising expectations. What used to impress and amaze people five years ago has become the status quo. People are now looking for that next leap in personal computer technology that will allow them to do their jobs better and increase their competitiveness in the marketplace.

As we have just seen, that next leap cannot be driven solely by the new hardware technology. An important question is how the user can exploit the current and coming hardware technology. To answer that question, we again have to look to the operating systems environment.

Users are expecting more function in order to increase productivity. One way to get more function is to allow more applications to run on the personal computer at the same time. However, it is important that this function be provided in a general way so that the kinds of applications you would want to run concurrently on the personal computer can all peacefully coexist. In addition, this environment must be presented to the user in a consistent and usable manner. As the power of the system increases, it becomes more and more important to make the system easy to use. If the system is too difficult to use, then people will revert to an environment with little personal flexibility. People will not believe that they have the freedom to make the personal computer a system tailored to fit their needs. Giving back one of the fundamental features of personal computing would not be acceptable.

Not only are users expecting to be able to run multiple applications, they are expecting to be able to run more sophisticated and powerful applications. As we will see, the new power of OS/2 allows more sophisticated applications to be written in such a way that they can coexist in a multiple applications environment. More powerful applications have been written in a DOS environment at the expense of going beyond the general features of DOS. Generally, this does not allow the application to work well in environments with other application programs that might also try to go beyond the power of DOS.

THE POWER OF OS/2

What are some of the more powerful features of OS/2? The following list offers a summary.

1. The DOS execution environment coexisting with the OS/2 execution environment.
2. Large real memory and virtual memory.
3. Memory overcommit.
4. Multiple applications.
5. Multitasking.
6. Interprocess communications.
7. Dynamic linked call/return interface. High level language support.
8. File system compatibility with DOS.
9. Interrupt driven device management.
10. Video, keyboard, mouse I/O subsystems.
11. National Language Support and message handling facilities.

The DOS Execution Environment and the OS/2 Execution Environment

The new and more powerful execution environment of OS/2 requires that applications be written to a different set of rules than the rules of the old DOS environment. Therefore, the DOS applications that we are familiar with cannot run in the new OS/2 execution environment. Because people will still need to run many of the old DOS applications until they are rewritten for OS/2, a DOS execution environment is provided with OS/2. This environment is similar to DOS 3.3 and is referred to as the "DOS execution environment." Users can switch between the DOS execution environment and the OS/2 execution environment. Applications that run in the OS/2 execution environment have all the power of OS/2 at their fingertips. While these OS/2 applications must conform to the new rules that go along with this new power, applications that run in the DOS environment are a subset of the DOS 3.3 application set.

The DOS application owns the screen and keyboard when the user is running the DOS execution environment. The user sees whatever the DOS application is doing to the screen, and the DOS application will get the keystrokes except for special key sequences that are system hot keys. These hot keys allow the user to do such things as suspend the DOS execution environment and allow the OS/2 execution environment to own the screen. When the DOS execution environment owns the screen and keyboard, it is in the **foreground**. When the user switches away from the DOS execution environment, it is moved to the **background**.

When the DOS execution environment is in the foreground, it is sharing the processor with the applications in the OS/2 execution environment. When the DOS application code is executing, the processor is in real mode. When the OS/2 applications are executing, the processor is in protect mode. The operating system and the device drivers are written to manage the fact that the system can be running in either real or protect mode. This is known as a **bimodal** environment. Although this characteristic of OS/2 has added complexity to the operating system and the device drivers that need to be written for OS/2, it was needed to support the DOS execution environment.

When the DOS execution environment is in the background, it is suspended and gets no processor cycles. This is why one of the restrictions on the DOS execution environment is that timing dependent and real-time applications are not supported. The OS/2 applications share the processor amongst themselves when the DOS environment is in the background. System performance is slower when the DOS execution environment is in the foreground because of the bimodal nature of that environment.

The user can choose the size of the DOS execution environment with a **CONFIG.SYS** parameter. CONFIG.SYS is a file that OS/2 reads when it is initializing. The contents of the file determine many of the characteristics of OS/2 that the user can set. The user can also choose not to have a DOS execution environment with a CONFIG.SYS parameter.

Some of OS/2, as well as all the OS/2 device drivers, reside below 640 KB, taking some of the available memory away from the DOS execution environment. Because the processor is in real mode when the DOS application is executing, the DOS application can bypass the system protection characteristics of OS/2 and execute forbidden instructions or write over system code/data (in memory below 640 KB) and system device drivers.

The OS/2 execution environment provides a new programming interface for applications along with a whole level of functionality above DOS. The user can switch between different OS/2 applications and the DOS environment with a hotkey sequence. The OS/2 Program Selector can be used to go directly to an application or to start a new application.

When an OS/2 application is in the foreground, it is sharing the processor with all the OS/2 applications that are currently active. The processor is in protect mode, so applications cannot access (without permission) another application's address space or do other nasty things such as disable processor interrupts or access I/O devices. Provisions have been made for special applications to enter a higher privilege level than normal applications so that they can get IOPL. (We discuss IOPL later in this chapter when we review the 80286 processor.) The user must explicitly allow IOPL applications in CONFIG.SYS. Preventing IOPL applications from loading can be useful during problem determination.

The rest of this book focuses on the new capabilities that OS/2 provides to OS/2 applications. It is good to know that many of the old DOS 3.3 applications are still usable in the DOS execution environment of OS/2. In this way, people can still benefit from their old software while they gradually switch to the new applications enabled by the powerful OS/2 execution environment.

Some DOS Application Restrictions and Considerations

DOS applications are not supported in the OS/2 execution environment. A subset of the DOS 3.3 application set is supported in the OS/2 DOS execution environment. No new OS/2 functionality is available to the DOS execution environment.

DOS applications that have timing dependencies are not supported in the DOS execution environment. Even when the DOS environment is in the foreground, *it is not getting 100 percent of the processor* as it would in a real DOS 3.3 environment. So an application that polls a device in a DOS 3.3 environment may not work in the OS/2 DOS execution environment due to timing considerations.

Applications that use undocumented DOS 3.3 function calls are not supported in the DOS execution environment. Applications that are sensitive to the DOS version number may not work because the version number for the DOS execution environment is 10.0. Applications that use DOS Network function calls also are not supported.

There are restrictions in the use of certain DOS and BIOS software interrupts in the DOS execution environment. Old DOS block device drivers are not supported, and there are significant restrictions on old DOS character device drivers. There are also differences between some of the DOS 3.3 utilities and commands and the utilities and commands that are supported in the OS/2 DOS execution environment.

OS/2 is responsible for the management of the system resources. This is the only way that multiple applications could share the same device (e.g., the disk). There are restrictions on which hardware interrupts DOS applications may own and which hardware devices they may try to program by going directly to the hardware.

DOS applications that go into spin loops to wait for certain hardware events to occur will not allow efficient distribution of the processor resource. DOS applications that do things like the following may run into trouble:

- Write into memory that they do not own.
- Go into a disabled spin loop.
- Reprogram the interrupt controller.
- Use or change the CMOS clock.

If the applications do any of the above, or in general try to use a system hardware resource without going through a programming interface, they run the risk of not running or can cause the entire system to stop functioning.

Large Real Memory and Virtual Memory

The 8088, or the real mode of the 80286 processor, supports addressability of real memory up to 1 MB. There is no virtual memory support in the 8088. By **real memory** we mean the physical memory in the system and the physical addresses that that memory has. By **virtual memory** we mean the addresses that the application uses and sees. In the real mode of the 80286, the real memory address is equivalent to the virtual memory address. The concept of virtual memory is not used when the real mode of the 80286 is discussed. Because the address space between 640 KB and 1 MB is reserved for memory mapped I/O adapters (and displays) and ROM BIOS, the real mode of the 80286 can support only application code and data up to 640 KB, less whatever the operating system takes up.

In a DOS system, one way to utilize memory above 1 MB is to have a virtual disk. This virtual disk is significantly faster than a hard disk and can be utilized by the application just like a regular disk (through the file system API). This use of memory above 1 MB has significant drawbacks, though. The application must manage its data on a virtual disk as a disk file, as opposed to data in memory. The application can only directly process whatever data is in memory below 640 KB. It must keep storing data and bringing new data in every time it needs to use data that is in the virtual disk instead of in memory. Application code residing on the virtual disk cannot be directly executed. Instead, it must be brought into memory like an overlay and then executed. This can cause unacceptable delays in real-time systems and adds significant complexity to the structure and design of the application.

Bank switched memory has also been used to try to remove some of the 640 KB bottleneck. This utilization of more than 640 KB of memory is better than nothing, but it is not a natural extension of the memory capabilities of the 80286 and does not allow applications to expand naturally into the architectural capabilities of the 80286 and 80386. It is essentially a way for 8088 systems to cope with the pressure to allow applications to utilize more than 640 KB of memory. 8088 systems have no other alternatives.

OS/2 provides an environment where the memory addressing capabilities of the 80286 protect mode can be exploited, not only by the operating system itself but by applications as well. In this environment, OS/2 and OS/2 applications can access a full 16 MB of physical memory directly without resorting to unnatural means such as a virtual disk or bank switching.

In addition, OS/2 utilizes the virtual memory capabilities of the protect mode environment of the 80286. In this sense, the addresses that the application sees are not equal to the physical addresses. This allows all the applications currently in the system to use much more memory than really exists in the physical system. The applications think that all the memory is really there, but in reality, it is not. OS/2 manages the fact that some of that memory is really on disk, and OS/2 will bring that memory into physical real memory when an application tries to access it. The application has no idea that the code or data was not really in physical memory when it tried to execute or access it. The application also has no idea how much physical memory there really is. This is called virtual memory support.

We discuss these concepts in greater detail when we review the 80286 architecture later in this chapter and in the chapter on Memory Capabilities (Chapter 2).

We have already discussed how important it is to have as much memory as possible available for applications. In addition, because OS/2 supports multiple applications concurrently, it is even more important for it to support large memory address spaces for each application. The virtual memory capabilities of the 80286 allow OS/2 to do this. By supporting the large real memory capabilities of the 80286 architecture, OS/2 allows direct and optimal utilization of the large real memory capabilities of the current and future personal computer systems.

Memory Overcommit

As we have just seen, OS/2 allows an application or applications to be larger than the amount of real memory in the system. This is called memory overcommit. OS/2 accomplishes this by **swapping** (moving) memory **segments** to disk when they are not being used. (We discuss segments in the 80286 architecture review in this chapter.) The **least recently used** segments are swapped to disk first. Once a segment is swapped out to disk, the real memory that it was occupying can be reused by another segment that may be brought in from the disk (swapped in). The segment is swapped in because either an application or the operating system decided to execute it or access it as data.

To get rid of the least recently used segments from real memory, certain segments may not have to be swapped out. Instead, they may be **discarded** (thrown away) because either

  □ The application created the data segment with the ability to be discarded.
  □ The segment cannot change because it is a code segment.

If the segment needs to be reused, it can be

  □ Brought back in from its original source.
  □ Recreated by the application. The application has given the system permission to discard the data segment.

Because segments can vary in size up to 64 KB, unused spaces in memory can begin to crop into the real address space as segments are discarded and swapped in and out. If there are two 32 KB spaces in real memory and a 64 KB segment needs to be swapped in, the system cannot swap that segment into two noncontiguous spaces in real memory. In cases like these, the system may decide to move some segments around in real memory in order to collect some of the spaces in real memory into bigger spaces. This is called **segment motion**.

Such use of the 80286 protect mode memory capabilities allows large applications to exist without any knowledge of the underlying physical memory availability or characteristics. This is a far cry from the overlay structures that large applications previously had to be aware of when they were bigger than the available memory. The applications had to plan to be of a certain size and to structure themselves in a certain way in order to bring executable code into a portion of their address spaces as it was needed. Applications using overlays also had to trade off address space for data against address space for executable code. In a memory overcommit environment with virtual memory support, applications don't need to bother understanding anything other than how many segments the system recommends that they should have, the maximum number of segments that the system supports, and the performance implications of the amount of swapping that the application will generate.

Multiple Applications

There are enhancements available to the DOS environment that support a multiple application environment. However, because it is a DOS environment, these enhancements come up against many of the limitations of the real mode of the 80286. It is very difficult to support useful multiple applications while fitting the enhanced environment, DOS, and the multiple applications all in 640 KB. Tricks can be used to move applications in and out of a virtual disk, but the resulting performance can be a problem in many environments. In addition, the real mode of the 80286 does not protect one application from another and does not protect the operating system from the applications.

These problems disappear in an OS/2 environment. OS/2 provides large virtual address spaces for each OS/2 application that is running in the system. OS/2 uses the protection mechanisms available in the protect mode of the 80286 to provide protection between applications and between the operating system and the applications.

OS/2 also provides the resource management and application rules necessary so that multiple sophisticated applications can coexist in the same system without problems. Applications can be given execution priority so that they obtain the required amount of processor resource.

OS/2 allows multiple applications to run concurrently. This means that users can significantly increase their productivity as they begin to use their machines in smarter ways. Data can be obtained from a remote source using a communications program while a large spreadsheet is being calculated and while the user has a text editor in the foreground where a memo is being typed in. The user can switch between applications as required to see what is going on.

OS/2 makes a much broader range of software choices available to the user because it provides an environment where multiple sophisticated applications can coexist and execute without interfering with each other. Previously, the user was forced to buy an integrated set of applications that could properly execute together in a DOS environment. In the new world of OS/2, the application development rules allow applications developed by different vendors to properly mesh together in the system. This will allow the user to choose the best application for each separate need.

Multitasking

Multitasking is when a system provides an application environment where an application can appear to the user to be doing more than one thing at the same time. Of course, since there is only one central processor in the system, the system cannot really be doing more than one thing at a time. However, there are many times that an application has multiple pieces of work to do that can be done in parallel, as long as there are some very well-defined synchronization points. There are also many times that the processor cannot continue doing a given piece of work because the work needs to wait for input to or output from a slow external device like the keyboard or the disk. Multitasking allows the pieces of work to be structured in such a manner that when one piece of work is waiting for something to happen in the system, another is allowed to use the processor. In a multiple application environment, each application has pieces of work that share the processor.

DOS is designed to be a single tasking environment, where the system can process only one piece of work at a time and only one application at a time. When an application is getting data from the disk, that application is waiting for the data and is doing nothing else in the meantime.

You may be asking yourself about certain programs in a DOS environment that appear to be multitasking. It is true that by bypassing the normal DOS interfaces an application can be implemented to have multitasking characteristics in a DOS environment. However, an application that does this will probably not work well with other applications, especially if those other applications also bypass the normal DOS interfaces to give themselves special characteristics.

The OS/2 multitasking capabilities allow each application in a multiple application environment to have multitasking characteristics. All the OS/2 applications will coexist and execute concurrently without interfering with each other. Of course, the more applications that there are, the less processing power each application will get per unit time. OS/2 has priority capabilities, so time-critical applications can be given higher priority than normal applications.

The basic unit of work that can be executed in OS/2 is called a **thread.** A thread consists of a series of program instructions that will execute in the system. A thread has similar characteristics to a simple DOS program. The basic unit of system resource ownership in OS/2 is called a **process**. Each process can consist of one or more threads. Multiple threads of the same process share a common set of system resources (except for things like a stack). These features are discussed in greater detail in the chapter on Multitasking and Multiple Applications (Chapter 3).

Multitasking is considered a necessity for the new systems environment of OS/2. Without it, it would not be possible to develop sophisticated high function applications that could properly coexist with each other in a multiple applications environment. Users expect applications that can respond quickly to keyboard input while continuing to process whatever else needs to be done. As the processors become more and more powerful, their relative speed will become even faster in relation to the external devices that they support. Communications subsystems and real-time applications require multitasking to be able to monitor external events while processing other pieces of work of lower priority. Without multitasking, none of the above would be possible in a general fashion in a multiple applications environment.

Interprocess Communications

Threads are the basic units of execution in the OS/2 environment. Multiple threads make up a process. In OS/2's multitasking environment, if all the threads that need to work together are part of the same process, then it is very easy for them to work properly together and synchronize at all the right times. The threads share the same system resources.

However, because different processes do not naturally share the same system resources, it is more difficult for multiple processes to pass information among themselves or to properly synchronize (if that is a requirement). This situation leads to the need for interprocess communications capabilities.

OS/2 provides many mechanisms for different processes to communicate with each other and to synchronize execution:

- RAM and System semaphores.
- Signal handlers (e.g., do something on keyboard CTRL-BREAK).
- Pipes.
- Queues.
- Shared memory.

We discuss these concepts in detail in the chapter on Multitasking and Multiple Applications (Chapter 3).

By having a rich set of interprocess communications capabilities, OS/2 provides an environment where applications as well as subsystems can be designed according to the function that they provide and the characteristics that they need to exhibit. If the different units of work are processes, then they are inherently protected from one another and only affect each other along very well-defined lines of communications.

Dynamic Linked Call/Return Interface. High Level Language Support.

There are six programming languages initially available from IBM for OS/2:

- IBM COBOL/2.
- IBM FORTRAN/2.

- IBM C/2.
- IBM Macro Assembler/2.
- IBM Pascal Compiler/2.
- IBM Basic Compiler/2.

These languages will run in either a DOS 3.3 environment or an OS/2 environment. Programs can even be written in such a way that the same code will be executable in either a DOS 3.3 or OS/2 execution environment if a certain subset of the OS/2 function calls are used and the code conforms to certain conventions. This subset of the OS/2 API is called the **Family Application Programming Interface**. The Family Application Programming Interface can be a powerful productivity tool for developing applications to run on either DOS 3.3 or OS/2 (as an OS/2 application in protected mode) *if the new features of OS/2 are not needed* for the applications and if the applications can use the Family Application Programming Interface.

The following three languages allow participation in the "Common Programming Interface" element of the IBM **Systems Application Architecture.**

- IBM FORTRAN/2.
- IBM COBOL/2.
- IBM C/2.

If you are interested in the computing environment and user interface capability that IBM's Systems Application Architecture provides, then the language you choose to implement a given application is an important consideration.

The call/return application programming interface (API) that OS/2 provides fits in more naturally with the structures that high level languages like to use. The dynamic linking nature of this interface adds a new dimension of flexibility to the operating system interface. The basic foundation of dynamic linking is very powerful. Applications that reference external dynamic link code as far calls do not actually access that code until the program is loaded into the system to be executed or until the program is actually running.

The operating system code that supports a given dynamic link interface can be changed while maintaining compatibility with existing applications *without having to recompile or relink the application*. In addition, the dynamic link interface is naturally extendable to services that subsystems or other applications may wish to provide to the general system. Other applications would use these services exactly as if the application were using system services. This is why the dynamic link nature of the OS/2 API is generally extendable and modular. Whole new sets of system services can be added and can be made to appear as if they are part of the system, even though they may be provided by an independent software vendor or a specialized group of a corporation. A good example of this would be a communications subsystem. The communications subsystem could be provided in such a manner that applications would treat it as a natural extension of the operating system.

The power of the dynamic link interface does not stop there. In the old DOS environment, when a program is linked with a set of code through external references, the external code becomes part of the program and stays with the program from then on. If the external code is changed after that, then the application would have to relink in order to make use of the new code. In addition, since the external code has essentially become part of the application after the link, it is like an extra set of baggage that must be carried around with the application after link time.

Dynamic linking changes all of that. After link time, the application is not bound to the externally referenced code to which it is dynamically linked. It is not until the application actually runs in the system that the code to which it is dynamically linked is used. This feature has valuable benefits that make the OS/2 dynamic link environment significantly superior to anything that has preceded it.

The function of a dynamic link interface can be enhanced while maintaining compatibility with old applications that have already been linked to the interface. The old applications do not have to be rewritten or relinked. The code behind the dynamic link interface can be totally changed to support a different systems environment, and the application still does not have to be relinked to run in that new environment. The only item that must remain the same is the information that makes up the external reference to the dynamic link library and routine within that library. This is because the application is not bound to the code that supports the interface until it is loaded to be executed or until it is actually executed.

Dynamic linking also avoids the baggage that the application carries around after link time. In the case of external references to a dynamic link interface, the executable form of the application does not actually contain the code that it is dynamically linking to. Instead, it contains only the references. The system will figure it all out at load or run time.

Because the external dynamic link code does not become part of the application until it comes time to actually use the application, if multiple applications in the system are linking to the same dynamic link interface, *only one set of the code that supports the dynamic link interface needs to be actually resident in the system.* This results in an enormous savings in the mass storage that is used to hold the applications themselves.

The system benefits do not end there. If the code that supports a given dynamic link interface is already resident in real memory due to use from a previous application, then when a new application tries to use the interface, *the system will recognize that the code that supports that interface is already in memory and will use the memory resident code instead of going out to disk to get it again.* This maximizes the system performance and memory utilization characteristics in a multiple application environment.

Applications can use dynamic linking in two different ways: **load time** and **run time.** Load time usage is what most people are familiar with. In this case, all the dynamic link references are resolved when the application is first loaded into the system to be executed. At this time, the dynamic link interface code may or may not be loaded into memory depending on the characteristics of its segments (**preload** or **load on demand,** to be discussed in Chapter 2) and how much available real memory there is to hold all the segments that need to be loaded. Essentially, the external references are all resolved when the program is first loaded.

Run time dynamic linking adds a new dimension to the flexibility of dynamic linking. When using run time dynamic linking, the application does not decide exactly which interface it wishes to use until the application code is actually executing. System interfaces exist to dynamically link to a given routine in a library during the execution time of the program. To illustrate the point, a program could be written to ask the user which dynamic link package should be used to accomplish a given function. The user could then type in the needed information while the program is actually executing, and the program could use that information to link to the external interface and pass control to it. This is a far cry from binding the application to all its call/return external interfaces at application link time.

File System Compatibility with DOS

OS/2 uses the File Allocation Table (FAT) file system, just like DOS. OS/2 also has similar support for fixed disk partitions, which is needed for fixed disks that are bigger than 32 MB. File system compatibility with DOS is an extremely important feature of OS/2.

With this capability, data can be moved from DOS to OS/2 with no transformation in between. If the user ran a DOS application that generated data on a hard disk or a diskette, then that data would be immediately usable as an OS/2 file. The file naming convention is also the same in both systems. This allows users to maintain a consistent system of naming files between the two operating systems.

Interrupt-Driven Device Management

External devices are supported in an OS/2 environment with **device drivers**. Devices can be supported in a **polled** fashion in a DOS environment because DOS is a single tasking single application environment. Polling means that when the application or device driver tries to get the device to do something, it will keep on asking the device in an infinite loop if it is done, until the device finally is done. No other work will get done in the system while this is going on. The program just sits there continually asking "are you done?" Polling wastes an incredible amount of processing power and could not possibly be compatible with a multitasking multiple application environment where it is important to use all the system resources as efficiently as possible.

The device driver model for OS/2 is structured to mesh well with a multitasking environment. The OS/2 device driver does not wait around for the device to finish doing what it was asked to do. Instead, the device driver tells the system to do other work, and the device driver waits for a device **interrupt**. Interrupts are a way for devices to hit the system over the head and force it to change the code it is executing. The system can be executing application code until the device requests service through the generation of an interrupt. We discuss interrupts again in the 80286 architecture section of this chapter and in the chapter on Interrupt-Driven Device Management (Chapter 6).

DOS does not provide a general mechanism for allowing application code to execute while the system is waiting for a device to complete an operation. The fact that OS/2 does do this plays a major role in its ability to use the hardware system resources in an optimal manner. Multiple devices can also be doing work for the same application or different applications at the same time. When the device driver returns control to the system and waits for a device interrupt, the application code can request service from a different device. The different device would be started up before the first device completed its operation. It is possible to have the diskette, the disk, the printer, the communications port(s), and so on, all functioning concurrently. This feature expands the power of the system well beyond the capabilities of DOS.

Video, Keyboard, and Mouse Subsystems

OS/2 provides systems support for the display, keyboard, and mouse console devices through a combination of device drivers and dynamic link interfaces. These console device subsystems are integrated into the user interface characteristics of the system, and they provide specialized interfaces that make it easier to use the console devices.

The video subsystem provides a high performance text-oriented superset of the BIOS Int 10h video interfaces available in the DOS environment. The keyboard subsystem allows an application to receive both scan code and ASCII representations of user keyboard input, and it is designed so that applications can yield the CPU when waiting on a keystroke. The mouse subsystem allows an application to generally manage the mouse device; it can control the way a mouse cursor is handled, and which types of mouse events are included as data in the mouse input buffer. Each of these subsystems also provides functions that allow an application or other subsystem to intercept the various function calls. By intercepting the video, keyboard, or mouse function calls, an application can extend or replace the base function provided by these subsystems.

National Language Support and Message Handling Facilities

We live in an international age. Companies expect to have the flexibility of providing software that can be used in many different countries, as their business needs warrant it. Independent software vendors would like to make their products available in multiple countries by making minimal changes for language and country-dependent information. This allows them to preserve their investment in the original software as much as possible.

OS/2 supports eleven languages with their associated keyboards. This means that the OS/2 screens, messages, and documentation are all translated to the appropriate languages and that the keyboard support is aware of the appropriate keyboard layout. The languages are as follows:

- Danish.
- Dutch.
- French.
- German.
- Italian.
- Norwegian.
- Portuguese.
- Spanish.
- Swedish.
- United Kingdom English.
- United States English.

OS/2 also supports six additional keyboards. They are as follows:

- Belgian.
- Canadian.
- Finnish.
- Latin American Spanish.
- Swiss French.
- Swiss German.

OS/2 also supports **code page** switching for certain displays and printers. A code page can be thought of as the device's (display or printer) character set or font. This support allows applications to select the display and printer character set that is appropriate for the given application. The appropriate code page for a specific application may not be the same as the language that the version of OS/2 is configured for. To handle this eventuality, OS/2 provides concurrent support for two code pages. The two code pages can be selected during the installation process. Either the user or the application can select the appropriate code page when necessary. The code pages that OS/2 can support are as follows:

- 437—PC ASCII, United States and other countries.
- 850—Multilingual, many European countries.
- 860—Portuguese.
- 863—Canadian French.
- 865—Nordic.

Besides the code page switching, what National Language Support features are provided by OS/2 that would make it easier for programs to be written for an international environment? That answer lies in the message handling facilities of OS/2. They can totally separate the messages that an application uses to interface with the user from the application itself. These messages reside in a separate file that can be independently translated by people who know nothing about computers but know a great deal about foreign languages. This is a very efficient way to develop software for different countries without recompiling or relinking the actual program. The translators themselves can create new message files using very simple file editing tools.

This translation technique can also be used by software designers to separate the language that is ultimately presented to the end user from what the programmers are working on. The programmers can continue to do what they do best while experts in human factors can concentrate on coming up with the best possible user messages. This partitioning of the work is a great help in developing user friendly software.

MIGRATION OF APPLICATIONS FROM DOS TO OS/2

An application that runs under DOS will not run in the OS/2 execution environment. At a minimum, the way the program interfaces with the system is different in the two environments. In DOS, programs use the INT interface, while in OS/2, programs use the dynamic link call/return interface.

To get a DOS application that is written in a high level language to run as an OS/2 application, the program would have to be recompiled and relinked. Source program changes would probably also be required, and they would definitely be required for assembler language programs. All INT calls to the system would have to be changed to dynamic link calls to the OS/2 application programming interface (API). Technical documentation available for OS/2 provides mapping suggestions from DOS INT function calls to the OS/2 application programming interface.

It makes sense to transform a DOS program to a program that can execute in the OS/2 execution environment *even if that program does not make use of any of the new capabilities of OS/2*. This is because the new OS/2 application can exist in the multiple applications environment of OS/2 and be used without regard to memory constraints.

Most applications can be significantly enhanced by taking advantage of the new functions available with OS/2. For example, spreadsheet programs can be upgraded to support huge amounts of data without moving data to and from disk. The spreadsheet would appear to the application to be totally in memory. In reality, if the system does not have enough physical memory, then OS/2 may swap some of the spreadsheet out to disk. The user could also buy more physical memory and avoid any swapping of the spreadsheet. Although the spreadsheet program itself has not been modified, its execution characteristics have significantly changed for the better.

Independent software vendors could improve the usefulness and competitiveness of their software by exploiting the new level of functionality available in the OS/2 execution environment. Between this pressure and the pressure of users just wanting applications that can run together in the OS/2 execution environment, it is expected that, over time, vendors will migrate most popular applications to the OS/2 execution environment.

OS/2 APPLICATION PROGRAMMING INTERFACE CHARACTERISTICS

We have already discussed that the OS/2 API is a call/return interface. The application issues a Far call to the function name. The application then passes all parameters to the function by pushing them onto the **stack**. Addresses of parameters can also be pushed onto the stack. All addresses are composed of a 16 bit **selector** (segment) and a 16 bit **offset** value (see the microprocessor overview section in this chapter). The number of parameters for a given function is always fixed.

On return from the function call, the return code is found in register AX (see the microprocessor overview section in this chapter). Parameters can also be returned by the function call. In this case, the application would push the address of the return parameter onto the stack before calling the function. The function always removes all the parameters from the stack. The function call preserves all the registers except for AX and the FLAGS register.

We do not present every detail of every API in this book. You can obtain such detailed information from the technical documentation available for OS/2. Instead, when we cover a given topic, we discuss the most important API functions for that topic at different levels of detail. In some cases, we discuss the parameters and functions at a very general level. In other cases, we give logical descriptions of all the parameters for a given function to show what the parameters represent. In still other cases, we show all the parameters for a given function down to the coding level of detail. We are providing the details of the API in this selective fashion to focus on the important points and to make it easier to comprehend what the level of function is for a given OS/2 capability.

80286 MICROPROCESSOR OVERVIEW

In this section we briefly review the most important 80286 microprocessor characteristics and functions. This overview should help you better understand the underlying support behind some of the new features of OS/2. OS/2 relies heavily on the new features of the 80286 to provide such functions as:

- Large real memory support.
- Virtual memory support.
- Application and operating system data protection.
- Protection from operating system improperly executing application code.
- System protection from applications executing certain processor instructions.

Before we explore the details of the 80286, let's briefly examine what a personal computer system looks like.

The Personal Computer System

Figure 1 contains a simple logical overview of a generic personal computer system. We can see that the microprocessor makes up only a small part of the personal computer system. The system bus is the highway over which the personal computer system components communicate. The system memory contains the instructions and data that the microprocessor accesses during execution. Input/Output devices communicate directly with the microprocessor or use DMA to place information in the system memory. Now, let's look at each of these components in more detail and introduce some important terminology.

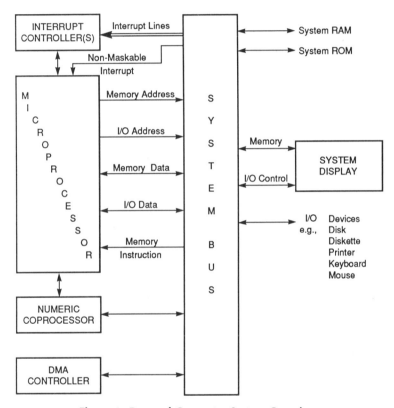

Figure 1. Personal Computer System Overview

System Bus

The **system bus** acts as the funnel for most of the communications that occur between the different components of the system. If you have ever installed additional adapter boards in your personal computer, you were plugging those adapter boards into the system bus. The bus defines the set of rules that the different parts of the system must obey so they can work well together. The characteristics of the system bus play a very important role in the overall behavior and performance of the system. This is why IBM has made the Micro Channel™ Architecture (the PS/2 system bus) an integral part of the Personal System/2 hardware announcement.

System Memory

Memory plays an integral part in the operation of the system. Data and processor instructions are stored in memory. The memory location that is used is selected by the **physical address** placed on the system bus. The size of the physical address that can be placed on the bus determines the maximum amount of physical memory that can be placed in the system.

There are three different types of memory that exist in a personal computer system:

□ RAM—random access memory.
□ ROM—read only memory.
□ Memory mapped I/O.

The system RAM forgets what was in it when the system is powered off. Data is written to and read from the system RAM. Program instructions that make up the applications that the user selects are read into the system RAM by the operating system from some other I/O (input/output) device and then executed by the microprocessor (by reading the instructions from RAM). Examples of devices that store these program instructions are diskettes and disks. Most of the memory that makes up a system is RAM.

The system ROM never loses its contents, even when the power is turned off. However, the system ROM can never be changed by the processor. The processor can only read the ROM. The ROM in the PS/2 systems contains the **BIOS** code and data of the system. BIOS stands for the Basic Input Output System. It is a layer of processor instructions and data that allows the processor to perform operations on the system hardware without directly accessing the hardware. This allows the operating system to be protected from certain changes in the hardware. The PS/2 has a BIOS called **Compatibility BIOS** which is the same kind of BIOS that is in the PC AT. This BIOS supports the real mode of the 80286. A new BIOS called **Advanced BIOS** was developed for the PS/2. This BIOS supports a system with multitasking characteristics and supports protect mode usage of the 80286. OS/2 and OS/2 device drivers utilize Advanced BIOS on the PS/2. The system BIOS code resides in part of the physical address space between 640 KB and 1 megabyte.

There are I/O (input/output) devices that have RAM as part of the device. This RAM is known as memory mapped I/O. A good example of this would be the IBM personal computer displays. The screen that the user sees is a direct representation of a section of RAM that is part of the display device. As the program modifies the display memory, different things appear on the screen. The processor modifies the control modes of the display device to control how the display RAM is interpreted by the display hardware. This RAM usually resides between 640 KB and 1 MB of the physical address space.

System Devices

Devices are usually accessed via I/O (input/output) addresses instead of memory addresses. The microprocessor has different instructions that cause I/O addresses to be generated and I/O data to be transferred. An I/O address will not cause memory to be accessed and a memory address will not cause an I/O address to be accessed. The system understands this difference between memory and I/O addressing because the system bus has special control lines to indicate whether an I/O or memory operation is in progress.

Devices usually have sets of control registers that are mapped to a set of I/O addresses. When the processor wants to cause a device to do something, it would output data to the correct I/O address for that device. That data would be placed in the control register of the device and would ultimately cause the device to perform some action. Normal data can also be output to the device in this manner. Device control registers are also read by the processor to get the current status of the device. For example, the processor may read a control register on the parallel printer port to see if the printer is ready to accept another data character. When the answer is yes, the processor then outputs the data character to a different I/O port, which contains the parallel port data register.

Certain devices in the system are block devices, which means that they do things with bunches (blocks) of data at one time instead of with one character (byte) of data at a time. For example, the disk on a PC AT or PS/2 does its read or write operation with 512 bytes at a time. This means that for a disk read operation the processor must transfer 512 bytes from the disk. Because there is no processor I/O instruction that says "read 512 bytes," the processor must execute a number of I/O read instructions for one or two bytes of data at a time. If the device uses **Direct Memory Access** (DMA) to transfer data to the system memory, then the processor does not need to be involved during the actual data transfer operation.

Direct Memory Access (DMA)

Certain devices are built to support the use of the system DMA controller to transfer data from or to system memory. If the DMA controller is moving the data from or to the system memory, then the processor does not have to keep on issuing I/O instructions to the device for each byte or couple of bytes of data that are transferred. Instead, the processor commands the DMA controller to move the data to or from a given physical address in memory and then tells the device to start moving the data. The processor can check to see when the operation is complete or the device can be programmed to generate an **interrupt** when the operation is complete.

The operation described above uses a single **DMA channel**. Most systems have more than one DMA channel. Block devices as well as character-at-a-time devices can be designed to utilize DMA. An example of a character device that has been designed to use DMA is SDLC. The data comes in a character at a time, but the processor does not get involved in the transfer of every character (byte) of data.

Disks and diskettes are examples of block devices that could use DMA.

On a Personal Computer AT, diskette data is transferred using DMA, but hard disk data is transferred using a series of processor I/O instructions. On the PS/2, diskette and hard disk data is transferred using different DMA channels.

When you use DOS, where only one thing at a time is going on, the fact that an operation is being done with DMA doesn't really buy you anything. The processor just sits there and waits for the DMA operation to complete because it has no other work to do anyway. In an OS/2 environment, the fact that the processor does not need to be tied up during the data transfer time can improve utilization of the processor. For example, on a PS/2, the disk and the diskette could be transferring data on two different DMA channels while the processor is doing something else (like servicing a timer interrupt).

As with everything else, you don't get something for nothing. If you go back to Figure 1, you can see how all the data must be transferred through that funnel called the system bus. If too many data transfers are going on at once, or if a single data transfer is using too much of the **bus bandwidth** for too long a period of time, then the DMA operations could interfere with each other or with the processor. The processor must get to the system memory even when it needs to fetch the next instruction that it will process. If the processor can't get to the system memory to fetch instructions, then it is essentially held up, waiting for the bus. The bus bandwidth defines how much data per unit time the bus can transfer. The bigger the bandwidth, the more data per unit time can be transferred through the funnel, so more DMA action can be supported concurrently with the processor also running. This is a very important consideration when designing hardware adapters that use DMA and are going to be used in a multitasking environment like OS/2.

Interrupts

Devices tell the microprocessor that they want to generate an interrupt by placing a signal on designated lines of the system bus. The interrupt controller interprets those signals and generates the interrupt that ultimately goes to the microprocessor. The interrupt controller supports multiple hardware interrupt lines on the system bus and translates what is going on on the system bus to special signals that the microprocessor can understand. Each interrupt line on the system bus corresponds to an interrupt level, and each line is prioritized. The interrupt controller also handles all the priority processing of the interrupt lines.

When the interrupt controller tries to generate an interrupt on the microprocessor, the microprocessor will respond if it is enabled to accept interrupts. The microprocessor will stop processing whatever stream of instructions it is currently executing and start executing a different stream of instructions. We discuss the way the new stream of instructions is determined later on in this section.

The new stream of instructions is generally called an **interrupt handler**. The interrupt handler is determined by what the interrupt level was. Since the interrupt level usually corresponds to a given I/O device, the interrupt handler is usually set up to handle interrupts for a specific device.

For example, the parallel printer device can be set up to generate an interrupt each time it is ready to accept a new character to be printed. The device driver will output a character to the parallel printer data register and then return control back to the system, allowing other useful work to be done. When that character has been printed, the parallel printer device will generate an interrupt. At 40 characters per second, that could be 25 milliseconds later. The printer device driver interrupt handler will eventually get control due to the interrupt. It will then check the parallel printer port to determine the cause of the interrupt (by reading an I/O port). It will see that it is ready to accept another character and it will output another data character to the parallel printer data port.

Interrupts are **edge triggered** on the PC AT and **level sensitive** on the PS/2. This is a description of the way the interrupt signal appears on the system bus and what kind of interrupt signal the interrupt controller is looking for. OS/2 supports only one device on a given interrupt level in the PC AT edge triggered environment. OS/2 supports multiple devices on the same interrupt level in the level sensitive environment of the PS/2. In a level sensitive environment, the device does not stop generating the interrupt signal to the interrupt controller until the device is serviced. In an edge triggered environment, the device generates one interrupt pulse that the interrupt controller detects. If the system chooses to reset the interrupt controller without servicing the device, then the interrupt could be lost and the device may never be serviced.

Numeric Coprocessor

The numeric coprocessor is essentially a hardware assist for the microprocessor. It allows the system to process certain kinds of instructions (like floating point operations) significantly faster than if they were emulated by a series of normal processor instructions. The system can be set up to detect when a numeric processor is not present and emulate those instructions when the main microprocessor tries to execute them.

The Microprocessor

The microprocessor fetches instructions from the system memory and executes (processes) those instructions. In the course of executing those instructions, the processor may decide to write data to memory, read data from memory, write data to an I/O address, or read data from an I/O address. Certain instructions (e.g., Conditional Jump) may cause the processor to execute an instruction other than the next instruction.

The microprocessor has some local memory within it. This local memory is called the microprocessor's **registers**. Instructions that use data in the processor's registers are usually more efficient and do not require that the microprocessor go out to the system bus to read or write that data. There are also internal registers within the microprocessor that are not used for general instruction execution but instead assist the microprocessor in its operation.

There are many characteristics of a given microprocessor that set it apart from other microprocessors, such as the following:

- The size (number of bits) and quantity of its general purpose registers.
- How powerful the instruction set is and how many bits of data the instructions can process at once.
- The amount of physical data that the processor can transfer at once on the system bus (number of bits).
- The different ways that the processor can address its data and whether those different ways are usable for most of the instructions.
- Whether there is a protection mechanism for use by the operating system and what it is.
- The processor's interrupt structure.

Now that we have seen a general overview of microprocessors, let's take a look at the 80286.

80286 State Description and Operation

Understanding the local memory of the 80286 and how it is used is the key to understanding how the 80286 works. Most of the local memory in the 80286 is referred to as registers. The contents of the registers and the local memory in the 80286 defines the "state" that the 80286 is in. From the current state, we can determine exactly what the 80286 is going to do next.

Take a look at Figure 2. It describes all the registers and other state variables that we are interested in understanding in the 80286. Before we explore, let us come to a very simple understanding of 80286 addressing for now. Each address is made up of two 16 bit values:

- The 16 bit value in one of the **segment registers.**
- A 16 bit **offset.**

The segment register value defines the **segment** that we are referring to. The offset value defines the offset within that segment. In an 80286, segments have up to 64 KB (65,536 bytes) in them (an offset of up to a 16 bit value ($2^{16} - 1 = 65,535$)). We discuss in the next section how the value in the segment register and the value of the offset are interpreted to form the physical memory address.

How does the processor know where to fetch the next instruction in memory from? The processor fetches the next instruction using CS as the segment register and IP as the offset. Certain instructions (like conditional jumps) modify the value

```
GENERAL PURPOSE REGISTERS              SEGMENT REGISTERS
-------------------------              ----------------


- Four 16 bit registers.              Four 16 bit registers.
  Each register can also be
  used as two 8 bit registers.
                                        CS - Code Segment
                                        DS - Data Segment
      AX = AH || AL                     ES - Extra Segment
      BX = BH || BL                     SS - Stack Segment
      CX = CH || CL
      DX = DH || DL


                                       SPECIAL REGISTERS
                                       ----------------

- Four more 16 bit registers.

      BP - Base Pointer                F - Flags
      SI - Source Index                IP - Instruction Pointer
      DI - Destination Index           MSW - Machine Status
      SP - Stack Pointer                     Word



              OTHER IMPORTANT INFORMATION
              ---------------------------


          - SEGMENT DESCRIPTOR CACHE REGISTERS
          - GLOBAL DESCRIPTOR TABLE (GDT) BASE & LIMIT
          - LOCAL DESCRIPTOR TABLE (LDT) BASE & LIMIT
          - INTERRUPT DESCRIPTOR TABLE (IDT) BASE & LIMIT
          - TASK REGISTER, TASK STATE SEGMENT BASE & LIMIT (*)


    (*) Beyond the scope of this book.
```

Figure 2. Simple 80286 State Description

of IP. If IP is not modified by the current instruction, then the size of the current instruction is added to IP so the next sequential instruction is executed. If IP is modified, then some other instruction within the segment defined by CS is executed. Certain instructions modify both CS and IP. This causes an instruction in a whole new segment of memory to be fetched.

The **stack** is a special section of memory that is used to store information when one of the following occurs:

- One procedure (set of processor instructions) calls another procedure.
- Some temporary storage area is needed and the program does not want to explicitly allocate data area for that temporary storage.

The current stack segment is defined by segment register SS. Registers SP or BP usually define the offset that is used (depending on what the stack is being used for). The processor usually gets its data from the segment defined by segment register

DS or ES. The offset for the data can be combinations of many different things. The offset can be explicitly coded into the instruction or it can be some arithmetic combination of one or two general purpose registers and an explicitly coded 16 bit value. There are some restrictions on which general purpose registers can be used (for offsets) in any given situation.

Most instructions have source and destination data targets. The source data can be explicitly coded in the instruction, can be in a general purpose register, or can be in memory. The destination target can be a general purpose register or memory location. Most instructions cannot operate on source and destination memory targets at the same time. However, some instructions are explicitly designed to do that. Those instructions tend to use the SI and DI as part of the source and destination offsets and DS and ES as the source and destination segments.

The **flags** register contains such information as the result of the last operation (e.g., sign bit, carry, overflow, etc.) and whether interrupts are enabled. The **machine status word** contains information about the processor such as whether it should be in real or protect mode. The details of these two registers are beyond the scope of this book.

The values placed in all these registers (and other local memory) when the microprocessor is powered up (reset) determines what the processor does at reset time. When the 80286 is reset, it is placed in real mode with CS = FOOOH and IP = FFFOH. As we will soon see, this causes the processor to begin fetching instructions at physical address location FFFFOH, just a little below 1 MB. The other three segment registers are 0 at this time.

80286 Addressing—Real Mode versus Protect Mode

Physical addresses produced by the 80286 are made up of two components: the 16 bit value in the segment register and the 16 bit offset value. The offset is determined by many different factors, depending on the situation.

The two 16 bit values are processed differently by the 80286 depending on whether the 80286 is in real mode or protect mode. When the 80286 is in real mode, it produces physical addresses the same as an 8088 or 8086 microprocessor. Let's take a look at Figure 3 to see how physical addresses are produced on the 80286 when it is in real mode.

Physical Address Generation in Real Mode

Spend some time studying Figure 3. This way of generating physical addresses has some very important characteristics. We have already discussed how the segment register determines the segment that the address will be in. Because the offset is a 16 bit value, each segment is 64 KB (65,536 bytes) big. The offset value ranges from 0 to 65,535. Segments also always start on 16 byte physical address boundaries. The physical address that is generated is a 20 bit value, so only 1 MB (OOOOOH–

1) Take the 16 bit segment register (value 0 - 65535 or
   0000H - FFFFH) and multiply by 16. In other words
   make it a 20 bit value by putting four 0 bits as
   the low order bits.

2) The value represented from the segment register is
   now 00000H - FFFF0H (0 - 1,048,650).
   Since the low order four bits are always 0, the value
   can only be every sixteenth possible number within
   that range.

3) Add the 16 bit offset to the 20 bit value.

4) Result is a 20 bit physical address ranging in value
   from 00000H to FFFFFH (overflow not considered).

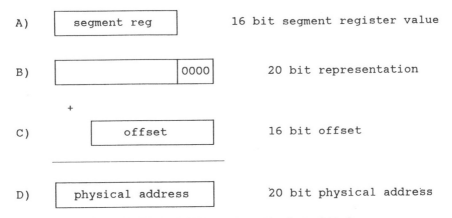

Figure 3. Physical Address Generation in Real Mode

FFFFFH) of physical memory can be accesssed using the real mode of the 80286.

Have you noticed the most important characteristic of all? By knowing the value that is in the segment register, *we know exactly where in physical memory the segment can be found.* Because the application program places values in the segment register, the application program can directly control which physical memory the application will be accessing. This is why it was previously stated that in a real mode 80286 environment the virtual address is equal to the real address. Remember, the virtual address is the address that the program sees and the real address is the physical address that is used to access the physical memory in the system.

Applications can also assume that if they add 1 to the value in the segment register, they will be accessing the same memory that they would have accessed if they increased the offset value by 16 (assuming no overflow).

These are the assumptions that programs in the DOS environment make all the time. This is one of the reasons why those programs cannot directly execute in the protect mode environment of the 80286.

Physical Address Generation in Protect Mode

By now we should at least have a clue as to what the protect mode scheme is. We have already discussed the following facts about generating addresses in the 80286 protect mode:

- □ Up to 16 megabytes of physical memory can be supported in the system.
- □ The virtual addresses are not equal to the real (physical) addresses. The value in the segment register does not directly correspond to a physical address.
- □ Virtual addresses that are not currently in memory (so they need to be brought into memory) are supported.
- □ Different virtual address spaces can be supported for different application programs.
- □ There is memory protection between the operating system and the applications.

The clue to the protected mode scheme is that the value in the segment register does not determine the base of the physical address of the segment as it did in real mode. Instead, the value in the segment register is called the **selector** when the 80286 is in protect mode. The selector acts as an index into a special table. This table has all the information about the physical memory segment. This information is called the **segment descriptor**.

Take a look at Figure 4 for an overview of how the selector value (which is found in the segment register) is interpreted. The lowest 2 bits of the selector have nothing to do with the generation of the physical address. Instead, they play a part in the protection mechanism. This role is discussed later.

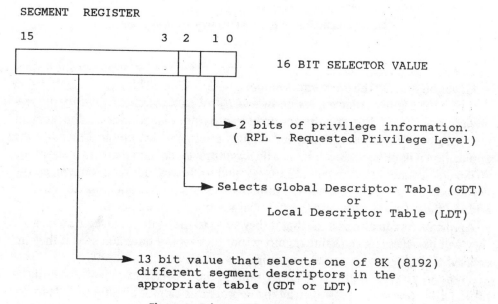

Figure 4. Selector Value Interpretation

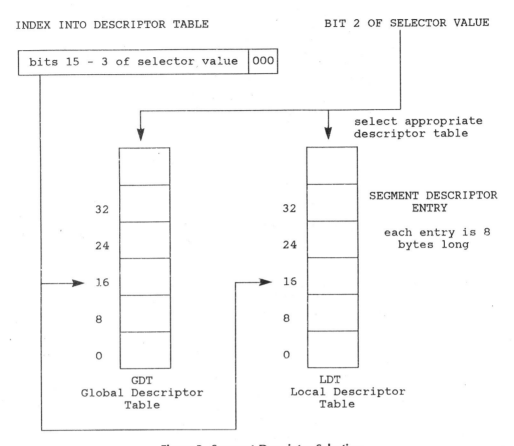

Figure 5. Segment Descriptor Selection

There are two different types of tables in the system that contain segment descriptors. They are the **Global Descriptor Table (GDT)** and the **Local Descriptor Table (LDT).** Bit 2 of the selector value determines which table is going to be accessed for the segment descriptor. Remember, the segment descriptor contains all the information that describes the physical memory that we are going after.

Figure 5 shows how the segment descriptor is chosen. After the correct table is chosen, bits 3–15 of the selector value select one of 8,192 different segment descriptors. Each descriptor is 8 bytes long.

The global descriptor table (GDT) usually contains segments that are used throughout the system, no matter which application is running. For example, the operating system code and data segment descriptors are usually found in the GDT. Sets of code that need to be protected from each other usually have their segment descriptors in different LDT tables. The operating system usually maintains a different LDT for each set of code that needs to keep its memory separate from other sets of code. In OS/2, each process has an LDT associated with it.

Take a look at Figure 6 to see what information about the segment is found in the segment descriptor. The information that we are interested in right now is the 24 bit physical base address. This 24 bit value determines where in physical memory

1) A 24 bit value which determines the base address of the physical segment. Allows access to 16 megabytes of real physical memory.

2) A 16 bit value which determines the size of the segment (up to 64 KB).

3) Whether the segment is currently present in physical memory.

4) Whether the selector value which corresponds to this segment descriptor was loaded into a segment register. Indicates that this segment was accessed.

5) Whether this is a code, data, or "special" (*) segment.

6) If code (executable instructions) segment then:
   - whether the processor may or may not read data from this segment.
   - whether this code segment is conforming (*).

7) If data segment then:
   - whether or not the processor may write into this segment.
   - whether the limit value corresponds to the segment growing up or down (*).

8) Privilege information (DPL - Descriptor Privilege Level).

(*) beyond the scope of this book

Figure 6. Information in a Segment Descriptor

the segment begins. The 16 bit offset value that makes up the other part of the address is added to the 24 bit physical address that we obtained from the segment descriptor to determine the final real (physical) address. Assuming that the segment grows up (instead of down, like a stack segment), if the offset exceeds the size of the segment, then the processor tried to access memory that is really not part of the segment. This produces an exception, which indicates that the program has made a mistake. There is also the potential for a protection exception when a program tries to access memory. The selector and the segment descriptor contain protection information.

This seems like a great deal of processing to have to do each time an address is accessed. If we go back to Figure 2, we can see what the segment descriptor cache registers are used for. The processor keeps the information (in the processor's local memory) for the current segment descriptors that are selected by the selector values currently in the segment registers. The processor does not need to access the GDT or LDT again unless a segment register is changed. This is why changing a segment register in protect mode is so costly in terms of performance. The processor also keeps the current value of the address and size of the GDT and LDT in its local memory.

Go back to the list of protect mode addressing features that are described at the beginning of this section. We can see how 16 megabytes of real memory are supported (instead of only 1 megabyte). We can see how different virtual address spaces are supported with different LDTs. The address that the program is using in the segment register has absolutely no correspondence to the real address that is being used.

Given the information presented in Figure 6, we can see how we would support virtual addresses that are not really in physical memory. If the segment is not really in memory, then the segment descriptor for that segment would say that it is not present. If the program loads a segment register with a selector value that corresponds to a segment that is not present, then the processor would get an exception condition for that operation. The processor would handle the exception with a special section of operating system code. This code would figure out where that segment is being stored on disk and then bring that segment into real memory and update the segment descriptor to show where the segment is in physical memory. If the processor needs to make room for the segment, then it might have to move some other segment out to disk. The segment that is moved out to disk is determined by the operating system, and it is usually the *least recently used* segment. The accessed information in the descriptor table helps the operating system determine which segments in the system are the least recently used.

Another important difference between real and protect mode is that in protect mode, segments have lengths associated with them. In real mode, all segments were 64 KB in length. In protect mode, programs allocate segments for just the size that they need. This helps conserve real memory and the virtual memory that is stored on disk. In addition, if a program makes a mistake and tries to access memory beyond the size of its segment, an exception is generated and the operating system knows that there is something wrong with that program.

We still have not completely covered the topic of memory protection. One of the key aspects of memory protection is privilege level, which is discussed in the next section.

Protection and Privilege

The 80286 has protection and privilege characteristics in protect mode. The real mode of the processor has no protection capabilities at all. This means that any program can access any physical memory (up to 1 megabyte) and can execute any processor instructions that are valid in real mode.

By having separate LDTs for each application, the operating system can ensure that each application is inherently protected from the other applications. Any selector value that an application generates cannot possibly get at a segment descriptor in an LDT that is not the current LDT.

By looking at Figure 6, we can see some of the protection mechanisms that are invoked whenever memory is accessed. Whenever a protection rule is violated, a processor **exception** is generated. This causes the processor to begin executing a special stream of instructions called an exception handler. It is a very similar situation to an interrupt, except that the processor did something to cause the exception while an interrupt is usually generated by a device. Generally, the operating system handles the exception. The processor is designed to usually allow the instruction that caused the exception to be retried after the exception condition has been removed.

The following are examples of operations that cause exceptions involving addressing problems of the program:

- The selector points to a segment descriptor beyond the current size of the descriptor table.
- The offset part of the address goes beyond the size of the segment.
- The privilege rules have been violated (to be discussed).
- CS (code segment register) was loaded with a selector value corresponding to a data segment descriptor. The processor is not allowed to execute instructions out of a data segment.
- The processor tries to write into a read only data segment.
- The processor tries to read from an execute only code segment.

In addition, if the processor tries to load a segment register with a selector that corresponds to a segment that is not present in memory, then an exception condition is created. This allows the operating system to find the segment on disk, bring it into real memory, change the segment descriptor to say that it is present at a given physical location, and resume execution at the instruction that caused the exception.

Without the concept of privilege, it would be very difficult to make much of this protection scheme useful. For example, a program knows that bit 2 of the selector value can be chosen to select the GDT. Since the GDT has many operating system segments, the program may try to use GDT selector values that it has no business using. How is the hardware set up to prevent programs from pulling stunts like that?

There are four levels of privilege in the 80286. They are numbered 0–3, with 0 being the most privileged and 3 being the least privileged. The operating system usually manages privilege. In OS/2, most applications run at privilege level 3, and the kernel of the operating system runs at privilege level 0. Applications that require I/O privilege (IOPL) can be written. We discuss IOPL later on in this section. In OS/2, when an application has IOPL, it is running at privilege level 2 and does not have all the OS/2 capabilities that it had at privilege level 3.

The basic concept behind privilege is that executing code can access data only at its privilege level or at less privileged levels. This prevents applications from accessing operating system data but allows the operating system to get at the application data that it needs. The privilege level of the code that is running is called the **current privilege level (CPL)** and is equivalent to the two low order bits of the CS segment register. The privilege level of the data that is being accessed is defined by two bits in the segment descriptor, called the **descriptor privilege level (DPL)**.

The execution environment can be set up in such a way that the application cannot play with its CPL. By giving the application a CPL of 3, the operating system can easily protect itself by giving all of its important data DPL values of 0. (In this example, 1 or 2 would work also.)

Normal Far Jumps and Calls can only be to code segments of equal privilege level. This prevents applications from directly calling operating system code segments. There are special segment descriptors called **gates** which are used to transfer control to different privilege levels and to change the current privilege level. Those details are beyond the scope of this book.

What is I/O privilege? The operating system can control which privilege levels are allowed to execute a certain set of instructions that are associated with I/O operations. Those instructions are as follows:

- Instructions that allow the processor to read data from or write data to the I/O address space.
- Instructions that disable and enable the ability of the processor to accept device interrupts.
- The LOCK (lock the bus) instruction (beyond the scope of this book).

These instructions have special privilege checks associated with them because they can do harm to the system if they are executed by an untrusted program. By explicitly requiring a program to ask for IOPL, the operating system can limit the scope of the set of application programs that may do harm to the system. The operating system can define the maximum value of CPL (the least trusted privilege level) that can have IOPL. On OS/2, the IOPL level is set to 2. General application programs run with a CPL of 3 so they cannot get IOPL. There is an API to allow applications to request IOPL. If the user sets up CONFIG.SYS a certain way, then those applications can get IOPL. There are restrictions on what applications can do in an OS/2 environment with IOPL. For example, applications cannot service device interrupts from an IOPL code segment. The preferred method for dealing with interrupt driven devices is via device drivers.

There are other instructions that may be executed only from privilege level 0 (CPL = 0), the most privileged level. These instructions do things like define how big and where the LDT and GDT are.

There are many instructions that are not available on the 8088 that are available on the 80286. Most of those instructions are also available in the real mode of the 80286. We have seen how rich the set of protection mechanisms are on the 80286.

Interrupt Handling

We have already discussed why devices need to generate interrupts. What we have left out is how it is determined what code gets control when the processor accepts the interrupt.

One possible interrupt that the system can get is called the **non-maskable inter-**

rupt (NMI). The processor cannot choose to ignore the NMI interrupt. It is generally used to tell the processor that something is very wrong with the system. A good example of this would be a memory failure.

There are fifteen possible hardware interrupt lines on the PC AT and the PS/2. They are handled by two interrupt controllers that are cascaded together. When OS/2 initializes the interrupt controllers, it chooses which interrupt numbers it will see for those fifteen possible hardware interrupt lines. The interrupt number that a given hardware interrupt line corresponds to is very important. It will determine which code gets control when the processor accepts the interrupt.

The interrupt controller manages the monitoring of the fifteen hardware interrupt lines. The interrupt controller is also responsible for managing the generation of the correct interrupt number in the processor. The interrupt controller will generate the appropriate interrupt number according to its interrupt priority rules. The processor can be disabled from accepting these kind of interrupts (external interrupts from the interrupt controller) at any given point in time by executing a disable interrupts instruction. The instructions to disable and enable processor interrupts require IOPL.

So how does the interrupt number correspond to what code gets control when an interrupt is accepted by the processor? To answer the question we need to introduce a new processor table called the **Interrupt Descriptor Table (IDT).** This table contains up to 256 entries that look very much like the segment descriptor entries we have already seen. The big difference is that they are "special" segment descriptors called **gates.** Each gate points to the appropriate interrupt handler for that interrupt number. Gates are beyond the scope of this book. However, when we were discussing code privilege, we mentioned that gates are used to allow the transfer of execution control from one privilege level to another.

The previous paragraph describes how the appropriate interrupt handler is chosen in protect mode. In real mode, the process of choosing the interrupt handler is very similar, except that a different kind of IDT is used. The IDT used in real mode has different size entries than the protect mode IDT. In addition, the real mode IDT entries are not gates. Instead, each entry in the real mode IDT is a real mode address, consisting of a 16 bit segment value and a 16 bit offset. This value corresponds to a real mode physical address, which will get control when the appropriate interrupt number is generated. The interrupt number corresponds to a given entry in the real mode IDT. Applications in the DOS environment of OS/2 should use DOS services to change the interrupt handler for a given interrupt number. They should not directly modify the real mode IDT.

The interrupt number causes the processor to transfer control to the code described by the IDT entry corresponding to the interrupt number. Stacks are used to make sure that the code that lost control can be resumed later on. There are many different types of gates that are used to accomplish different kinds of things. NMI interrupts cause an interrupt number of 2 to be generated.

Software can explicitly generate interrupts by executing the processor INT instruction. OS/2 does not support application usage of the INT instruction in protect mode. Exception conditions (like protection exceptions) also cause interrupts that the processor cannot disable. The operating system must handle the exception conditions.

The chapter on Interrupt Driven Device Management (Chapter 6) discusses how OS/2 or user installed device drivers can be set up to handle device interrupts. OS/2 manages the IDT and the initial handling of the interrupts. It is the responsibility of the device driver to manage the interrupt at the device and to reset the interrupt at the device and at the interrupt controller.

SUMMARY

We have covered a tremendous amount of material in this chapter. By now you should have a very good understanding of the general functions of OS/2 and a basic background in the way the 80286 works. It is time to start getting into the details of how to utilize some of the functions we have discussed. In the next chapter we discuss the memory capabilities of OS/2 and how programs can use that capability via the API.

2

OS/2 Memory Capabilities

WE HAVE DISCUSSED how the system memory plays a very important role in the operation of the computer system. The operating system's code and data as well as the user's applications' code and data reside in the system memory. The system microprocessor fetches the code from the system memory and executes it. During the execution of that code the microprocessor may also fetch data from the system memory.

One of the cornerstone advances that OS/2 provides (over DOS) is that it exploits the additional memory capabilities of the 80286 microprocessor. In the previous chapter we reviewed in detail how much more capability the 80286 has over the 8086 in the area of system memory utilization.

In summary, the 8086 addresses the real physical memory directly from the address that the application uses. The address used by the application is a direct representation of the physical address. 8086 addresses consist of a 16 bit segment and a 16 bit offset. The 16 bit segment defines a 64 KB segment in physical memory. The 16 bit offset defines which address within the 64 KB segment is to be used. Up to 1 MB of physical memory can be accessed directly with the 8086.

On the 80286, the address used by the application is not a direct representation of the physical address. This is why the address is called a virtual address. The address consists of a 16 bit selector and a 16 bit offset. The 16 bit selector is used to obtain a segment descriptor from a table in memory. This descriptor contains all the important information about the real physical memory segment, including such things as the following:

□ Where it is in physical memory (up to 16 MB of physical memory can be accessed), or information that the segment is not in physical memory.
□ How big it is (segments don't all have to be 64 KB in size).
□ Protection, privilege, and type of use (e.g., execute only) information.

43

MAJOR BENEFITS

As a result of exploiting the new memory capabilities of the 80286, OS/2 provides the following major functional advances:

- ☐ Supports systems with up to 16 MB of physical memory. With DOS, only 640 KB of memory is directly usable by applications. With OS/2, applications and the operating system can execute code and fetch data directly from up to 16 MB of physical memory. The area between 640 KB and 1 MB is still used by the system for BIOS and memory mapped I/O.
- ☐ Supports application usage of memory greater than 640 KB and memory greater than the physical memory in the system. Applications can be written to utilize more than 640 KB of memory. In addition, OS/2 provides support to allow segments of memory to be not present in physical memory. Instead, the segment is kept on disk and brought into memory when it is used. This is called memory overcommitment.
- ☐ Supports multiple application usage of memory greater than the physical memory in the system. In addition, different Local Descriptor Tables are used, allowing applications to be protected from one another.
- ☐ OS/2 itself uses the memory capabilities of the 80286. This allows the operating system to be protected from applications and also allows operating system code and data to take part in the memory overcommit characteristics of the system. OS/2 does not consume as much physical memory as it would require if all of OS/2 needed always to be present in physical memory.

OS/2 provides protection between different applications and between applications and the operating system. In addition, OS/2 allows the user to run an application or a group of applications that use a great deal of memory. More than 640 KB of memory and even more memory than can be physically found in the system can be utilized.

These large memory capabilities translate directly into substantial benefits for the user. Applications can do the following:

- ☐ Solve more sophisticated problems.
- ☐ Be easier to use.
- ☐ Provide more data handling capabilities.
- ☐ Provide more detailed visual feedback.

Applications can offer these benefits if they are not constrained by too little physical memory or too little system address space. But more importantly, the user can now run more than one application at a time without worrying about the system running out of physical memory. Complete subsystems and their applications can be in use without the need for every instruction and piece of data to be resident in physical memory.

As with everything else, there are performance and execution time tradeoffs that must be made. Applications need to be structured to minimize the movement of memory between the physical memory of the system and the disk. The user must provide enough physical memory to allow a reasonable response time for the desired execution environment.

MEMORY OVERCOMMITMENT

Support of physical memory of up to 16 MB is easy to understand. The segment descriptor arrangement explicitly allows a physical address of up to 16 MB to be generated.

However, when we say that more memory can be in use than actually physically exists in the system, what do we mean? When an address is used on the 80286, the segment descriptor may say that the segment is not present in memory. The address that exhibits this behavior looks like any other memory address used by the application or the operating system. It is just that when the microprocessor tries to determine where that address is in physical memory, it turns out that the address is not available in physical memory at that time. This causes the processor to generate a "not present" exception. The operating system must handle this exception and figure out where the memory segment is.

OS/2 keeps "not present" segments in the swap file, which resides on disk. OS/2 provides the memory overcommitment capability by utilizing three techniques:

- □ Segment swapping.
- □ Segment discard.
- □ Segment motion.

Segment swapping describes the movement of the memory segments between physical memory and the swap file on disk. A **least recently used (LRU)** algorithm is used to determine which segments are removed from physical memory. When a memory segment must be brought in from the disk, then physical memory must be made available for it. It may be necessary to remove a memory segment from physical memory in order to free up the space. OS/2 tries to avoid moving to disk those segments that are used frequently and recently. It is a good bet that those segments will be used again and soon. If a popular segment is moved out to disk, it will just have to be brought back into physical memory. This would generate unnecessary system overhead and affect system performance.

OS/2 also generates room in physical memory through **segment discard**. Segments that are code do not have to be moved out to disk. Instead, when they need to be removed from physical memory, they can be thrown away. When it comes time to use them again, they are brought back from their original location on disk. Certain data segments can also be discarded. When a data segment is created, it can be created as discardable. When the application is busily using the segment, it "locks" the segment so it won't be discarded. Applications that allow segments to be discarded help the operating system to more efficiently provide a memory overcommit environment.

Let's say a 64 KB segment needs to be swapped in from disk. There may not be 64 KB of contiguous physical memory available to move it to. This is where the **segment motion** capabilities of OS/2 become important. OS/2 moves segments around in memory to collect small areas of unused physically contiguous memory into one large area of unused physically contiguous memory.

We have included a memory overcommitment example program in Chapter 4. In this example, we show how a memory programming interface called DosAllocSeg is used. The program is designed so that the person running the program can specify the amount of memory to be allocated. In this way, you can experiment with allocating different amounts of memory and observe the differences this makes in the behavior of the system. We describe the different memory programming interfaces later on in this chapter.

MEMORY PROTECTION

Applications (processes) are protected from each other because they have different Local Descriptor Tables (LDTs). OS/2 creates a different LDT for each process in the system. The selector component of the memory address used by the application will index into a *specific* LDT for the segment descriptor. There is no way for one application to get the segment descriptor of a different application because it cannot cause the 80286 to access the other application's LDT. Therefore, applications cannot read or destroy a different application's memory.

Sometimes applications wish to share a portion of memory. This need arises when one application wishes to communicate with another by using a common piece of memory. OS/2 provides this capability through the memory application programming interface. Memory segments that are shareable can be created by an application. Certain kinds of memory segments that are shared are called **name-shared segments**. We explain these segments in the application programming interface section of this chapter.

OS/2 applications run at privilege level 3. OS/2 applications that have IOPL run at privilege level 2 while they have IOPL. OS/2 itself and the device drivers run at privilege level 0. Privilege level 0 is the level with the most privilege. The privilege level feature of the 80286 allows the operating system to be protected from applications. It also allows the operating system to require applications that wish to have IOPL to conform to special rules.

SYSTEM MEMORY CHARACTERISTICS

OS/2 maximizes the amount of memory available for the DOS execution environment by keeping only part of the resident portion of OS/2 below 640 KB. This resident portion of OS/2 is not swapped. In addition, all the device drivers in the system reside below 640 KB. The device drivers also are not swapped. The remainder of the area below 640 KB is available for the DOS execution environment.

An additional resident portion of OS/2 is found immediately above the 1 MB memory address. Besides the resident portions of OS/2, there is also a portion of OS/2 that is swappable, just like applications. This allows more efficient use of the system's physical memory.

SEGMENT PRELOAD VERSUS LOAD ON DEMAND

Application segments are defined as **preload** or **load on demand**. When a segment is preload, it is loaded into memory as soon as the application is started. This means that the segment will try to use physical memory, but it may be swapped out if there is not enough physical memory.

When a segment is characterized as load on demand, the segment is not loaded into memory until it is actually accessed by the application. A load on demand segment will not put a strain on the system memory resource until it is actually used. A load on demand segment may never take up physical memory or space on the swap file. Application segments that may not be used are good candidates to be set up as load on demand segments.

Usage of load on demand versus preload segments is an important mechanism that applications must consider in order to reduce the system overhead that they generate when they first are loaded and when they execute.

USER SETTABLE CHARACTERISTICS

The user has the ability to determine many of the system memory usage characteristics through parameters in the CONFIG.SYS file.

The user can remove the availability of physical memory from applications by setting up a virtual disk or by setting up a disk cache. The user must weigh the benefits of having a virtual disk or a disk cache versus the additional system overhead that will be generated when there is less physical memory in the system available for applications to use.

The user can disable all swapping and/or segment motion in the system. A user may want to do this for a special time-critical application environment where the application may not work properly if it has to wait for code or data to become available because memory is being swapped or moved.

The user can choose the size of the DOS execution environment to be smaller than the maximum that would be available if all the remaining memory below 640 KB were used for the DOS environment. The user may also choose not to have a DOS execution environment at all. Users who do not need to run any applications in the DOS execution environment should make sure that none is created. This will leave more physical memory available for the applications that the user cares about.

The user can decide where the swap file will reside. If there is the possibility that the swap file will grow and use up the whole disk, then the user may wish to put the swap file into a separate disk partition.

MODULE DEFINITION FILE SEGMENT CHARACTERISTICS

We describe the **Module Definition File** in the chapter on Advanced Programming Concepts (see Chapter 7). An application writer uses the Module Definition File to determine many of the segment characteristics that an application code or data segment needs to have. Some of those segment characteristics are as follows:

- Whether the segment is preload or load on demand.
- If it is a code segment, whether it is read as data and executed or just executed. If an execute only code segment is read, then an exception would be generated by the 80286.
- If it is a data segment, whether it is read from and written to or just read from. If a read only data segment is written to, then an exception would be generated by the 80286.

PERFORMANCE AND SYSTEM CONSIDERATIONS

As we discussed earlier, applications should be structured to reduce the amount of swapping and segment motion that they generate in the system. This can be done by structuring the code and data segments so that the most probably used code and data are grouped together in common segments. The least probably used code and data (e.g., user help or error processing) should be grouped in separate segments.

The segments should then be defined as preload or load on demand depending on how likely they are to be used and their usage performance requirements.

It is also important for the application writer to consider the size of the segments. Larger segments are good for data and code that will be used frequently. But the larger the segment, the more system overhead is generated when it is moved or swapped, and the more physical memory it takes up. Mixing frequently and infrequently used code or data in the same segment is undesirable and wastes the system's physical memory.

Applications should be structured to trade off the following:

- Segment sizes.
- Number of segments.
- Number of segments that would need to be present in physical memory during normal application processing.
- Amount of swapping that would occur during a memory overcommit situation.

It is very important for the application writer to consider that the user will have other applications present in the system at the same time. The application writer should not try to optimize the application's segment structure for a one-application environment. For example, all the application's segments should not be made preload in order to make the application run faster (if the system had enough physical memory to run the one application). Instead, the application writer must structure the application to behave well in a multiple application environment. The user will appreciate applications that work well together in a multiple application environment. Conversely, the user will not use an application that causes unnecessary performance problems for the rest of the system.

MEMORY PROGRAMMING INTERFACES

You do not need to be application writers in order to want to understand the memory capabilities of OS/2. In fact, you need to understand these capabilities in order to be sure that you can do the following:

- □ Set up your systems properly (through CONFIG.SYS).
- □ Understand how the amount of physical memory you have affects the system performance you will observe with a given set of application programs.

If you use a high level language to write a simple application, you would not necessarily have to explicitly use any of the OS/2 memory programming interfaces. However, by reviewing the capabilities that the OS/2 memory API provides, you will gain a much better insight into how OS/2 applications can exploit these large memory capabilities.

In discussing the memory programming interfaces, we use the term "process." For now, think of a process as an application. It is a program entity in OS/2 that owns system resources. One of those resources is the right to access a memory segment. An application can consist of one process or many processes.

Capabilities of the Memory Programming Interfaces

Of course, OS/2 allows processes to allocate segments of memory. When a segment is allocated using the API, a 16 bit selector is returned to the process. The process uses the selector value to access the segment of memory. The process can create memory segments of any size up to 64 KB. It can also change the size of the memory segment if it wishes to, which allows the process to make more efficient use of system memory. In addition, the process can tell OS/2 that it doesn't want to use the memory segment anymore. This allows OS/2 to free up that particular LDT entry and stop swapping the memory segment.

Processes can create memory segments that can be shared with other processes. One method of doing this causes the shared memory segment to be given a "name." This name is then used by the other process to gain addressability to the segment. Another method allows a process to explicitly enable a different process to ask to use the shared memory segment without the use of a logical name to identify it.

Processes can create memory segments that are discardable by OS/2. When the process wishes to use the segment, it explicitly tells OS/2 that it cannot discard the memory segment at this time (lock the memory segment). Then, when the process doesn't need the segment for a while, it tells OS/2 that the segment is now discardable (unlock the memory segment). If OS/2 needs to create room in physical memory it may discard the memory segment. When the process needs to use the memory segment again, it tells OS/2 that it is now not discardable (lock). If OS/2 has already discarded the memory segment, then the process is told (via the return from the lock function) and the process needs to recreate the memory segment. Even though this discard technique appears to be extra work, it can be very useful for processes that require lots of temporary memory and don't want to burden the system with all the swapping overhead that that memory would require when it is not in use.

One of the interesting aspects of the way DOS programs access memory is that the physical address corresponds directly to the 16 bit segment address that the process uses. This allows processes that need more than 64 KB of memory to address a large data structure by moving through the entire data space without having to look up new segment base addresses. OS/2 provides a way for applications to allocate multiple 64 KB segments that all have selector values derived from the previous selector value. The next selector is derived by adding a fixed value to the current selector. This allows an application to request a large (bigger than 64 KB) memory area and access the whole area directly just by knowing the value of the selector of the first memory segment that describes the large memory area.

OS/2 provides a way for a process to create a code selector for a data area. With this code selector, a process can execute code that is also considered data and that might have been written to by a process.

There may be cases where a process needs many little pieces of memory. If the process creates separate memory segments for each few bytes of memory that it needs, then a great deal of unnecessary system overhead is generated. OS/2 provides a mechanism that processes use to carve up a segment of memory into many smaller pieces. OS/2 then keeps track of which memory is currently unused within the single memory segment. The process makes requests for small pieces of memory within the memory segment, and OS/2 returns the correct offset into the memory segment that the process should use. This feature of OS/2 is called the **Memory Suballocation Package,** and it is provided as a set of dynamic link routines.

Managing Memory Segments

OS/2's programming interface provides a mechanism to create, change the size of, and free up memory segments. A data segment can be turned into an executable code segment.

DosAllocSeg Creates a memory segment of any size up to 64 KB. The interface returns the 16 bit selector value that the process uses to access the memory segment just created by the system. The new memory segment is movable and swappable.

The process may request that the created segment be given the following characteristics:

- ◻ The segment may be shared by means of the current process giving access to this segment to another process. See DosGiveSeg.
- ◻ The segment may be shared by means of a different process getting access to this segment. See DosGetSeg.
- ◻ The segment is discardable. This could happen if the system has a low memory situation. The process must explicitly tell the system when it is using and finished using this segment. DosLockSeg and DosUnlockSeg indicate use of the segment. When the segment is first created it is considered "locked" and the application may use it. If this characteristic is not requested, then the segment is not discardable.

DosReallocSeg Changes the size of a memory segment that is already created by passing the selector of the segment and the new size desired to the interface. If the segment is shared, then the size of the segment may only be increased. If the segment was created as discardable, then this system request also performs the same function as DosLockSeg.

DosFreeSeg Allows a process to free up a memory segment that it previously created or obtained access to. If the memory segment is shared, then the memory segment will be deallocated (freed) only after all processes that obtained access to or created the segment have issued this system request.

DosLockSeg A process may make a segment discardable when it creates the segment. If it does, then each time it wishes to use the segment (except after the segment is first created) it must use this programming interface. Use of this interface tells the operating system that the application will now use the segment, and the system may not discard the segment at this time. If this call fails, then the process knows that the segment was discarded and it must recreate the segment with DosAllocSeg.

DosUnlockSeg tells the system that it is permissible to discard the segment. DosLockSeg and DosUnlockSeg calls can be nested. In other words, if N DosLockSeg calls are issued, then N DosUnlockSeg calls must be issued before the system will be able to discard the segment.

The system can still move or swap a segment that is locked.

DosUnlockSeg Tells the system that a locked discardable memory segment is now available for discarding. Segment discard is a way that processes can allow the system to make better use of the available physical memory. For example, if the process is using a great deal of temporary memory, then this is a useful technique that it can use to lessen the impact of the use of all that memory.

DosCreateCSAlias Creates a valid Code Segment selector from a DS, ES, or SS data segment selector. The segment must be exclusively owned by the process (not shareable) and may not be part of a large chunk of memory allocated by DosAllocHuge. A process loads a valid section of executable code into a data segment and uses this system call to make it possible for the process to call this memory segment as a code segment.

Sharing Memory Segments

The programming interface allows the process that created the memory segment to share access to it with other processes in the system.

DosGiveSeg Allows the process that created the memory segment to enable another process to access the same memory segment. For the DosGiveSeg request to work properly, the process explicitly tells the system that it is going to do this when the segment is created.

The process that created the segment with DosAllocSeg passes the segment's selector and the Process ID (see next chapter) of the desired sharer of the segment to the system. The system returns the segment selector that the other process should use to access the same memory segment. The caller passes this selector to the other process by using some form of interprocess communications.

DosGetSeg Gets access to a memory segment created by another process. The process that created the memory segment must enable another process to gain access to the segment via this system interface. The other process passes the selector of the desired memory segment to this system interface, and the system enables that other process to access the memory segment.

Name-Shared Segments

Logical names can be given to memory segments when they are created. This allows other processes in the system to gain access to the created memory segment by knowing the name of the memory segment.

DosAllocShrSeg Creates a memory segment of any size up to 64 KB that is identified with a name. The process passes the size and the name to the interface. The selector that the process should use to access the memory segment is returned to the caller.

The name that the process wishes to give to the segment has the same format as an OS/2 file name. The name must be in the subdirectory \sharemem\, so all names start with the character string \sharemem\. The DosGetShrSeg system interface allows another process to get access to the same memory segment by using the name that the creator gave to the segment.

DosGetShrSeg Gets access to a memory segment that was created with the DosAlloc-ShrSeg system function. All the process needs to know is the name that was given to the memory segment when it was created. The process passes the name of the memory segment to the system and gets back the selector to use for access.

Managing Huge Memory Segments

If you require a memory area greater than 64 KB, you should consider this feature of the application programming interface.

DosAllocHuge Allocates a chunk of memory that is bigger than the maximum size of a memory segment (64 KB). The process tells the system how many 64 KB segments it wants and how big it wants the last segment to be (up to 64 KB). The process also tells the system the maximum size it would ever want this chunk of memory to reach. The system returns the selector value of the first memory segment of this large chunk of memory. The process uses DosGetHugeShift to figure out the selectors that correspond to the following memory segments in the large chunk of memory.

Look at the example in Figure 7. The process asks for a memory area of 140 KB. Selector value "1024," which points to a 64 KB segment, is returned. By issuing the DosGetHugeShift call, the process discovers that it needs to add 8 to the first selector value (1024) to get the value of the selector (1032) that points to the second 64 KB of memory in the 140 KB memory area. By adding 8 to 1032, the value of

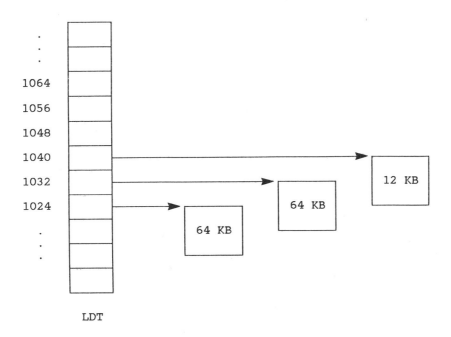

Figure 7. Allocating "Huge" 140 KB of Memory

the third selector value (1040) is computed. The third selector points to a memory segment that contains 12 KB. The three segments add up to 140 KB of memory.

Memory allocated this way can be enabled for DosGiveSeg, DosGetSeg, and segment discarding. The only difference between this and memory allocated with DosAllocSeg is that only the first selector value is used with the appropriate calls, and the function (e.g., DosGiveSeg) is done for the entire large chunk of memory.

DosGetHugeShift Obtains the value that must be added to the first selector that is returned due to a call to DosAllocHuge. By adding this value to the first selector, the second selector that the process should use to access the second 64 KB of memory is determined. Each subsequent selector is computed the same way.

DosReallocHuge Changes the size of a large chunk of memory that was originally allocated by DosAllocHuge. The size can be increased only to the maximum limit set in the original DosAllocHuge call.

Memory Suballocation Package

OS/2 provides a set of programming interfaces that the processes use to allocate small pieces of memory out of a single segment of memory. This feature is important because it is very inefficient to create a new memory segment for each little piece of memory a process requires.

DosSubSet Tells the system to prepare a segment of memory for the memory suballocation package to use. This interface must also be used if the size of the memory is increased with DosReallocSeg. The memory suballocation package uses memory segments created with DosAllocSeg or DosAllocShrSeg.

DosSubAlloc Allocates a block of memory within a memory segment that has already been created and initialized with DosSubSet. The process passes the size of the desired block and the selector of the memory segment to the programming interface. On return, the offset of the block (within the memory segment) is given to the process.

The largest block that may be allocated is 8 bytes less than the size of the memory segment. All blocks are allocated in multiples of 4 bytes.

DosSubFree Frees up a block of memory that was allocated by DosSubAlloc. The selector of the memory segment, the size of the block, and the offset of the block within the segment is passed to the programming interface. If the information is not consistent with the layout of the block within the memory segment, the system generates an error.

DEVICE RELATED MEMORY MANAGEMENT CAPABILITIES

In the introduction, we discussed memory mapped I/O devices and DMA driven devices. The memory management application programming interface that we have covered in this chapter does not contain enough function to support these devices. The function covered does not allow an application to request access to a specific physical address. While an application can create and access memory segments, none of the function that we have covered allows the application to tell the system to place that memory or allows access to system memory at a specific physical address.

Memory Mapped I/O Devices

In order to use these I/O devices, an application must be able to gain access to physical memory at a specific physical address. Chapter 6, which discusses Interrupt-Driven Device Management, covers how a device driver can create memory selectors that the application can then use to access the physical memory on the I/O device.

DMA Devices

Devices that use DMA to move data to or from system memory always require the physical memory address of the system memory. But, as we have discussed, the application is not aware of the physical address of the memory segment that it is using for a data buffer. Chapter 6 explains how a device driver gets addressability to this physical memory.

3

Multitasking and Multiple Applications

IN THE LAST CHAPTER, we explored how OS/2 provides sufficient memory space for almost any imaginable workstation application or set of applications. Another major advancement of OS/2 over DOS is the ability for applications to have multitasking capabilities and for the user to employ more than one application at the same time.

Only one application can be run at a time in the world of DOS. This means that the user must complete all the processing required for program A before program B can be run. Why is it important to be able to run more than one application at a time?

If we were going to do some chores around the house under the rules of only one activity at a time, then our day would go by very inefficiently. We would load up all the dishes in the dishwasher and then start up the dishwasher. Unfortunately, we could not do anything else until the dishwasher finished. Then we would put all the dishes away. We would then load up the washing machine with dirty clothes. After waiting for the wash to finish, we would then load up the dryer and run the dryer. If we had any more clothes to wash, we couldn't do anything about it until the dryer finished. We would then wash some more clothes. Not a very good use of our time. If we could run the dishwasher, washing machine, and dryer all at the same time, then the total elapsed time would be much less and we could get to other work that needs to be done.

The same holds true for workstation users. A user might wish to run a few programs that do not require very much interaction but take a long time to finish. Following are a few examples of programs with these characteristics:

- Large spreadsheet calculation.
- Compiling a program.

□ Obtaining data via a communications link.
□ Printing a file.

While all these activities are going on, the user may wish to employ a program that requires a great deal of interaction, such as a text editor or word processor. By overlapping all these activities, the user can increase productivity significantly. The elapsed time of running many programs in parallel is usually not equal to the sum of the times that it would take to run the applications separately. This is because most applications do not need to use the processor 100 percent of the time. Usually the application needs to wait for data to be read in or written out to an input/output device. While the application is waiting for this activity to take place, the system processor can accomplish other useful work. OS/2's multitasking and multiple application support is based on making the most efficient use of the system processor. The operating system will continuously try to find useful work for the processor to do.

Under DOS, the potential of the system processor to perform useful work is limited because the DOS environment forces the system processor to "wait" for input/output operations to complete before it can process the next piece of work. The system processor does not literally enter a "wait" state. Instead, it continuously asks whether the input/output operation is complete until the answer is yes. This kind of operation is also known as a **spin loop**.

Sometimes, keeping multiple copies of the same application active can be very useful. Users may wish to have multiple copies of a text editor active so that different notepads can be active on different subjects. By having multiple instances of the same application active, the user does not need to go through the process of saving one file and bringing in another. It is essential that the method for switching from one application to another be very quick and easy.

We can easily understand the benefit of having the ability to run more than one application at the same time. But what about multitasking? OS/2 uses its general multitasking support to enable the multiple application environment. The need for multitasking is there even for a single application.

Multitasking support allows an application to do more than one thing at a time. Because there is only one processor in the system, the application is not really doing more than one thing at a time. However, the system uses the processor in a manner that gives the appearance of more than one thing happening at a time.

In a DOS system, an application can do only one task at a time. A task can be thought of as a piece of work that needs to be done by the processor. Applications must do their tasks **synchronously**. This means that each task must follow a previous task. For example, after asking to read a disk file, a DOS application cannot do anything else until the read completes and the data is read into memory from the disk. A DOS application might ask the system whether there are any characters from the keyboard to read. This is called **polling**. The reason for this is that after the application reads the keyboard, if there are no characters to read, the application becomes stuck waiting for keyboard input.

In a multitasking environment, an application does not have to execute tasks one at a time or synchronously. Instead, the application can have more than one task active at a time. It can have one task reading the keyboard and another task reading data from the disk. While data from the disk is still waiting to be read in, the application can be using the processor to get input from the keyboard and do whatever else is needed. Because the timing relationship between all the tasks is not known at every point in time, the tasks are said to be executing **asynchronously**.

Because of the complex nature of the multitasking environment, the system provides many services to ensure that an application or set of applications can be written properly. For example, the tasks in the application must be able to do the following:

- Start, stop, and control tasks.
- Communicate with each other.
- Synchronize activities.
- Serialize use of system resources.

Without these capabilities, the multitasking environment would be chaotic, and it would not be possible to accomplish any useful work. In this chapter, we explore the way the OS/2 application programming interface supports a multitasking environment.

The term "task" is not used in the OS/2 environment. Instead, the following three terms are used to describe the entities of work that apply to the OS/2 multitasking and multiple application environment:

- Session.
- Process.
- Thread.

We describe the multitasking capabilities of OS/2 from the perspective of sessions, processes, and threads.

MULTIPLE APPLICATIONS

From the user's perspective, an application generally consists of a program that reads keyboard and/or mouse input, displays data on the screen, and does data processing. In OS/2 terminology, this is called a **session**.

The application that is currently receiving keyboard input and displaying data on the screen is called the **foreground** session. The rest of the programs in the OS/2 system are called **background** sessions. OS/2 sessions that are in the background still receive processor time and continue to execute. A background session is still able to do everything that a foreground session does. The only difference is that the user can communicate only with one session at a time: the foreground session.

It doesn't make much sense to allow every program running in the system to write to the screen at the same time. If every program in the system received the same keyboard input every time the user typed a keystroke, then the system wouldn't work very well. When a background session tries to write data to the screen, the data is placed in a section of system memory that is a logical representation of the screen.

The data is not actually placed on the screen. This memory area is called a **logical video buffer**. When a session is placed in the foreground, the logical video buffer that belongs to that session is placed on the screen. The previous image on the screen is saved as the logical video buffer of the previous session. Likewise, when the user types on the keyboard or moves the mouse, the data goes only to the foreground session. The background sessions think that the keyboard and/or mouse is unused.

The DOS execution environment gets processor time only when it is the foreground session. When the DOS execution environment becomes a background session, it does not receive any processor time and is essentially frozen until it is brought back into the foreground. This is because applications in the DOS execution environment are "ill behaved." For example, a DOS application in a background session might write directly to the physical screen, writing over the user viewable screen that belongs to the foreground session.

Multiple Sessions—A User's Perspective

How is the session concept translated to what the user can control? The OS/2 **Program Selector** and **session manager** accomplish this task.

The Program Selector provides a full screen menu that allows the user to do the following:

- Select from a list of programs to start.
- Start a command processor.
- Switch the screen to a program that has already been started.

The user's choice becomes the foreground session. The user can also add (or delete) new programs to the list of programs that can be started.

If a DOS execution environment is provided as part of the system configuration, then the user can choose that environment from the list of programs that have already been started. If the user does select the DOS environment, the screen comes up with the DOS prompt and the DOS command processor (COMMAND.COM) active. The user can also choose the OS/2 command prompt from the list of possible programs to be started. When chosen, the OS/2 command prompt is displayed and the OS/2 command processor (CMD.EXE) is active in the current foreground session. OS/2 programs can be started from the OS/2 command prompt, just as a DOS application can be started from the DOS command prompt. The user can set up a special file called a **batch file** which contains a sequence of commands normally entered at the command prompt. This allows a complicated sequence of commands to be set up in advance for a less sophisticated workstation operator.

The session manager provides a key sequence so the user can switch to the next session (running program). A different key sequence allows the user to immediately select the Program Selector menu. With this capability, the user easily changes which program he or she interacts with. It is also very easy for the user to start up new programs or directly choose which session is to become the foreground session.

The power of the session manager would be limited if user interaction were the only way for the session manager to be invoked. The next section describes the OS/2 session manager programming interface. This interface allows a program running in a session to start and control another session. This powerful OS/2 feature can be used to automatically start new sessions for the user and control which sessions appear to the user as the foreground session.

Session Programming Interfaces

DosStartSession Creates and starts a new program in a different session. The new program interacts with the user totally independently of the program that started it.

The caller specifies the title of the program, the "fully qualified" name of the program to be started (program name), and any "input arguments" that need to be passed to the new program. The title of the program appears on the full screen menu of already started programs that is part of the Program Selector. The program name contains the drive letter and directory path of the program as well as the name of the file that contains the program. The input arguments are the set of input parameters that are passed to a program when it is started in an OS/2 execution environment. The started program defines input parameters that tell it how to operate when it is invoked.

In addition, this interface is used to start the OS/2 command processor as the program name (CMD.EXE) to be started in another session. The input arguments are the application that the OS/2 command processor should start. The command processor is set up either to terminate the session when the application completes or to leave the session running with the command processor prompt when the application completes. Of course, by making the program name the application to be started, the application is started without using the OS/2 command processor.

If the program issuing the DosStartSession request is in the foreground session, then it can request that the program it is starting be made the foreground session. Otherwise, the program that is started must be a new background session.

The new program can be started as a totally independent entity from the program that started it. However, the caller can request that a parent/child relationship be established between the caller's session and the new program's session. The caller becomes the parent session and the new program becomes the child session. This parent/child relationship should not be confused with the process parent/child relationship that is discussed with the DosExecPgm programming interface. By making the new session its child, the parent session can control the child session with the other session manager programming interfaces. The parent session may control only its direct child sessions. It may not control the descendants of its child sessions (i.e., any sessions started by its child sessions). If a parent session is terminated, then all its child sessions are also terminated.

If the caller establishes a parent/child relationship, then the Session ID of the child returns to the parent. This ID is used in the other session manager programming interface calls. In addition, the caller can set up an area of memory for determining when the child session ends and what the return code from that session was. The OS/2 queuing mechanism accomplishes this. We discuss the OS/2 queuing functions later on in this chapter.

DosSelectSession A parent session makes one of its child sessions the foreground session. This happens only if the parent session or one of its descendants is currently the foreground session. The parent uses the Session ID to identify the child session that it wishes to become the foreground session. With this interface, the session that the user is currently interacting with can be controlled automatically.

The caller may also request that its own session be made the foreground session. The action will take place if one of its descendants is currently the foreground session.

DosSetSession A parent session can set some characteristics of a child session. The parent uses the Session ID of the child to identify the child session.

The parent session can make a child session selectable or nonselectable by the user from the Program Selector menu. The child session can still be set to the foreground session through the use of DosSelectSession.

The parent session can bind one child session to itself. This means that if the user selects the parent session, the child session will automatically become the foreground session. Only one child can be bound to the parent session at a time. This binding affects selections made by the user but does not affect selections made through DosSelectSession. The parent session can also unbind the child session.

DosStopSession A parent session can terminate a specific child session by using the appropriate Session ID, or it can terminate all its descendants. Even if this function request completes, the caller cannot assume that the child session has terminated until it receives notification through the queueing mechanism that it set up when the child session was started with DosStartSession.

PROCESSES AND THREADS

One of the responsibilities of OS/2 is to manage the use of system resources. We now know that access to the keyboard and the screen is managed as a session. The foreground session owns the physical screen and keyboard.

There are many other kinds of resources in the system. Access to a given memory segment or a file (by using a file handle) are examples of system resources. A process owns a local descriptor table (LDT) that allows it to access all the memory resource that the process owns. A process also has a set of files, pipes, queues, and system semaphores associated with it. The entity that owns system resources in OS/2 is called a **process**.

An application is started as a process within a session. For example, the command processor allows a user to start an application from the command line of a session. The reason why an application is not synonymous with a process is that the original process that makes up the application can start additional processes that are also part of the application. All the processes of the application may share the same keyboard and display because they are in the same session. However, they cannot share the same memory (except if explicitly enabled through shared memory segments), nor would they necessarily share access to the same files. This separation of system resource ownership implies that a well-defined barrier exists between processes.

This "wall" between the processes can be very useful for large and complex applications. The wall, which is really the concept of system resource ownership, allows the design of the application to be broken down into smaller pieces that can interact with each other only in some very well-defined ways.

Different processes provide a mechanism to enhance the integrity of the different pieces of the application. One process does not automatically get the ability to alter the contents of another process's data or files. This can be useful in protecting sensitive data from different pieces of the same application. The operating system keeps track of the system resources that a process owns and helps recover the system resources if the process does not gracefully end.

The OS/2 process allows large complex applications to be broken down into smaller pieces that can affect each other only in well-defined ways. By designing the application as separate processes, we can reduce the overall complexity of the application. Different people or groups could implement the different processes with a very clear design of how they would interact. The OS/2 process architecture drives this clear design.

The wall between the different processes requires explicit mechanisms to enable the processes to interact with one another. This interaction is called **interprocess communications** and is covered in this chapter. We already know how different processes can share access to the same memory segment. Processes that interact with each other through these mechanisms do not necessarily have to be part of the same application.

A process also owns "units of execution." A unit of execution is called a **thread**. It can be thought of as a series of program instructions that are executed one after the other. We can equate an application in the DOS environment to a single thread of execution because the entire program executes synchronously from beginning to end. In the DOS environment, there can never be two sets of program instructions being executed "at the same time" or asynchronously. In OS/2, all the sets of program instructions that execute independently of one another (asynchronously) are called threads.

A process is made up of at least one thread but can consist of many threads. All the threads of a process equally share the system resources owned by that process. For example, two threads of the same process have access to the same memory segments, and there is no way for one thread to remove the ability of the other thread to access those segments. When a process consists of multiple threads, those threads are considered "tightly coupled" because they must cooperate very closely. If they do not cooperate, then they will end up stepping on each other and changing the same system resource without being aware of what the other threads are doing.

When two threads are executing asynchronously to each other, it means that each thread does not know what the other thread is currently doing. For example, one thread of a process could be reading from the keyboard and writing to the display and another thread of the same process could be reading from a file and writing to the display. The ability to have multiple threads of execution is very valuable because it allows a process to continue doing useful work even though it may also be waiting for another part of the system to complete a request. Even if the file I/O takes a long time to complete, the user will still see the application respond to the keyboard input. The only complication in this example is that both threads are updating the screen. If each thread goes to a different portion of the screen, there is no problem. If they both update the same portion of the screen, then the two threads must, at certain well-defined points in their execution, synchronize their actions with one another.

Even though a process is the entity in OS/2 that owns system resources, the system still needs to keep track of certain things on a per thread basis:

- Thread ID. As each thread of the process is created, it receives a unique Thread ID. This Thread ID is used by other threads in the process to identify a specific thread in their process.
- Stack. Each thread of the process requires a separate save area for its registers.
- Processor registers (if not currently executing). Each thread of the process has a separate set of processor registers that must be kept track of.
- Dispatch state. For each thread, the OS/2 scheduler needs to know whether the thread can be executed or whether the thread is currently waiting for something in the system to happen before it can execute.
- Priority (to be discussed). Each thread has a unique priority associated with it.

OS/2 requires these items in order to manage different units of execution (threads).

It is less costly for a process to start a new thread than it is to start a new process. A new thread is just a new unit of execution within the same process environment. Basically, the new thread requires the creation of a small thread environment. On the other hand, a new process needs the creation of a new process environment, including a new local descriptor table (LDT) and a new set of file handles.

The structure of an application that consists of a single process and multiple threads is such that there are multiple units of execution that all execute asynchronously. All these separate units of execution equally share the same system resources, such as access to memory segments or file handles. The structure of an application that consists of multiple processes is the same as the previous example except that the separate units of execution have separate sets of system resources and cannot access each other's system resources (e.g., memory segments or files) unless specifically enabled.

Chapter 4 contains two programming examples illustrating processes and threads. The first example shows a simple thread model using a RAM semaphore and some of the semaphore programming interfaces to signal an event and synchronize the execution of the threads. The second example builds upon this thread model by introducing a separate process. In this example, the pipe interprocess communications mechanism is demonstrated by passing data between the processes. We describe the various programming interfaces related to processes and threads later on in this chapter.

Process Programming Interfaces

In OS/2, a program is started as a new process. When a new program is started, it is passed an **environment segment** that it uses to figure out what it should be doing. The environment segment is similar to the Program Segment Prefix (PSP), which is what is passed to a DOS program on startup.

A process uses DosExecPgm to create and start a new process. When a new process is created, it is passed a set of **argument strings** and **environment strings** which are part of the environment segment. The created process determines what the structure of the environment segment should be. The creator process determines the contents of the environment segment. The OS/2 command processor will always pass the program name and whatever is entered on the command line by the user to the created program as argument strings. The user can set up the environment strings through the SET environment variables command. An application program can set up a convention that if the user sets an agreed upon environment variable, then the program will act a certain way. OS/2 maintains certain environment variables that the user can change. For example, the PATH environment string determines the file paths that are searched for executable files.

When one process creates another process, then the creator process is called the parent process and the created process is called the child process. The parent/child relationship between processes should not be confused with the parent/child relationship between sessions.

A child process **inherits** certain characteristics of its parent process. For example:

- Handles to
    files.
    pipes.
    standard devices (e.g., input and output).
    character devices.
- Environment segment.
- Priority.
- Session.

Because a child process will inherit the standard input and output file handles, and the parent can control where those file handles really point to, the parent process can control where a child process sends its input and output (assuming it uses the appropriate file handles). The system uses this implication of inheritance to orchestrate **redirection**. For example, the user can start an application via the command processor that receives its input from a given file and then cause the output of the application to go to another given file or to another application.

A process can control another process by creating it and its environment segment, terminating it, changing its priority, controlling its inheritance to handles, and interacting with it via the OS/2 interprocess mechanisms.

A process can set up a section of program code that is executed when the process terminates. This is called an exitlist routine. A process uses this ability to determine how its system resources are cleaned up before the system terminates it. A dynamic link library uses this ability to clean up any resources that it uses on behalf of the application process.

A process can have several exitlist routines registered to execute when it terminates. There are restrictions on what an exitlist routine can do. For example, an exitlist routine cannot start other programs, and it must terminate as quickly as possible.

DosExecPgm   A program is created and started as a child process. The parent process identifies the file containing the program as either a fully qualified (contains entire drive:directory path) file name or just a file name. If it is not a fully qualified file name, then the current environment string for PATH will be searched until the appropriate file name that contains the program is found. The program name is also passed to the child process.

A new process environment is created for the child process. As discussed above, the child process inherits certain characteristics from its parent process. The parent process controls the inheritance of some of those characteristics. If the parent process wants to control the environment segment that the child inherits, then it gives the child process a pointer to a set of argument strings and a pointer to a set of environment strings (environment segment).

The parent process controls how the child process executes with respect to the parent. For **synchronous** execution, the thread of the parent process will not continue executing from the point of the DosExecPgm function call until the child process completes. The termination code and the result code of the child process are returned to the parent process. The child process specifies the result code when it completes. The termination code tells the parent process whether the child process completed normally, abnormally, or was prematurely terminated by another process.

For **asynchronous** execution, the thread of the parent process continues to execute "at the same time" that the child process executes. When the DosExecPgm call completes, the Process ID of the child process is returned to the parent and the thread of the parent process continues to execute while the child process is executing. The parent uses the Process ID of the child to identify it when controlling the child with the programming interface. If the parent process wants the result code of the child, then it requests that it be made available for return by way of the DosCwait programming interface.

DosCwait A thread of the parent process waits for the completion of a child process. The child process needs to be started asynchronously with DosExecPgm, with the option to return status to DosCwait.

The parent thread chooses between waiting until the child process completes or continuing to execute if no completion status is available at the time of the call to DosCwait.

The parent chooses to wait for a specific child process or any child process. In addition, the parent can also wait for the descendants of a child process to complete.

The result code and termination code of the completed child process are returned to the parent process.

DosKillProcess A process can terminate a child process or a child process and all of its descendants.

DosKillProcess generates a SIGTERM signal to the process(es) that is being terminated. A process can choose to set up a SIGTERM signal handler that takes control when another process tries to terminate it with DosKillProcess. We discuss signal handling later on in this chapter.

DosExit Allows a thread to terminate itself. The thread can also request that all the threads in its process be terminated in order to terminate the process. When a process wants to terminate, even if it thinks there is only one thread active, it should issue a DosExit call requesting that all the threads of the process be terminated. This will terminate any threads that the operating system started on behalf of the process that the process does not know about. When the process is terminated, any exitlist routines registered with the DosExitList function call are executed.

DosExitList Allows a process to register sections of code that are invoked when the process terminates. These exitlist routines can free up resources that may be required by other processes. For example, a process may own a system resource when it is abnormally terminated. A process exitlist routine is then invoked and can release this system resource so other processes can use it. Otherwise, a deadlock can occur. Using this mechanism, the resource does not force other processes to wait forever for it to become available.

In addition, an exitlist routine uses DosExitList to invoke other exitlist routines that are registered for the same process. Each exitlist routine must complete its activity as quickly as possible. Otherwise, the process cannot be completely terminated by the operating system.

Thread Programming Interfaces

A thread can create and start up other threads within the same process. A thread in a process can suspend or resume another specific thread within the same process. A thread can also prevent other threads in its process from executing during a critical section of its execution.

DosCreateThread A thread can create and start a new thread that belongs to the same process. The new thread executes asynchronously to the current thread of execution. The Thread ID of the new thread is returned to the caller.

The caller passes a pointer to the code that will receive control via a far jump to start the execution of the new thread. The caller also passes a pointer to the new thread's stack. The operating system sets up the processor registers and creates and starts the new thread at the caller's priority.

DosSuspendThread The caller suspends another thread within the same process by specifying that particular Thread ID. The suspended thread will not execute any more application instructions, but it may execute a little while longer if it is currently executing within the system and holds a system resource.

DosResumeThread The caller restarts a previously suspended thread (of the same process) by specifying the appropriate Thread ID.

DosEnterCritSec Allows a thread to prevent any other threads in its process from executing. A count is maintained of the number of times that this call is made (16 bit value). It can be done to ensure that no other threads in the process access a resource that the requesting thread wishes to serialize on.

This call will not prevent a process signal handler from getting control.

DosExitCritSec Is used to negate the effect of a previous DosEnterCritSec. If multiple DosEnterCritSec calls were made, then the same number of DosExitCritSec calls must be made to allow other threads in the process to execute.

Priority Programming Interfaces

The priority of a process or thread indicates how important it is that that process or thread have a chance to execute. It is much more important for a thread that keeps up a communications link to run than it is for a thread that updates the time on the screen. The user does not care if the time is updated at the exact instant that it changed. However, if the communications link is disrupted because the communications thread could not respond, then the user will not be very pleased.

The application programming interface gives an application the ability to set its priority to whatever it wishes. It is important that an application not abuse this ability and make itself the highest priority application in the system. If every application does this, then the system will not function properly.

If multiple threads have the same priority, then OS/2 will **timeslice** between the threads. When timeslicing, the operating system allows each thread to execute for a specified amount of time. This is called **round robin** scheduling, and it allows multiple threads that have the same priority to share the processor fairly. The user has control over the length of the timeslice with a CONFIG.SYS parameter, TIMESLICE.

If a thread does not have the opportunity to execute for a given length of time, then it is given a boost in priority. The user has control over the length of time that it takes to get the boost in priority with a CONFIG.SYS parameter, MAXWAIT.

The priority of a thread is made up of one of three priority classes and a priority level. The three classes are

- □ Time Critical.
- □ Regular.
- □ Idle.

Each priority class has 32 priority levels (0–31). The higher the number, the higher the priority. The Time Critical Class has a higher priority than the Regular class, and the Regular class has a higher priority than the Idle class. OS/2 will execute higher priority threads before lower priority threads.

Appropriately named, the Time Critical priority class is intended for a thread with an activity that depends on executing within a very short period of time from the occurrence of some event. If the time critical activity does not execute, then the application or environment will not work. The operating system does not vary the priority level of any of the threads in the Time Critical priority class (static scheduling). The operating system performs round robin scheduling of Time Critical threads in the same priority level.

The Idle priority class is used for threads that execute only when there is no other work to do in the system. This is a good way to optimally use the processing power in the system to do work that does not need to be done at any specific time. The operating system does not vary the priority level of any of the threads in the Idle priority class (static scheduling). The operating system performs round robin scheduling of Idle priority class threads in the same priority level.

The Regular priority class is where most of the threads in the system run. The operating system varies the priority level of the threads in the Regular priority class. These changes depend upon what the thread is doing and how the rest of the system is behaving. Examples of the types of things that can affect the priority level include the thread performing I/O in the foreground or the thread being "starved" and not getting a chance to execute.

DosSetPrty Changes the priority class and priority level of the following:

- □ A process and all of its threads. The process is identified by its Process ID. The current process can also be chosen.
- □ A specific thread within the current process or the current thread.
- □ A process (and all of its threads) and all its descendant processes (and all of their threads). The chosen process must be the current process or a descendant of the current process.

The caller may choose to change only the priority class or only the priority level of the affected thread(s), or both class and level. The requested change to the priority level is relative to whatever the current value of the priority level is. For example, the caller requests that the priority level be increased by five. If the priority class is changed, then it is a changed to a specific priority class. For example, the caller requests to change the priority class to the Time Critical priority class.

When a thread is created, it inherits the same priority as its parent thread.

DosGetPrty A thread asks for the priority class and priority level of the initial thread or a specific thread (by using the Thread ID) of its process.

INTERPROCESS COMMUNICATIONS

When an application consists of a single process with multiple threads of execution, it is very easy to see how the different threads can communicate with each other. They share all the same resources (e.g., memory). In this situation, the real challenge is to make sure that the different threads do not interfere with each other.

We already know how the programming interface allows threads to control the execution of other threads in the same process. They can explicitly suspend them, restart them, or stop all the other threads from running.

When an application consists of multiple processes or when a process from one application needs to communicate with the process of another application, the fact that the processes do not share system resources is an important consideration. The operating system must supply special functions to give the processes the ability to pass or share data with each other:

- Shared memory.
- Pipes.
- Queues.

We already know how a process creates a memory segment so it can be accessed by another process. Pipes and queues are two different mechanisms that processes use to pass or share data.

In addition, processes may wish to control or serialize access to a shared resource or function or to communicate the occurrence of certain events to each other. This is accomplished through the following interprocess communications mechanisms:

- Signals.
- Semaphores.

Pipes

Two or more related processes can communicate through a pipe. Related processes are all processes that can inherit characteristics from a common ancestor. For example, two processes that are children of the same parent process are related. If a process creates a pipe, then any child processes that the parent creates can inherit the ability to read from or write to the pipe.

Communicating via a pipe is similar to reading or writing to a file. The only difference is that the pipe is in memory instead of on disk. When the pipe is created, the creator determines how big the pipe is, up to 64 KB in size.

The process reads data from the pipe in a First-In-First-Out (FIFO) order. There is no way to change the order of the data in the pipe. Moreover, once a process reads data from the pipe, it cannot reread the data. The operating system keeps track of the data and free space in the pipe. If a thread writes to a pipe and the pipe has no more room in it, the operating system makes the writer wait until enough data is read from the pipe so that more data can be put in.

The data that the processes pass between them is actually copied between the writer and the pipe and then again between the pipe and the reader. This can be inefficient if too much data needs to be transferred.

DosMakePipe   A process creates the pipe. The caller determines how big the pipe will be. The pipe can be read from or written to with the standard file I/O calls, DosRead and DosWrite. Two handles are returned to the caller: one for DosRead and the other for DosWrite.

Child processes have the right to read to or write from the parent process's pipe if they inherit and know the appropriate handles to use.

Access to the handles is terminated with the file I/O call, DosClose. When all processes using the pipe issue a DosClose on their handles, then the pipe is destroyed.

Pipes are very simple mechanisms that closely related processes can use to communicate with one another. Pipes are best used with small amounts of data because the data is copied multiple times. The order in which the receiving process reads the data is always the order in which the data is written to the pipe.

Queues

A queue is another mechanism that processes can use to pass or share data. A queue is more powerful and flexible than a pipe.

When two processes communicate with a queue, the actual data is not moved between the two processes. Instead, a pointer to the data and the length of the data is passed in a **queue element**. This makes a queue more efficient than a pipe because the data is not copied. Instead, the necessary information to find the data is moved through the queueing mechanism.

All processes using a queue must have addressability to the memory segments that hold the actual data. So, when a process reads a queue element and tries to access the memory segment containing the data, it must have the permission and the capability to get to that memory segment. This means that a queue must be used in conjunction with shared memory.

The queue elements may be read from the queue with or without being destroyed. The process can also read the queue elements in First-In-First-Out (FIFO) order,

Last-In-First-Out (LIFO) order, or in priority order. If element priority order is chosen, then the writer to the queue specifies the relative priority of the queue element (0–15). Queues are clearly more flexible than pipes, where the destructive FIFO read mechanism is the only way to read from the pipe.

The creator (owner) of the queue is the only process that may read queue elements from the queue. All threads of the owner process can read from the queue. Other processes can obtain access to write to the queue. Of course, all the threads within the writer processes can write to the queue. In summary, a queue has a single reader process and multiple writer processes.

The process that reads from the queue performs the following actions:

- □ Creates (DosCreateQueue) the queue.
- □ Peeks (DosPeekQueue) or Reads (DosReadQueue) from the queue.
- □ Closes (DosCloseQueue) the queue.

The processes that write to the queue perform the following actions:

- □ Open (DosOpenQueue) the queue.
- □ Write (DosWriteQueue) to the queue.
- □ Close (DosCloseQueue) the queue.

DosCreateQueue Creates the queue. The caller (process that owns the queue) gives the queue a name, which looks just like a fully qualified file name. The name must begin with \QUEUES\. When another process wishes to open the queue for writing, it uses this name.

The caller chooses the kind of queue element ordering that will be used for the queue. The choices are FIFO, LIFO, or priority ordering.

The caller obtains a handle to use for the other queue-related programming interfaces. The calling process is the only process that is allowed to read queue elements.

DosOpenQueue Opens the queue for writing. A queue must be created before it can be opened. Once the queue is created, it has a name that other processes use to open it. The name is a fully qualified file name that begins with \QUEUES\.

The Process ID of the owner of the queue is returned to the caller. The write handle for the queue is also returned to the caller. Once a process has opened the queue, it may write to the queue.

DosWriteQueue Adds a queue element to the queue identified by a queue handle. The queue element contains the following:

- □ The address of the data.
- □ The length of the data.
- □ A separate word of information that can be used to describe the data that the queue element points to. The meaning of the word is part of a predetermined convention between the reader process and writer processes of the queue.

The caller specifies the priority of the queue element. Elements with the same priority are passed in FIFO order.

DosReadQueue Allows any thread of the process owner of the queue to read queue elements from the queue. The handle obtained during the queue creation identifies the queue to read from. The queue element is removed from the queue when it is read.
   The caller receives the following:

   □ Queue element (size, data address, and word of information).
   □ Process ID of the process that wrote the queue element to the queue.
   □ Priority of the queue element.

   The reader of the queue can choose to override the normal ordering of the queue elements by using DosPeekQueue. The previous queue element viewed with DosPeek-Queue can be read with DosReadQueue.
   The caller can do one of the following:

   □ Wait until there is at least one element on the queue.
   □ Not wait, even if there are no elements on the queue.

If the caller chooses the Wait option, then the caller must specify a semaphore handle. If multiple threads of the owner process are reading from the queue, then they all must use the same semaphore handle. We discuss semaphores later on in this chapter. The semaphore enables the process to understand when data is written into the queue and to act accordingly.

DosPeekQueue Performs the same function as DosReadQueue with one major exception. The peeking process (which must be the queue owner) uses this interface to look at a queue element without removing it from the queue. This allows the owner process to search through the queue elements until it finds a specific element. Then, the process uses DosReadQueue to remove that specific element from the queue.

DosQueryQueue Allows both reading and writing processes to find out how many elements are currently in the queue. The queue handle identifies the queue.

DosPurgeQueue The queue owner deletes all the queue elements in a queue identified by a queue handle, leaving the queue empty.

DosCloseQueue Terminates the ability of a process to access a queue. If the queue owner closes the queue, then the queue is destroyed. At this point, any writers to the queue get a return code saying that the queue has been terminated.

   Queueing is a powerful mechanism which processes that share memory use to pass data to each other. Large quantities of data can be passed efficiently because the data is not actually copied; instead, a queue element is transferred from one process to another. The order in which a process transfers the queue elements is very flexible. The reading process can choose to read queue elements (peek) without removing them from the queue.

Signals

We now know how processes can communicate with one another by sending and receiving data. There is still the need for a mechanism that enables a process to tell another process to do something *now*, something like the way software interrupts work. A software interrupt directly invokes a software interrupt handler.

A process registers a handler for an event, termed a **signal**. The handler, when invoked, is executed by the initial thread of the process. This initial thread is created when the process is created with DosExecPgm. If the process is using the reception of signals for other than exception kinds of events, then it should keep the initial thread around to handle the signals instead of having the initial thread do normal work. Additional threads can be created with DosCreateThread to do normal work.

Either the operating system or a process can send a signal to a particular process. When the signal handler is given control, it is passed the return address and the kind of signal that occurred. The sender of a Flag signal can also pass information to the Flag signal handler.

A process can register a signal handler for the following kinds of events:

- □ Control-Break key pressed (SIGBREAK).
- □ Control-C key pressed (SIGINTR).
- □ Program terminated (SIGTERM).
- □ Flag A (SIGPFA).
- □ Flag B (SIGPFB).
- □ Flag C (SIGPFC).

If a process does not establish a signal handler for SIGBREAK, SIGINTR, or SIGTERM, then the operating system will terminate that process if any of those signals are sent to the process. A process can choose not to be terminated by those signals by establishing a signal handler for them.

A process sends another process any of the FLAG signals by using the DosFlagProcess interface. A process makes another process believe that the user has entered the Control-Break or Control-C key sequence with the DosSendSignal interface.

The signal handling functions are powerful mechanisms that a process can use to execute special code when any of the above events occur. By keeping the initial thread of a process idle, a process can easily handle any of the signals that it may want to receive to perform its job.

The DosKillProcess function call is used to send the SIGTERM signal to another process.

DosSetSigHandler Allows a process to specify the action that takes place for a particular signal. The process requests one of the following actions for the signal:

- □ The system default action takes place for the signal.
- □ The signal should be ignored.
- □ The routine at the address provided with the call should get control when the signal is received. This is how the process installs a signal handler.
- □ If another process tries to signal this process with the signal, then the signalling process should receive an error.
- □ A signal handler notifies the operating system that it is finished processing the signal and is ready to process another one.

When a process installs a signal handler, the caller is returned the address of the previous signal handler and the action that previous signal handler wanted to take with the signal. If the process does not wish the current signal handler to be active anymore, it can restore the previous signal handler with this information.

DosHoldSignal Allows a process to suspend the processing of signals for a very short period of time. For example, a dynamic link library may need to allocate a resource for a process and not be able to handle the termination of the process for a short period of time. This function call allows a process to disable and re-enable signal handling. These calls can be nested.

   The system will remember that the signal was generated and will give the process the signal as soon as it re-enables signal processing. The amount of time that signals may be disabled should be kept to a minimum, just as the amount of time that hardware interrupts may be disabled must be kept to a minimum.

DosFlagProcess A process can send a Flag signal (A, B, or C) to another process or to another process and all of its descendants. This means that one or more signal handlers will be invoked. The caller may specify an argument that the target process's signal handler receives. If the target process has not installed a signal handler for the appropriate signal, then the signal will be ignored. The target process can also specify that the caller receive an error when trying to signal the desired signal type with DosSetSigHandler.

   The caller passes the desired Process ID and the signal type to the system.

DosSendSignal A process sends a Control-C or Control-Break signal to the last process in the command subtree of a desired Process ID. The system looks for an installed signal handler by searching parent processes until it finds the handler.

Semaphores

Semaphores are a very important communications mechanism. They allow threads to serialize their use of a resource or a function in terms of semaphore "ownership." Semaphores also enable a thread to signal another thread of the occurrence of an event. Threads of a single process or different processes can use semaphores.

There are two different types of semaphores:

- System semaphores.
- RAM semaphores.

A System semaphore must be explicitly created with DosCreateSem. The creating process gives the semaphore a name. Other processes then gain permission to access the System semaphore by opening the semaphore with the name established at its creation. Whenever a process creates or opens a System semaphore, the process receives a System semaphore handle. Processes use this handle along with the other system semaphore programming interfaces of the operating system.

System semaphores require more system overhead than RAM semaphores. System semaphores are easily used between different processes. The operating system provides a publicly accessible open mechanism (DosOpenSem) so that other processes can gain access to the System semaphore without having to share memory. Instead, the different processes just need to agree on the name of the semaphore. The operating system also manages the termination of a process that owns a System semaphore. Other processes are never left waiting for a terminated process to free up a System semaphore because the operating system manages the System semaphore.

A RAM semaphore is really just a double word of system memory. The RAM semaphore handle is the address of the location in memory that contains the RAM semaphore. RAM semaphores do not need to be created or opened, but they should be initialized into a known state. All processes using the same RAM semaphore need to be able to access the segment of memory that the RAM semaphore is in.

RAM semaphores require much less overhead than System semaphores. However, RAM semaphores are best used between different threads of the same process. The system takes no actions to manage RAM semaphores. For example, if the owner of a RAM semaphore is terminated without freeing up the semaphore, the system takes no action to tell another process that the owner of the RAM semaphore is never going to free it up.

System Semaphore Interfaces

Processes can create System semaphores or gain access to System semaphores already created.

DosCreateSem Allows a process to create a System semaphore. The creator gives the semaphore a name. The name consists of a fully qualified file name that begins with \SEM\. The creator receives a semaphore handle that it can use with the other semaphore programming interfaces.

The creator determines whether the semaphore will be an **exclusive** System semaphore or a nonexclusive System semaphore. Exclusive System semaphores are best used when semaphore ownership functions are required. A **thread** obtains ownership to a System semaphore by issuing a DosSemRequest. If the System semaphore was created with the exclusive attribute, then once a thread owns the semaphore, *no other threads may modify the state of the semaphore*. This prevents any other threads from freeing up ownership of the System semaphore from the thread that currently owns it. Only the thread that owns an exclusive System semaphore may free up an exclusive System semaphore.

If the System semaphore is used for signalling purposes, then it should be created as nonexclusive. The nonexclusive attribute allows any thread to modify the state of the semaphore. Most signalling situations require this capability.

DosOpenSem Allows a process to gain access to a System semaphore that was created by another process. The current process needs to know the name that was given to the System semaphore when it was created. The process then receives the semaphore handle. The process that creates the System semaphore does not need to issue this function call.

When a process creates new processes (DosExecPgm), the new processes inherit the open semaphore handles. The child processes do not own the semaphores even if the parent process owned the semaphore during the time that the child process was created.

DosCloseSem Is used when a process does not wish to use the System semaphore anymore. The process passes the handle of the System semaphore that it wishes to close to the programming interface. When all the processes that are using a System semaphore issue this call, the System semaphore is removed from the system.

If a process does not close a System semaphore when it terminates, then the system automatically closes it. If the process terminates while holding the System semaphore, then the system notifies any threads in other processes that were blocked waiting on the System semaphore that a process terminated while owning the System semaphore.

Semaphore Ownership Interfaces

These interfaces apply to both System semaphores and RAM semaphores. Exclusive System semaphores are usually used for semaphore ownership functions. Once a thread owns an exclusive System semaphore, it is the only thread that is allowed to change the state of the semaphore.

DosSemRequest Allows a thread to claim ownership of a semaphore identified by the semaphore handle. If the semaphore is unowned, then the calling thread will own the semaphore. If the semaphore is already owned by another thread, then the current thread can choose to do the following:

- □ Continue executing without getting the semaphore.
- □ Wait forever until it can own the semaphore.
- □ Wait for a specified amount of time to try to own the semaphore and then give up if the semaphore is not available for ownership.

If the thread decides to wait until it can own the semaphore, the operating system will perform a "level sensitive" check of the semaphore. This means that the state of the semaphore will be checked at the same time that the operating system tries to execute the thread. If the semaphore is not in the correct state, then the operating system will not execute the thread. The system does not consider that the semaphore may have been unowned. The thread is not executed if the semaphore becomes unowned but another thread executes and establishes ownership before the current thread gets a chance to execute. The semaphore needs to be unowned at the time that the system tries to execute (dispatch) the waiting thread.

If the semaphore is a System semaphore and is created with the "exclusive" attribute, then the owner can issue recursive DosSemRequest calls and the system will keep track of the number of times that the thread requested the semaphore. When the semaphore is owned, other threads cannot issue any semaphore calls that would change the state of the semaphore (e.g., DosSemClear, DosSemSet, etc.).

This request is also used with Ram semaphores and nonexclusive System semaphores for signalling purposes.

DosSemClear A thread releases ownership (unowns) of the semaphore. A thread owns a semaphore due to a call to DosSemRequest. If the System semaphore is created as "exclusive," and DosSemRequest is issued multiple times, then DosSemClear must be issued the same number of times by the thread before the System semaphore becomes unowned. If the System semaphore is created as nonexclusive, then any thread can issue this request to free up ownership of the semaphore.

This call is also used with DosSemWait, DosSemSetWait, and DosMuxSemWait to clear the semaphore for signalling purposes.

Semaphore Signalling Interfaces

These interfaces apply to both System semaphores and Ram semaphores. Exclusive System semaphores are usually *not* used for signalling purposes.

If DosSemRequest and DosSemClear are used for signalling with nonexclusive System semaphores or RAM semaphores, then a thread will normally wait for a DosSemRequest to complete. It will wait because the thread is currently in a set (owned) state. It does not matter who set the semaphore. Any thread can signal the waiting thread by using DosSemClear.

The programming interfaces reviewed below are used to set semaphores and wait for them to be cleared. DosSemClear is used to clear semaphores.

DosSemSet Sets a semaphore for signalling purposes. It is the opposite of DosSemClear, which clears a semaphore for signalling purposes.

DosSemWait The calling thread waits until the semaphore is clear or until a given amount of time has elapsed. If the semaphore is already clear, then the caller will not have to wait for it to be cleared. The caller chooses either to get control immediately if the semaphore is set or to wait forever until the semaphore is cleared. The calling thread does not establish ownership of the semaphore.

As with DosSemRequest, the operating system checks in a level sensitive manner to see if the semaphore is cleared. The state of the semaphore is not important except at the point in time when the operating system is attempting to restart the execution (dispatch) of the thread.

DosSemSetWait Performs the same function as DosSemWait except that the semaphore is set by this call. The caller must wait for the semaphore to be cleared unless the caller has asked to be returned to immediately, regardless of the state of the semaphore.

As with DosSemWait, the operating system checks the semaphore in a level sensitive manner.

DosMuxSemWait The calling thread waits until one of many semaphores is clear. The caller chooses a timeout value so that even if none of the semaphores are clear, the system will still be able to dispatch the caller. The caller can choose to get control immediately even if no semaphores are clear or not to get control until one of the semaphores is cleared.

There is a significant difference between this call and the previous signalling function calls. The caller can specify a list of semaphores that should be monitored. If *any* of the semaphores are cleared, then the caller will be dispatchable. In addition, the check of each semaphore is done in an "edge triggered" manner. This means that if the semaphore is cleared and then set again (before the operating system tries to execute the thread that called DosMuxSemWait), the thread will still be dispatchable (executable).

TIMER SERVICES

OS/2 provides a number of programming interfaces that perform services relating to the following:

- Getting and setting the date and time.
- Waiting for a specified amount of time.
- Starting and stopping interval timers.

Many of the interfaces provide inputs or outputs in units of milliseconds. It is important to note that the accuracy of the system is less than that. The operating system maintains a system timer that currently counts at a rate of about 32 HZ. This means that the system keeps track of the time about every 1/32 of a second. This amount of time is called the clock **tick**. Time intervals are accurate to about one or two clock ticks. This means that currently the accuracy for the functions discussed is about 50 milliseconds. This does not account for the fact that even if a thread becomes executable with an accuracy of about 50 milliseconds, the operating system may not dispatch (execute) it immediately.

The system time that is maintained will keep an accurate count of hours, minutes, and seconds. Over a long period of time, the system does not maintain an accurate count of milliseconds. Programs that keep track of long periods of time should take this into account.

DosGetDateTime The caller gets the following:

- Time in hours, minutes, seconds, and hundredths of seconds.
- Date in month, day, and year.
- Time zone in relation to Universal Time.
- The day of the week.

DosSetDateTime Allows the caller to set the system information that is returned with DosGetDateTime. The day of the week cannot be set.

DosSleep Allows a thread to suspend itself from execution for a specified period of time. The period of time is specified in milliseconds and is rounded up to the next clock tick.

The caller must take into account that the accuracy of the call is only to one or two clock ticks and that normal priority scheduling considerations may keep the thread from executing once its sleep interval has elapsed.

Programs should not use this interface to keep track of time.

DosTimerAsync Is the asynchronous equivalent of DosSleep. The caller continues to execute after issuing the call. The calling thread passes a semaphore handle to the system. When the timer interval elapses, the system clears the semaphore. By setting the semaphore before making this call, the calling process can detect when the interval has elapsed by noting that the semaphore has been cleared.

A timer handle is returned to the caller. This handle is used to stop the timer function before it completes.

DosTimerStart Is equivalent to DosTimerAsync except that instead of asking for notification of a single time interval's elapse, this interface asks for a periodic timer.

Once the system clears the semaphore, it automatically starts another time interval. The process must set the semaphore again before the next interval interval elapses if it is to detect the elapse of that interval. It is possible to miss an interval by not setting the semaphore again before another time interval has elapsed.

DosTimerStop Is used to stop a timer that is started with DosTimerStart or DosTimerAsync. The timer handle returned with either call is used to stop the timer. The semaphores that are used with the calls will be in an undetermined state when the timer is stopped.

GLOBAL AND LOCAL INFOSEG

The operating system maintains a global information segment that contains information applicable to the entire system. There is also a local information segment that is maintained for each process in the system. Applications may wish to use this information but should be aware that the information segment may be updated while the application is reading it.

A process obtains the ability to read the global information segment and its local information segment by using the **DosGetInfoSeg** programming interface.

Information contained in the local infoseg includes:

- □ The Process ID of the current process.
- □ The Process ID of the parent of the current process.
- □ The priority class and the priority level of the current thread.
- □ The Thread ID of the current thread.
- □ The Session ID that the current process is part of.
- □ Whether the current process is in the foreground.

Information contained in the global infoseg includes:

- □ Time and date information.
- □ The version information for the system.
- □ Parameters that the system uses to schedule threads for execution.
- □ The block device number that the system booted from.
- □ The Process ID of the foreground process.
- □ Whether the system has a DOS execution environment.

4

Illustrating Concepts in Programming Examples

THIS CHAPTER IS FOR THE READER who wishes to delve a little deeper into the technical details involved in exploiting the function of OS/2. In this chapter, we look at some simple examples demonstrating the use of the OS/2 Application Programming Interface (API). We begin with a review of the tools necessary to build a program for the OS/2 environment. Then we develop several programming examples that demonstrate the use of the OS/2 API.

The OS/2 programmer needs a workstation with OS/2, the Operating System/2 Toolkit, and a compiler and/or assembler. Chapter 1 lists the languages provided by IBM for use with OS/2. The compilers, assemblers, and other tools supplied with these languages are family applications that can execute on OS/2 or DOS 3.3. These language products can also generate code for either operating system.

The examples we use in this book are written in C. We chose C not only because of its increasing popularity, but also because its data types, control structures, and standard run time libraries enable us to convey the essence of the OS/2 API with minimum language distractions. In all cases, the programming style used in the examples is optimized to portray the OS/2 API and to make the program easily readable. For example, most variables in these example programs are declared as global variables at the beginning of the program for ease of reference. Naturally, in a software production environment, one would strive to minimize the scope of variables to only those routines that need to access them. Also, in these example programs we do not check the ErrorCode returned from the OS/2 function calls. In some cases we have even shortcut certain fundamental concurrent programming principles, resulting in race conditions where multiple threads are used. There are many programming guides for multitasking and concurrent programming, and the reader who intends to develop programs in C for the OS/2 environment should consult one of the many books on C that discuss techniques for program clarity, maintainability, and portability.

The Operating System/2 Toolkit has important information to assist the OS/2 programmer. In addition to guidelines for using the linker, it contains standard OS/2 macro definitions, function declarations, and error equates for the IBM Assembler/2 and IBM C/2 languages. These tools, in conjunction with the sample programs supplied with the Toolkit, can have a programmer generating running code in a very short period of time.

Before we proceed, let's review compiling, linking, and some C source coding conventions for the benefit of the reader whose high level language of choice is something other than C.

C PROGRAMMING CONVENTIONS AND SYNTAX REVIEW

In this section, we discuss compiling and linking and review a small part of the C language syntax to assist the non-C programmer in reading the examples. We also discuss the common data types used to call OS/2 functions with IBM C/2.

Compiling

A C program consists of one or more source files. Source files in C are named with the letter "c" as their file name extension (xxxxxxxx.c). Common declarations and equates that are used in many different C programs are usually separated into include files. Include files (also known as header files) follow the naming convention of having a file name extension of the letter "h" (xxxxxxxx.h).

Every source file in a program must be run through the C compiler. The output from this process is an object file. The object file is the machine language code along with the necessary external reference information for the linker, as well as the relocation information for the operating system loader. The compiler can also generate listing files in various formats that record the results of the compilation process. The IBM C/2 compiler can be invoked from the OS/2 command line by typing

cc

and then following the compiler prompts to enter the necessary file names and options. If you choose to use the CC command, you will probably want to build a batch file (.bat file in DOS, .cmd file in OS/2) and run the compiler directly from the command line. The syntax to run the compiler from the command is

cc sourcename [,[objectname]] [,[listingname]][;]

In general, what this means is that you must provide a source file name; the compiler will default object file and listing file names if you do not provide them; and any other compiler options must appear before the semicolon.

A sample command line invocation of the IBM C/2 compiler is

cc testprog.c,testprog.obj,/Fs testprog.lst /G2;

This command line causes the compiler to do the following:

- Compile the source file called testprog.c.
- Name the resulting object file testprog.obj.
- Create a listing file called testprog.lst.
    The /Fs option in front of the listing file name indicates to generate a source program listing. The /G2 option indicates to generate code for the 80286 microprocessor.

Note that the option switches are case sensitive and must be entered exactly as shown.

Although this sample command line invocation of the C compiler demonstrates only two of the available options, there are many more that can be used to control the compilation process. Some of these other capabilities of the IBM C/2 compiler that make it a powerful program development tool allow the programmer to do the following:

- Use environment variables to direct the compiler to search separate default directories for files such as executable files, include files, and library modules.
- Set options for compatibility with the IBM Personal Computer C Compiler 1.00.
- Control the types of listing files generated.
- Set controls that affect the C preprocessor.
- Specify various methods of handling floating-point operations.
- Set the level of warning/error messages to be reported.
- Specify different optimization goals, including memory size or execution speed.
- Have several different memory models, including Small, Medium, Compact, Large, and Huge.
- Generate object files with the characteristics necessary for use with the debugging program provided with the compiler.

This brief summary of the options available with the IBM C/2 compiler is intended to give you a feel for its power and flexibility. There are more advanced options available. You should refer to the IBM C/2 publications for additional details on the compiler defaults and options.

Linking

Once you have successfully compiled your program, it is ready to be linked. As with the IBM C/2 compiler, the OS/2 linker will prompt you for the necessary input if you do not provide it on the command line. Alternately, the linker can read an input file, called a response file, that specifies the options and file names to use. Although we give a sample invocation of the linker below to help us get started, we cover the syntax for the linker in more detail in Chapter 7.

An important part of the link process for C programs is to establish addressability to the appropriate C standard run time libraries. Many functions commonly used with C programs are not actually part of the language, but they still are somewhat standardized across various C implementations. For example, there are C standard run time functions for I/O and for string manipulation. There are different C/2 run time libraries for the different memory models and different operating system environments. Usually, if you execute the linker in the same environment in which you intend to execute the resulting program, the appropriate libraries are used by default.

As with the compiler, we will focus on the use of the linker from the command line. A sample command line invocation of the OS/2 linker is

link testprog.obj,testprog.exe,testprog.map,slibc.lib slibc5.lib doscalls.lib;

This command line causes the linker to do the following:

- Link the object file testprog.obj.
- Name the resulting executable file testprog.exe. This is the file that contains the OS/2 executable program.
- Create a link map called testprog.map that lists the segments in the exe load module.
- Use slibc.lib which is the DOS-independent portion of the C run time libraries.
- Use slibc5.lib which is the OS/2-dependent portion of the C run time libraries.
- Use doscalls.lib which is the library used to resolve external dynamic link references to OS/2 function calls.

The IBM C/2 publications and the OS/2 Technical Reference contain documentation for the linker defaults and options. We continue our discussion of the linker in Chapter 7.

Compiling and Linking in One Step

IBM C/2 has a command that allows the programmer to compile and link a program in one step. This command is called the "CL" command. An example of the CL command, used to compile and link the first example program in this chapter, called name.c, follows.

cl /Fs name.c /F 2000

This command line directs the compiler and linker in the following ways:

- □ The /Fs option indicates to generate a source program listing.
- □ "name.c" is the source file name.
- □ The /F 2000 option allocates an 8 KB stack.

Most of the options available with the CC command are also available with the CL command.

As you can see, the command line syntax for the CL command is very convenient. We used the CL command to compile and link the examples in this book.

Reading an OS/2 Program Written in C

As mentioned previously, common declarations and equates that are used in different C programs are usually separated from the programs in include files. Common OS/2 function declarations for IBM C/2 are provided with the OS/2 Toolkit. These declarations are accessed via the include statement:

#include < doscall.h >

Figure 8 is an example of an OS/2 function declaration for IBM C/2 using the hypothetical function call "DosGenericCall."

First, we see in Figure 8 that comments are delimited at the beginning by "/*" and at the end by "*/" and can span multiple lines. This example shows the C program declaration for an external OS/2 generic function. The terms "unsigned far pascal" indicate the return value type and size (which is the error code returned from the function call), along with the function calling convention. Following the function name is the argument type list with comments to help document the required function parameters.

The "extern" storage class specifier is required for the declaration of all external functions. It means that storage for linkage to this function is to remain allocated throughout the life of the program (static), and that its name is known to the linker.

```
/* This is a comment */

/***    DosGenericCall - Read Character from device
 *
 *      Return a character from the device
 */

extern unsigned far pascal DosGenericCall (
        struct DeviceData far *,        /* Buffer for device data */
        unsigned,                       /* Function parameter */
        unsigned );                     /* Device handle */
```

Figure 8. OS/2 Function Declaration for IBM C/2 Provided with Toolkit

The term "unsigned" means that the return value is an unsigned integer, which in IBM C/2 is a 16 bit (80286 word) value. The term "far" indicates that the function should be accessed via a far call, and "pascal" defines the convention for placing parameters on the stack.

The argument type list is contained within the parentheses of the function declaration. In addition to two arguments that are unsigned integers, we see the C syntax to define an argument that is a far pointer to a structured data type. Remember from our discussion of the 80286 microprocessor that an address is made up of two 16 bit parts. In real mode, the address is a 16 bit segment and a 16 bit offset. In protected mode, the address is a 16 bit selector and a 16 bit offset. If a C program makes a data reference, it can use one of two types of pointers. If the data item is in the currently active data segment, then a near pointer that specifies only the offset from the current data segment can be used. If the data item is in some other data segment, then a far pointer that specifies both the selector (segment in real mode) and the offset must be used.

To complete our sample function declaration, let's look at Figure 9, which shows a structure declaration for DeviceData in the DosGenericCall function.

Although these function and structure declarations are only hypothetical examples, they portray the format of the standard IBM C/2 declarations available as include files with the OS/2 Toolkit. These include files greatly facilitate your getting started in developing OS/2 programs using C.

The structure declaration shown in Figure 9, called DeviceData, has three members of various types. The most common data types in IBM C/2 programs for parameters passed to OS/2 functions are:

char	8 bit character (–128 to 127)
unsigned char	8 bit unsigned character (0 to 255)
int	16 bit integer (–32,768 to 32,767)
unsigned	16 bit unsigned integer (0 to 65,535)
long	32 bit long integer (–2,147,483,648 to 2,147,483,647)
unsigned long	32 bit unsigned long integer (0 to 4,294,967,295)
unsigned far *	32 bit (segment/selector:offset) pointer to an unsigned integer
char far *	32 bit (segment/selector:offset) pointer to a character

Let's look at some simple examples that demonstrate the use of the OS/2 API.

```
/***    DeviceData - structure that contains device data */

struct DeviceData {
        unsigned char device_code;     /* raw device code */
        unsigned char ascii_code;      /* ASCII mapping of code */
        unsigned long time;            /* time stamp of data */
        };
```

Figure 9. OS/2 Structure Declaration for IBM C/2 Provided with Toolkit

I/O WITH VIDEO AND KEYBOARD

The OS/2 video and keyboard functions provide a high performance replacement for the BIOS functions that are available under DOS. Programmers can use these functions to develop responsive text-based applications. In this section, we look at an example of how a text-based application can utilize the video and keyboard API.

Figure 10 shows the high level logic for the first program we use to illustrate some simple OS/2 Video and Keyboard function calls. Figure 11, on page 90, contains the actual sample program.

Describing the Sample Program

Obviously, the simple program shown in Figure 11 does not exploit the total flexibility of the OS/2 video and keyboard functions. It is intended to introduce you to the conventions for making calls to OS/2. Let's walk slowly through this first program, describe what it's doing, and define the OS/2 functions it uses.

After the comments at the beginning of the file which name the program, we see the #include preprocessor directives. These statements direct the preprocessor to include the declarations for the OS/2 API library and the C string functions standard run time library.

The remainder of the program is defined in a procedure called "main." In the C language, procedures are called "functions," although the terms are used synonymously in this book. Every C program must have a function called main, since the first executable statement in main is defined as the primary entry point into the C program. The body of the main function is contained within left and right braces ({}). This body consists of a declaration list of variables local to main, and a series of statements known syntactically in C as a "compound statement."

To assist in reading the program, we have grouped the variable declarations. In the first set of variables, we see the declaration of an unsigned integer called Error-Code. The C language allows us to initialize this variable in its declaration, and we have initialized ErrorCode to 0. The next set of variables are used for calling the OS/2 KbdStringIn function. First, we see a 32 byte array of characters called CharBuffer. Next, is a variable called KbdLength. KbdLength is a structured data type called KbdStringInLength. The structure KbdStringInLength is conveniently defined in the include file "doscalls.h" furnished with the OS/2 Toolkit. The definition of this structure is based on the OS/2 API definition for KbdStringIn as specified

```
Clear the screen
Display "Please Enter Your Name"
Read a string of characters from the keyboard
Display string just read
Exit
```

Figure 10. Sample Program Logic—VIO and KBD calls

```
/**************************************************************************************/
/*  Video and Keyboard Sample Program                                               */
/**************************************************************************************/

#include <doscall.h>                                  /* OS/2 API declarations     */
#include <string.h>                                   /* C string functions        */

main()                                                /* Start of C main routine   */
{

/* General Variables - used throughout the program *******************************/

    unsigned  ErrorCode = 0;                          /* Value returned by OS/2 calls */
    int       RowCounter = 0;                         /* Variables used in "for" loop */
    int       ScreenLength = 25;                      /* to clear the display      */

/* KbdStringIn Variables - used to input user's name *****************************/

    char      CharBuffer[32];                         /* Character buffer          */
    struct    KbdStringInLength KbdLength;            /* Length table(from doscalls.h)*/
    unsigned  IOWait;                                 /* Indicate if wait for char */
    unsigned  KbdHandle;                              /* Reserved word of zeros    */

/* VioWrtTTY Variables - used to clear display and display prompts ***************/

    char far *TTYCharStr = "\r\n";                    /* Blank line string         */
    int      TTYLength;                               /* Length of TTY string      */
    unsigned VioHandle;                               /* Reserved word of zeros    */

/* DosExit Variables ************************************************************/

    unsigned  ActionCode=1;                           /* Exit all threads in process */
    unsigned  ResultCode=0;                           /* Result saved for DosCWait */

/* Start of executable program **************************************************/

    for(RowCounter =0; RowCounter <= ScreenLength; RowCounter++)   /* Clear the 25 line screen  */
                                                      /* by writing 25 blank lines. */
      ErrorCode = VIOWRTTTY(TTYCharStr = "\r\n",      /* VioWrtTTY moves the cursor */
                      TTYLength = strlen(TTYCharStr), /* as though the output was to */
                      VioHandle = 0);                 /* a teletype device.        */

    ErrorCode = VIOWRTTTY(TTYCharStr = "Please Enter Your Name: ",  /* Output prompt to the user  to*/
                      TTYLength = strlen(TTYCharStr), /* enter their name.         */
                      VioHandle = 0);

    KbdLength.Length = 32;                            /* Read the user's name into a */
                                                      /* 32 character keyboard input */
    ErrorCode = KBDSTRINGIN((char far *)CharBuffer,   /* buffer.                   */
                      (struct KbdStringInLength far *)&KbdLength,  /* The default ASCII keyboard */
                      IOWait = 0,                     /* input mode is used.       */
                      KbdHandle = 0);

    CharBuffer[KbdLength.LengthB] = '\0';             /* Concatenate the user's name */
    TTYCharStr = strcat("\r\nOS/2 Says Hello To ",CharBuffer);  /* with a "Hello" message.   */

    ErrorCode = VIOWRTTTY(TTYCharStr,                 /* Output the resulting message.*/
                      TTYLength = strlen(TTYCharStr),
                      VioHandle = 0);

    DOSEXIT(ActionCode,                               /* Notify OS/2 of termination */
         ResultCode);

}                                                     /* End of C main routine     */
/**************************************************************************************/
```

Figure 11. Sample Program—VIO and KBD calls

in the OS/2 Technical Reference, Volume 2. The two remaining variables used with KbdStringIn are unsigned integers.

We have defined three variables for use with the VioWrtTTY function. The first is a far pointer to a character string called TTYCharStr. The pointer is initialized to point to a blank line string. The \r and \n are the escape sequences for the carriage return and line feed characters, respectively. TTYLength and VioHandle are defined as integer and unsigned integer, respectively.

Finally, two variables for the parameters required on the DosExit function are defined as unsigned integers and initialized.

OS/2 Function Calls

Before continuing, let's look in some detail at the three OS/2 function calls introduced in the sample program shown in Figure 11.

VioWrtTTY

VioWrtTTY outputs text strings to the display as though it were a teletype device. The output starts at the current cursor position and wraps to the next line if the end of the line is reached. The function also automatically scrolls the screen when a new line is needed at the bottom of the display. This function is extremely convenient when line-oriented output is desired.

There are three parameters with this function call.

CharStr Is a far pointer to the string to be written.

Length Is an integer specifying the length of the output string.

VioHandle The video handle is not currently used in the OS/2 Vio API, but the programmer is required to provide a word of zeros for this parameter.

The characters in the output character string are sent to the display, with the exception of the carriage return, line feed, backspace, tab, and bell characters. These characters are treated as commands and are acted upon as appropriate.

KbdStringIn

The KbdStringIn function reads a character string from the keyboard. The behavior of this function is affected by the keyboard mode setting. Although a detailed description of the keyboard modes is beyond the scope of this book, some important modes are ASCII versus Binary, and Echo On/Off.

The KbdStringIn function has four parameters.

CharBuffer Is a far pointer to the character string input buffer.

Length Is a far pointer to a length table (structure) with two members. The first member in the table is passed by the caller and contains the length of the input buffer. The second member is the length of the received input that is returned by the KbdStringIn function.

IOWait Has different meanings depending on the keyboard mode setting. In ASCII mode, this parameter is always set to zero to indicate that the function should wait for the user to press carriage return. In Binary mode, a zero for this parameter indicates that the function should wait until the input buffer is full before returning. IOWait set to one in Binary mode means to return immediately with as many available characters as can fit into the input buffer.

KbdHandle Specifies either the default keyboard or a logical keyboard. An application can open multiple logical keyboards as part of the support for multiple code pages. (See Chapter 8 for a discussion of code pages.) In our example, we specify the default keyboard by setting KbdHandle equal to zero.

In our example, we use the default keyboard mode, which is ASCII with Echo On.

DosExit

The DosExit function indicates to the operating system that the thread or process is terminating.

There are two parameters with this function call.

ActionCode Indicates whether to terminate just this thread (ActionCode = 0), or all of the threads in the process (ActionCode = 1).

ResultCode Is the termination code that is passed to any thread in the parent process that has issued a DosCwait (wait for child process to terminate) for this process. For a child process with multiple threads, only the last DosExit termination code is returned to the thread waiting with DosCwait.

If a process is about to terminate, the last thread in the process is used to execute the routines in the DosExitList list. When a process terminates, all resources that are tracked by the system and owned by this process are released. Termination of a process should always specify an ActionCode equal to one, since the system may automatically create threads on behalf of the process for some types of operations.

Completing the Description of the Sample Program

We begin the executable portion of the video and keyboard program shown in Figure 11 by clearing the display. We use VioWrtTTY in a "for" loop to output 25 blank lines to the screen. Because of the case sensitivity of C programs, the OS/2 function calls are coded as all capital letters. We will continue to use mixed case when discussing the calls to improve readability. The expression "RowCounter++" in the for loop means to use the value in RowCounter and then increment it by one.

Notice that the length of the output string is obtained by using the standard C string length function (strlen).

The next step is to output a prompt to the user to enter his or her name. In preparation for calling the KbdStringIn function, we initialize the input buffer length member of the keyboard input length structure to the size of the input buffer. We then call KbdStringIn.

Notice that we never defined a buffer pointer to pass as a parameter for this call. Instead, we explicitly typecast the expression in the KbdStringIn function expression list. In C, the value of an array identifier is equivalent to a pointer to the first element (array index equal to zero) of the array. Since we are compiling this example as a small model program, data pointers are by default only 16 bit offsets into the data segment. The OS/2 KbdStringIn function requires a far pointer to the character string input buffer, so we explicitly cast the function expression to a far pointer to a character with the syntax "(char far *)."

Similarly, the pointer to the input string length structure is cast in the expression for the second argument. This can be read in the program source code as "a far pointer to a structure of type KbdStringInLength located at the address of KbdLength."

The final output for this simple program is constructed by placing a null byte in the input buffer at the end of the string that the user entered. This null byte turns the string into an ASCIIZ string that can be passed to the string concatenation (strcat) function. The user's name is then concatenated with a hello message, and the resulting string is output to the display using the VioWrtTTY function again.

The last step of the program is to call DosExit to tell the system that the program is terminating. Notice that we initialized ActionCode to one to tell OS/2 to terminate any threads that it may have started on our behalf.

This program illustrates how easy it is to get code running under OS/2. With this in mind, let's move on to an example that begins to exploit some of the new features of OS/2.

MULTITASKING—ONE PROCESS WITH TWO THREADS

As you saw in Chapter 3, OS/2 provides a robust set of multitasking functions. Let's look at a simple program illustrating the use of a single process with two threads employing an InterProcess Communications (IPC) mechanism to synchronize themselves.

One important characteristic of threads that we want to illustrate is the benefit of their tightly coupled nature. By tightly coupled, we mean that all threads within a process share equal access to the resources owned by that process. Since memory allocated to the process is one of the resources that is shared by the threads, we use a simple RAM semaphore as the IPC mechanism to synchronize the threads.

Our simple program models an application that uses one thread to execute a pro-

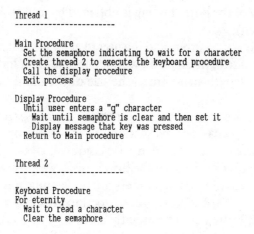

```
Thread 1
-----------------------

Main Procedure
    Set the semaphore indicating to wait for a character
    Create thread 2 to execute the keyboard procedure
    Call the display procedure
    Exit process

Display Procedure
    Until user enters a "q" character
       Wait until semaphore is clear and then set it
       Display message that key was pressed
    Return to Main procedure


Thread 2
-------------------------

Keyboard Procedure
For eternity
    Wait to read a character
    Clear the semaphore
```

Figure 12. Sample Program Logic—Two Threads

cedure that takes data from the keyboard, and another thread to update the screen. Figure 12 shows the high level logic for our dual threaded program.

Notice in Figure 12 that we never explicitly terminate Thread 2. That is because we have set ActionCode equal to one on the DosExit function call. This setting tells the system to exit the process, causing all threads within that process to be terminated. In this way, Thread 2 is also terminated.

Figures 13 and 14 show the actual program for our multiple threads example.

```
/**************************************************************************/
/*  Process with 2 Threads Sample Program                                */
/**************************************************************************/

#include <doscall.h>                                  /* OS/2 API dynamic link library*/
#include <stdio.h>                                    /* C standard I/O run time lib  */

/* General Variables ******************************************************/

    unsigned        ErrorCode = 0;                    /* Error code return from OS/2  */
                                                      /* function calls               */
/* Semaphore Function Variables *******************************************/

    unsigned long       RamSemaphore;                 /* Storage for RAM semaphore    */
    unsigned long far   *SemHandle = &RamSemaphore;   /* Pointer to RAM semaphore     */
    unsigned long       Timeout = -1;                 /* Set for infinite timeout     */

/* KbdCharIn Variables ****************************************************/

    struct KeyData      KeyStructure;                 /* Key structure defined in     */
                                                      /* doscalls.h                   */
    unsigned            IOWait;                        /* Indicate if wait for char    */
    unsigned            KbdHandle;                     /* Reserved word of zeros       */

    struct KeyData far *KeyStructurePointer = &KeyStructure;  /* Pointer to key structure  */

/* DosExit Variables ******************************************************/

    unsigned        ActionCode=1;                     /* Exit all threads in process  */
    unsigned        ResultCode=0;                     /* Result saved for DosCWait    */

/**************************************************************************/

    void            DisplayProcedure();               /* Function decarations         */
    void far        KeyboardProcedure();
```

Figure 13. Multiple Threads (Part 1)—Declarations

```
main()                                                       /* Start of main procedure      */
{
/* DosCreateThread Variables *********************************************************************/

    unsigned          ThreadIDWord;                          /* New thread ID                */
    unsigned char     NewThreadStack[2000];                  /* New thread stack             */

/* Start of executable program ******************************************************************/

    ErrorCode = DOSSEMSET(SemHandle);                        /* Initialize semaphore as set. */

    ErrorCode = DOSCREATETHREAD(KeyboardProcedure,           /* Create thread 2 for keyboard */
                    (unsigned far *)&ThreadIDWord,           /* procedure.                   */
                    (unsigned char far *)&NewThreadStack[1998]);

    printf("Created separate thread (thread 2) for the Keyboard procedure.\n"  /* Display status message   */
           "Initial thread (thread 1) is executing the Display procedure.\n"
           "Press any alphanumeric key, press q to quit.\n");

    DisplayProcedure();                                      /* Call the display procedure   */
                                                             /* with thread 1.               */
    printf("Issuing DosExit with ActionCode set to terminate all threads.");  /* Display the ending status  */
                                                             /* message.                     */
    DOSEXIT(ActionCode,                                      /* Notify OS/2 of termination   */
            ResultCode);

}                                                            /* End of C main routine.       */
/***********************************************************************************************/
void DisplayProcedure()                                      /* Display procedure.           */
{
  do{
    ErrorCode = DOSSEMREQUEST(SemHandle,                     /* Block on the SemRequest until*/
                    Timeout);                                /* a key press causes the       */
    printf("%c key was pressed, press q to quit.\n",KeyStructure.char_code);  /* Keyboard procedure to issue */
  }while(KeyStructure.char_code != 0x71);                    /* a SemClear.                  */
  return;
}                                                            /* End of Display procedure     */
/***********************************************************************************************/
void far KeyboardProcedure()                                 /* Keyboard procedure.          */
{
  for(;;){                                                   /* Infinite loop blocks waiting */
    ErrorCode = KBDCHARIN(KeyStructurePointer,               /* for a character and then     */
                    IOWait = 0,
                    KbdHandle = 0);
    ErrorCode = DOSSEMCLEAR(SemHandle);                      /* signals the Display procedure*/
  }                                                          /* via SemClear                 */
}                                                            /* End of Keyboard procedure.   */
/***********************************************************************************************/
```

Figure 14. Multiple Threads (Part 2)—Main Procedure

OS/2 Function Calls

We will assume at this point that we do not need to dwell on the variable declarations for the remaining sample programs. Let's go directly to the definitions of the OS/2 function calls. The multiple threads example shown in Figures 12 through 14 uses five new OS/2 function calls.

DosSemSet

This function call sets a semaphore. It has one parameter.

SemHandle Is a double word value that has different meanings depending upon whether it is referring to a System semaphore or a RAM semaphore. For a System semaphore, the handle is returned on either the DosCreateSem or DosOpenSem request. For a RAM semaphore, the handle is the semaphore memory address (far pointer to the semaphore).

The function sets the semaphore regardless of whether it was previously set or clear. In our sample program, it is used to initialize the semaphore.

DosSemClear

DosSemClear clears the semaphore. It wakes up any threads blocked on the semaphore. There is one parameter with this function call.

SemHandle (see DosSemSet).

The function clears the semaphore regardless of whether it was previously set or clear. It is used with DosSemRequest, DosSemSetWait, DosSemWait, and DosMuxSemWait to support both resource sharing and signalling.

DosSemRequest

This function call obtains ownership of a semaphore. By ownership, it is meant that the function successfully changes a semaphore from clear to set. In our sample program, we use DosSemRequest with a nonexclusive semaphore for event signalling. If the nonexclusive semaphore is set when this function accesses it, the requesting thread is placed in a wait state until the semaphore is cleared. The requesting thread can specify a timeout period that interrupts the wait state and returns the thread to the caller.

DosSemRequest has two parameters.

SemHandle (see DosSemSet).

Timeout Is a double word value indicating the number of milliseconds the thread is willing to wait on the semaphore. The caller can indicate an infinite timeout by setting this parameter to minus one.

This function can also be used with System semaphores to serialize the use of a resource. As part of this resource serialization facility, System semaphores can be created for exclusive ownership. This means that when one thread establishes ownership of the semaphore, no other thread can clear or otherwise alter the state of the semaphore. Multiple DosSemRequest calls to an exclusively owned semaphore are counted by the operating system. The semaphore will not become unowned until the corresponding number of DosSemClear requests are made. A more complete discussion of the use of exclusive semaphores appears in the Semaphore section of Chapter 3.

DosCreateThread

DosCreateThread creates a separate execution thread within the current process. It has three parameters.

PgmAddress Is a far pointer to the address of the program to receive control under the new thread.

ThreadIDWord Is a far pointer to the address of a word in which DosCreateThread will place a number that identifies the new thread. This number can be used to control the thread with certain other function calls (e.g., DosSuspendThread, DosResumeThread).

NewThreadStack Is a far pointer to the address of the end of the new thread's stack. The programmer is responsible for allocating stack space for each new thread of a process. The minimum stack size depends on the OS/2 function calls made by the thread. It is a good idea to provide at least a 2 KB stack.

The system creates a new dispatchable entity (thread) and makes a far call to the address specified in the PgmAddress parameter. All resources of the parent process are concurrently accessible to the new thread and all other threads in the process.

KbdCharIn

KbdCharIn returns a set of information upon receiving a character from the keyboard. This set of information is generally referred to as a character data record. There are three parameters with this function call.

CharData Is a far pointer to the address of a buffer to place the character data information. The information returned for each character is quite extensive. The character data record includes fields for the following:

  □ ASCII character code.
  □ Scan code from the keyboard of the key pressed.
  □ Status information on the state of the character.
  □ Reserved field for National Language Support shift status.
  □ Shift state field for all of the shift keys.
  □ Time stamp of the keystroke.

IOWait Indicates whether to wait for a character (IOWait = 0) or return immediately if no character is available (IOWait = 1).

KbdHandle Identifies either the default keyboard or a logical keyboard.

A character data record is returned whenever a character is received or the keyboard shift state changes. Also, keystroke data may be modified by a keyboard monitor before the data reaches the application.

Description of the Multiple Threads Sample Program

We see in this program how easy it is to spawn an independent thread of execution in an OS/2 application. Since we are using a RAM semaphore to synchronize the operation of the two threads, we have explicitly initialized this semaphore to the set condition before starting the second thread. We then call the OS/2 DosCreateThread function. Notice that even though this is a C small model program, we only have to specify the function identifier for KeyboardProcedure. This is because we declared it as a far procedure (void far KeyboardProcedure).

After returning from the DosCreateThread call, we use the C standard output function "printf" to display a status message. We then call DisplayProcedure, which immediately goes into a wait state since it is requesting the semaphore that was previously initialized to the set condition. When the semaphore is cleared, the printf function is used to output a message that a key was pressed. The "while" condition is tested to see if the character pressed was a "q" (hexadecimal 71). If the character is not a q, then the procedure loops and issues the DosSemRequest again. Otherwise, we return to the main procedure, display an exit message, and terminate the process.

The keyboard procedure is a very simple function that contains an infinite "for" loop with two OS/2 function calls. The first call is the KbdCharIn function with the IOWait parameter set to wait for a character to come in. When the character arrives, KbdCharIn completes, and the DosSemClear function is issued to signal the display procedure.

MULTITASKING—TWO PROCESSES WITH MULTIPLE THREADS

As we can see from the previous example, multiple threads can be used very easily within an application to gain concurrency. Multiple threads can also be used to simplify the program structure by partitioning the application functions into separately executed procedures. It is important to keep in mind the tightly coupled nature of multiple threads within a process. While this tightly coupled characteristic of threads can simplify their use, it can also be detrimental to a modular program design.

Since all threads in a process have equal access to the process's resources, a problem in one thread can destroy data or otherwise interfere with the execution of another thread in that process.

A fundamental principle of structured design is to limit the scope of data and resource ownership of independent functions. The goal of this principle is to reduce the complexity of a large application by decomposing it into a system of independent modules. The resulting application is easier to develop and maintain. One technique an OS/2 application programmer can use to limit the scope of data and resource ownership is through the use of OS/2 processes.

Let's build upon our previous example by enhancing the hypothetical application that it represents. Suppose that we wanted to maintain a database to log the occurrence of various events. In the previous example, the simple event that we were monitoring was the user pressing a key on the keyboard. Let's pretend that this is just one of several types of events that we would want to log in our database. Furthermore, let's assume that maintaining the integrity of this database is vital to our business.

We now have defined an application that can be logically partitioned into two independent modules. One module is responsible for monitoring an event (keep in mind that in a real application there would probably be more than one event monitoring module). A separate module is responsible for logging the event in a data base. Our OS/2 application will implement these modules as processes and use an InterProcess Communications (IPC) mechanism to communicate between them. The IPC mechanism in this example will demonstrate passing data in messages using the OS/2 pipe mechanism.

By separating event monitoring from event logging, we have simplified the application. The application is simplified because we have partitioned the problem into two smaller problems (divide and conquer approach). The execution of this application in the OS/2 multitasking environment is advantageous because the processes can execute concurrently. Also, the data integrity of the database logging process is improved since the event monitoring process does not have access to the data and resources (files) of the database process. The interaction of the two processes is limited to the well-defined IPC pipe mechanism. This exemplifies how OS/2 facilitates the application of structured programming principles. Applications can be designed in a modular fashion with minimum coupling between the modules using a well-defined IPC interface. Finally, our example using separate processes demonstrates that if a thread in the event monitoring process terminates abnormally, we do not have to worry about abnormally terminating the database process.

There is one more point about our hypothetical example. To simplify the example and give it more visible operating characteristics, we simulate writing records to a database file by writing them in a window of the display screen.

The high level logic for this multiprocess, multithreaded application is shown in Figure 15.

Figures 16 through 25 contain the source code for our multiple process example.

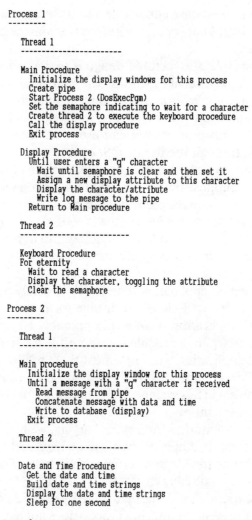

```
Process 1
---------

    Thread 1
    -----------------------

    Main Procedure
      Initialize the display windows for this process
      Create pipe
      Start Process 2 (DosExecPgm)
      Set the semaphore indicating to wait for a character
      Create thread 2 to execute the keyboard procedure
      Call the display procedure
      Exit process

    Display Procedure
      Until user enters a "q" character
        Wait until semaphore is clear and then set it
        Assign a new display attribute to this character
        Display the character/attribute
        Write log message to the pipe
      Return to Main procedure

    Thread 2
    -----------------------

    Keyboard Procedure
    For eternity
      Wait to read a character
      Display the character, toggling the attribute
      Clear the semaphore

Process 2
---------

    Thread 1
    -----------------------

    Main procedure
      Initialize the display window for this process
      Until a message with a "q" character is received
        Read message from pipe
        Concatenate message with data and time
        Write to database (display)
      Exit process

    Thread 2
    -----------------------

    Date and Time Procedure
      Get the date and time
      Build date and time strings
      Display the date and time strings
      Sleep for one second
```

Figure 15. Sample Program Logic—Two Processes with Multiple Threads

OS/2 Function Calls

The multiple process example shown in Figures 15 through 25 uses eight new OS/2 function calls.

VioScrollUp

VioScrollUp scrolls up an area of the display buffer. There are seven parameters with this function call.

TopRow Is a word value containing the top row of the area to scroll.

LeftCol Is a word value containing the leftmost column of the area to scroll.

```
/******************************************************************************/
/*  Multiple Processes with Multiple Threads - Process 1                      */
/******************************************************************************/
#include <doscall.h>                              /* OS/2 API dynamic link library*/
#include <stdio.h>                                /* C standard I/O run time lib  */
#include <string.h>                               /* C string library             */

/* General Variables **********************************************************/

    unsigned           ErrorCode = 0;             /* Error code return from OS/2  */
                                                  /* function calls               */
/* Semaphore Function Variables ***********************************************/

    unsigned long      RamSemaphore;              /* Storage for RAM semaphore    */
    unsigned long far  *SemHandle = &RamSemaphore;/* Pointer to RAM semaphore     */
    unsigned long      Timeout = -1;              /* Set for infinite timeout     */

/* KbdCharIn Variables ********************************************************/

    struct KeyData     KeyStructure;              /* Key structure defined in     */
                                                  /* doscalls.h                   */
    struct KeyData far *KeyStructurePointer = &KeyStructure;  /* Pointer to key structure */

/* VioScrollUp Variables ******************************************************/

    unsigned           TopRow;                    /* Upper left hand corner       */
    unsigned           LeftCol;
    unsigned           BotRow;                    /* Bottom right hand corner     */
    unsigned           RightCol;
    unsigned           NumLines;                  /* Number of lines to scroll    */
    char               FillChar[2] = {0x20,0x1F}; /* Fill character to use        */
    unsigned           VioHandle = 0;             /* Reserved word of zeros       */

    char               NewFillChar[2] = {0x00,0x0F};  /* Another fill character   */

/* VioWrtCharStrAtt Variables - used to display text prompts and messages ****/

    char far           *CharStr;                  /* String to be written         */
    unsigned           VioLength;                 /* Length of character string   */
    unsigned           Row;                       /* Starting position - row      */
    unsigned           Column;                    /* Starting position - column   */
    char far           *Attribute;                /* Display attribute            */

/* DosExit Variables **********************************************************/

    unsigned           ActionCode=1;              /* Exit all threads in process  */
    unsigned           ResultCode=0;              /* Result saved for DosCWait    */
```

Figure 16. Multiple Processes: Process 1 (Part 1)—Declarations

BotRow Is a word value containing the bottom row of the area to scroll.

RightCol Is a word value containing the rightmost column of the area to scroll.

Lines Is a word value containing the number of lines to scroll up. It indicates the number of lines that will be inserted at the bottom of the scroll area.

Cell Is a far pointer to the address of a structure containing the character and attribute to be used on the lines inserted in the scroll area.

VioHandle Is reserved for future use and must contain a word of zeros.

The row and column numbers on the screen are zero-based.
In addition to scrolling, this function is a fast and convenient mechanism for clearing the screen.

```
/* Display window character definitions ****************************************************/

    char far *Thread1Window[12] = {"┌───┐",          /* An array of strings used to  */
                                    "│   │",          /* outline the Thread 1 display */
                                    "│   │",          /* window                       */
                                    "│   │",
                                    "│   │",
                                    "│   │",
                                    "│   │",
                                    "│   │",
                                    "│   │",
                                    "│   │",
                                    "│   │",
                                    "└───┘"};

    char far *Thread2Window[3] = {"┌───┐",            /* An array of strings used to  */
                                  "│   │",            /* outline the Thread 2 display */
                                  "└───┘"};           /* window                       */

    int               RowCounter = 0;                 /* Variables used in "for" loop */
    int               Window1Length = 12;             /* to output arrays of strings  */
    int               Window2Length = 3;

/* DosExecPgm Variables ********************************************************************/

    char              ObjNameBuf[64];                 /* Object name buffer            */
    char              ArgumentString[64];             /* Argument string buffer        */
    struct ResultCodes ReturnCodes;                   /* DosExecPgm ResultCode struct  */
    char              ProgramName[] = "proc2.exe";    /* Program name string           */

    char far          *ObjNameBufPointer = ObjNameBuf;       /* Object name buffer pointer   */
    unsigned          ObjNameLength = 64;             /* Object name buffer length     */
    unsigned          ExecFlags = 1;                  /* Execute asynchronously        */
    char far          *ArgPointer = ArgumentString;   /* Argument string pointer       */
    char far          *EnvPointer = 0x0000;           /* Environment strings pointer   */
    struct ResultCodes far *ReturnCodesAddress = &ReturnCodes;  /* Return code structure pointer*/
    char far          *PgmPointer = ProgramName;      /* Program to exec filename ptr  */

/* DosMakePipe Variables ******************************************************************/

    unsigned          ReadHandle;                     /* Pipe read handle - returned   */
    unsigned          WriteHandle;                    /* Pipe write handle - returned  */
    unsigned          PipeSize;                       /* Requested pipe size           */

/* DosWrite Variables *********************************************************************/

    unsigned          BufferLength = 2;               /* Write output buffer length    */
    unsigned          BytesWritten;                   /* Bytes written - Returned      */

/* String variables - used for general string manipulation *******************************/

    int               StringIndex;
    int               Arg1Index;
    int               Radix = 10;
    char              HandleString[8];
    char              *HandleStringPointer;

/*****************************************************************************************/

    void              DisplayProcedure();             /* Function declarations         */
    void far          KeyboardProcedure();
```

Figure 17. Multiple Processes: Process 1 (Part 2)—Declarations

VioWrtCharStr and VioWrtCharStrAtt

These function calls write a character string to the display. With VioWrtCharStr, the characters in the string assume the display attributes of the characters they replace. VioWrtCharStrAtt has an additional parameter that allows the programmer to specify a single display attribute to use for displaying the string.

There are five and six parameters respectively with these function calls.

```
main()                                                             /* Start of main procedure    */
{

/* DosCreateThread Variables *************************************************************************/

    unsigned        ThreadIDWord;                                  /* New thread ID              */
    unsigned char   NewThreadStack[100];                           /* New thread stack           */

/* Start of executable program **********************************************************************/

    ErrorCode = VIOSCROLLUP(TopRow=0,                              /* Clear the screen           */
                   LeftCol=0,
                   BotRow=-1,
                   RightCol=-1,
                   NumLines=-1,
                   (char far *)FillChar,
                   VioHandle = 0);

    ErrorCode = VIOWRTCHARSTR(CharStr = "OS/2 (TM) Standard Edition",    /* Title the display     */
                   VioLength = strlen(CharStr),
                   Row = 1,
                   Column = 27,
                   VioHandle = 0);

    ErrorCode = VIOWRTCHARSTR(CharStr = "Multiple Processes/Threads Example",   /* Include the program name  */
                   VioLength = strlen(CharStr),
                   Row = 3,
                   Column = 22,
                   VioHandle = 0);

    ErrorCode = VIOWRTCHARSTR(CharStr = "(Press q to Quit)",       /* Display how to exit program */
                   VioLength = strlen(CharStr),
                   Row = 23,
                   Column = 30,
                   VioHandle = 0);

    ErrorCode = VIOWRTCHARSTRATT(CharStr = "PROCESS 1",            /* Label area of screen used  */
                   VioLength = strlen(CharStr),                    /* for Process 1              */
                   Row = 5,
                   Column = 16,
                   Attribute = "\034",
                   VioHandle = 0);

    for(RowCounter = 0; RowCounter < Window1Length; RowCounter++)  /* Display Thread 1 window     */

        ErrorCode = VIOWRTCHARSTRATT(Thread1Window[RowCounter],
                       VioLength = strlen(Thread1Window[RowCounter]),
                       Row = 7 + RowCounter,
                       Column = 19,
                       Attribute = "\034",
                       VioHandle = 0);

    for(RowCounter = 0; RowCounter < Window2Length; RowCounter++)  /* Display Thread 2 window     */

        ErrorCode = VIOWRTCHARSTRATT(Thread2Window[RowCounter],
                       VioLength = strlen(Thread1Window[RowCounter]),
                       Row = 20 + RowCounter,
                       Column = 19,
                       Attribute = "\034",
                       VioHandle = 0);

    ErrorCode = VIOSETCURPOS(Row = 21,                             /* Place cursor inside the    */
                   Column = 20,                                    /* Thread 2 window            */
                   VioHandle = 0);
```

Figure 18. Multiple Processes: Process 1 (Part 3)—Initialize the Display

CharStr Is a far pointer to the character string to be written to the display.

Length Is a word value containing the length of the character string in bytes.

Row Is a word value containing the row number (zero-based) where the first character in the string will be written.

```
ErrorCode = DOSMAKEPIPE((unsigned far *)&ReadHandle,              /* Create the pipe that will   */
                        (unsigned far *)&WriteHandle,             /* be inherited by Process 2   */
                        PipeSize = 16);

for(StringIndex = 0; StringIndex <= strlen(PgmPointer); StringIndex++)   /* Put the child process program*/
    ArgumentString[StringIndex] = ProgramName[StringIndex];             /* name in the first argument   */
                                                                        /* string                       */
ArglIndex = StringIndex;

HandleStringPointer = itoa(ReadHandle,HandleString,Radix);        /* Convert the read handle to a */
                                                                  /* string                       */
for (StringIndex = 0; StringIndex <= strlen(HandleStringPointer); StringIndex++)
    ArgumentString[ArglIndex + StringIndex] = HandleString[StringIndex];  /* Make read handle string the */
                                                                          /* second argument string      */

ErrorCode = DOSEXECPGM(ObjNameBufPointer,                         /* Exec Process 2               */
                       ObjNameLength,
                       ExecFlags,
                       ArgPointer,
                       EnvPointer,
                       ReturnCodesAddress,
                       PgmPointer);

ErrorCode = DOSSEMSET(SemHandle);                                 /* Initialize semaphore as set. */

ErrorCode = DOSCREATETHREAD(KeyboardProcedure,                    /* Create thread 2 for keyboard */
                           (unsigned far *)&ThreadIDWord,         /* procedure.                   */
                           (unsigned char far *)&NewThreadStack[98]);

DisplayProcedure();                                               /* Call the display procedure   */
                                                                  /* with Thread 1                */
ErrorCode = VIOSETCURPOS(Row = 24,
                         Column = 0,                              /* Move the cursor before exit  */
                         VioHandle);

printf("Issuing DosExit with ActionCode set to terminate all threads.");   /* Display the ending status    */
                                                                           /* message.                     */
DOSEXIT(ActionCode = 1,
        ResultCode = 0);                                          /* Notify OS/2 of termination   */
}                                                                 /* End of C main routine.       */
/****************************************************************************************************/
```

Figure 19. Multiple Processes: Process 1 (Part 4)—Remainder of Main Functions

Column Is a word value containing the column number (zero-based) where the first character in the string will be written.

Attribute (VioWrtCharStrAtt only) is a far pointer to the attribute to be used with each character in the string.

VioHandle Is reserved for future use and must contain a word of zeros.

If the string is longer than the current line then the remainder of the string is continued on the next line until the end of the screen is reached. If the operation reaches the end of the screen, the function terminates.

VioSetCurPos

VioSetCurPos sets the position of the cursor. There are three parameters with this function call.

```
void DisplayProcedure()                                    /* Display procedure executed by*/
{                                                          /* Thread 1                    */
  do{
    ErrorCode = DOSSEMREQUEST(SemHandle,                   /* Block on the SemRequest until*/
                       Timeout);                           /* a key press causes a        */
                                                           /* SemClear in Thread 2        */
    NewFillChar[0] = FillChar[0];
    if (NewFillChar[1] > 0x70) NewFillChar[1] = 0x0F;      /* Calculate next display      */
    else NewFillChar[1] = NewFillChar[1] + 0x10;           /* attribute to use            */

    ErrorCode = VIOSCROLLUP(TopRow=8,                       /* Display new character and   */
                       LeftCol=20,                         /* attribute                   */
                       BotRow=17,
                       RightCol=20,
                       NumLines=1,
                       (char far *)NewFillChar,
                       VioHandle = 0);

    ErrorCode = DOSWRITE(WriteHandle,                       /* Write the character and     */
                       (char far *)NewFillChar,            /* attribute to the pipe so that*/
                       BufferLength,                        /* Process 2 gets it           */
                       (unsigned far *)&BytesWritten);

                                                           /* Repeat until a "q" character */
  }while(KeyStructure.char_code != 0x71);                  /* is received                 */
  return;
}                                                          /* End of Display procedure    */
/********************************************************************************************/
void far KeyboardProcedure()                               /* Keyboard procedure.         */
{
  int ToggleSwitch = 0;
  for(;;){                                                 /* Infinite loop blocks waiting */
    ErrorCode = KBDCHARIN(KeyStructurePointer,0,0);        /* for a character and then    */
                                                           /* signals the Display procedure*/
    FillChar[0] = KeyStructure.char_code;                  /* via SemClear                */
    if(ToggleSwitch == 0){
      FillChar[1] = 0x0F;                                  /* ToggleSwitch switches between*/
      ErrorCode = VIOSCROLLUP(21,20,21,20,1,(char far *)FillChar,0);  /* normal and inverse video to */
      ToggleSwitch = 1;                                    /* make it easier to see       */
    }                                                      /* Thread 2 reading keyboard   */
    else{                                                  /* input                       */
      FillChar[1] = 0x70;
      ErrorCode = VIOSCROLLUP(21,20,21,20,1,(char far *)FillChar,0);  /* This thread terminates as a */
      ToggleSwitch = 0;                                    /* result of Thread 1 issuing  */
    }                                                      /* a DosExit with ActionCode set*/
                                                           /* to 1                        */
    ErrorCode = DOSSEMCLEAR(SemHandle);
  }
}                                                          /* End of Keyboard procedure.  */
/********************************************************************************************/
```

Figure 20. Multiple Processes: Process 1 (Part 5)—Display and Keyboard Functions

Row Is a word value containing a row number (zero-based) where the cursor will be placed.

Column Is a word value containing the column number (zero-based) where the cursor will be placed.

VioHandle Is reserved for future use and must contain a word of zeros.

DosMakePipe

DosMakePipe creates a pipe for interprocess communications. There are three parameters with this function call.

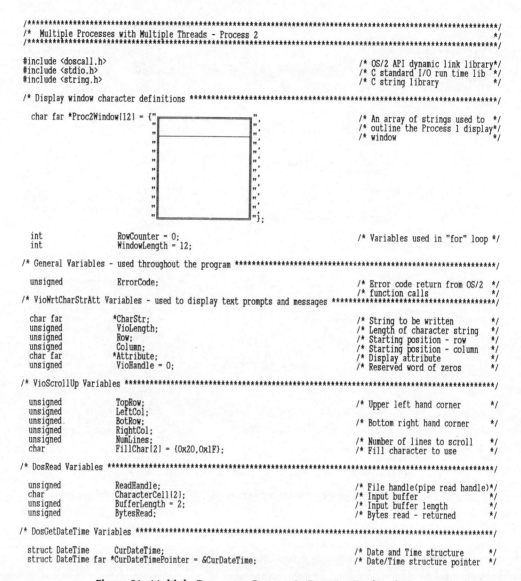

```
/****************************************************************************************/
/*  Multiple Processes with Multiple Threads - Process 2                               */
/****************************************************************************************/

#include <doscall.h>                                  /* OS/2 API dynamic link library*/
#include <stdio.h>                                    /* C standard I/O run time lib  */
#include <string.h>                                   /* C string library            */

/* Display window character definitions ************************************************/

    char far *Proc2Window[12] = {"                     ",   /* An array of strings used to */
                                 "                     ",   /* outline the Process 1 display*/
                                 "                     ",   /* window                      */
                                 "                     ",
                                 "                     ",
                                 "                     ",
                                 "                     ",
                                 "                     ",
                                 "                     ",
                                 "                     ",
                                 "                     ",
                                 "                     "};

    int              RowCounter = 0;                   /* Variables used in "for" loop */
    int              WindowLength = 12;

/* General Variables - used throughout the program *************************************/

    unsigned         ErrorCode;                        /* Error code return from OS/2  */
                                                       /* function calls               */
/* VioWrtCharStrAtt Variables - used to display text prompts and messages **************/

    char far         *CharStr;                         /* String to be written         */
    unsigned         VioLength;                        /* Length of character string   */
    unsigned         Row;                              /* Starting position - row      */
    unsigned         Column;                           /* Starting position - column   */
    char far         *Attribute;                       /* Display attribute            */
    unsigned         VioHandle = 0;                    /* Reserved word of zeros       */

/* VioScrollUp Variables ***************************************************************/

    unsigned         TopRow;                           /* Upper left hand corner       */
    unsigned         LeftCol;
    unsigned         BotRow;                           /* Bottom right hand corner     */
    unsigned         RightCol;
    unsigned         NumLines;                         /* Number of lines to scroll    */
    char             FillChar[2] = {0x20,0x1F};         /* Fill character to use        */

/* DosRead Variables *******************************************************************/

    unsigned         ReadHandle;                       /* File handle(pipe read handle)*/
    char             CharacterCell[2];                 /* Input buffer                 */
    unsigned         BufferLength = 2;                 /* Input buffer length          */
    unsigned         BytesRead;                        /* Bytes read - returned        */

/* DosGetDateTime Variables ************************************************************/

    struct DateTime  CurDateTime;                      /* Date and Time structure      */
    struct DateTime far *CurDateTimePointer = &CurDateTime;  /* Date/Time structure pointer */
```

Figure 21. Multiple Processes: Process 2 (Part 1)—Declarations

ReadHandle Is a far pointer to the address of a word where the read handle for the pipe is returned. This handle is used on subsequent calls to DosRead to read data from the pipe.

WriteHandle Is a far pointer to the address of a word where the write handle for the pipe is returned. This handle is used on subsequent calls to DosWrite to write data into the pipe.

Pipesize Is a word containing the number of bytes the system is to reserve for data in the pipe.

```
/* DosSleep Variables ***********************************************************************/

    unsigned long      TimeInterval;                           /* Sleep time duration      */

/* String variables ************************************************************************/

    char               TimeHour[3];                            /* String variables used to */
    char               *TimeHourPointer = TimeHour;            /* build the time string    */
    char               TimeMinutes[3];
    char               *TimeMinutesPointer = TimeMinutes;
    char               TimeSeconds[3];
    char               *TimeSecondsPointer = TimeSeconds;
    char               Time[9] = "  :  :  \0";
    char               *TimePointer = Time;

    char               DateDay[3];                              /* String variables used to */
    char               *DateDayPointer = DateDay;              /* build the date string    */
    char               DateMonth[3];
    char               *DateMonthPointer = DateMonth;
    char               DateYear[5];
    char               *DateYearPointer = DateYear;
    char               Date[9] = "  /  /  \0";
    char               *DatePointer = Date;

    char               LogString[20];                          /* This string is output by the */
    char               *LogStringPointer = LogString;         /* thread that is logging the   */
                                                               /* event                        */
    int                Radix = 10;                             /* Used by the itoa function    */

/* DosExit Variables ***********************************************************************/

    unsigned           ActionCode=1;                           /* Exit all threads in process */
    unsigned           ResultCode=0;                           /* Result saved for DosCWait   */

/*****************************************************************************************/

    void far           DateTimeProcedure();                    /* Function declarations       */
    void               BuildTimeString();
    void               BuildDateString();

/*****************************************************************************************/
```

Figure 22. Multiple Processes: Process 2 (Part 2)—Declarations

DosWrite

This is the file system function call to write data to a file. This function also applies to pipes and devices that support the file system interface (e.g., DosWrite to LPT1, where LPT1 is the reserved name for printer number 1). The function moves the specified number of bytes from the output buffer to the file/pipe/device and then returns to the caller.

There are four parameters with this function call.

FileHandle Is a word value containing either the file or device handle obtained on the DosOpen, or the pipe's write handle returned on the DosMakePipe Function call.

BufferArea Is a far pointer to the caller's output buffer.

BufferLength Is a word containing the number of bytes to be written from the buffer.

BytesWritten Is a far pointer to the address of a word where the number of bytes actually written will be returned.

If a file or device has been opened as read-only, then the DosWrite will not be performed.

```
main(argc, argv, envp)                                               /* Start of C main routine   */
int argc;                                                            /* argc is count of argument */
char *argv[ ];                                                       /* strings                   */
char *envp[ ];                                                       /* argv array contains argument */
                                                                     /* strings                   */
{                                                                    /* envp is environment strings */
/* DosCreateThread Variables ***********************************************************************/

    unsigned          ThreadIDWord;                                  /* New thread ID             */
    unsigned char     NewThreadStack[1002];                          /* New thread stack          */

/* Start of executable program ********************************************************************/

    ErrorCode = VIOWRTCHARSTRATT(CharStr = "PROCESS 2",              /* Label area of screen used */
                                 VioLength = strlen(CharStr),        /* for Process 2             */
                                 Row = 5,
                                 Column = 55,
                                 Attribute = "\032",
                                 VioHandle = 0);

    for(RowCounter =0; RowCounter < WindowLength; RowCounter++)      /* Display the Process 2 window */
        ErrorCode = VIOWRTCHARSTRATT(Proc2Window[RowCounter],
                                 VioLength = strlen(Proc2Window[RowCounter]),
                                 Row = 7 + RowCounter,
                                 Column = 48,
                                 Attribute = "\032",
                                 VioHandle);

    ErrorCode = DOSCREATETHREAD(DateTimeProcedure,                   /* Create Thread 2 for date and */
                                (unsigned far *)&ThreadIDWord,       /* time procedure            */
                                (unsigned char far *)&NewThreadStack[1000]);

    ReadHandle = atoi(argv[1]);                                      /* Get the pipe read handle from*/
                                                                     /* the second argument string */
    do{
                                                                     /* Top of loop that continues */
        ErrorCode = DOSREAD(ReadHandle,                              /* reading character cells from */
                            (char far *)CharacterCell,               /* the pipe until a "q"      */
                            BufferLength,                            /* character is received     */
                            (unsigned far *)&BytesRead);

        ErrorCode = VIOSCROLLUP(TopRow=10,                           /* Scroll the window with the */
                                LeftCol=49,                          /* new attribute             */
                                BotRow=17,
                                RightCol=69,
                                NumLines=1,
                                (char far *)FillChar,
                                VioHandle = 0);

        LogString[0] = CharacterCell[0];                             /* Build the log string      */
        LogString[1] = 0x00;
        LogStringPointer = strcat(LogStringPointer," ");
        LogStringPointer = strcat(LogStringPointer,TimePointer);
        LogStringPointer = strcat(LogStringPointer," ");
        LogStringPointer = strcat(LogStringPointer,DatePointer);

        ErrorCode = VIOWRTCHARSTRATT((char far *)LogStringPointer,   /* Display the new log string */
                                VioLength = strlen(LogStringPointer),
                                Row = 17,
                                Column = 49,
                                Attribute = &CharacterCell[1],
                                VioHandle);
    }
    while(CharacterCell[0] != 0x71);                                 /* Test for a "q" character  */

    DOSEXIT(ActionCode,                                              /* Notify OS/2 of termination */
            ResultCode);
}
/*************************************************************************************************/
```

Figure 23. Multiple Processes: Process 2 (Part 3)—Main Function

```
void far DateTimeProcedure()
{
  for(;;){                                                 /* Begin endless loop          */
    ErrorCode = DOSGETDATETIME(CurDateTimePointer);        /* Get the date and time       */
    BuildTimeString();                                     /* Call BuildTimeString        */
    ErrorCode = VIOWRTCHARSTRATT(TimePointer,              /* Display the time string     */
                         VioLength = strlen(TimePointer),
                         Row = 8,
                         Column = 51,
                         Attribute = "\032",
                         VioHandle);

    BuildDateString();                                     /* Call BuildDateString        */
    ErrorCode = VIOWRTCHARSTRATT(DatePointer,              /* Display the date string     */
                         VioLength = strlen(DatePointer),
                         Row = 8,
                         Column = 60,
                         Attribute = "\032",
                         VioHandle);

    ErrorCode = DOSSLEEP(TimeInterval = 1000);             /* Sleep for about a second    */
  }                                                        /* This thread terminates when */
                                                           /* the process terminates      */
}
/***********************************************************************************************/
void BuildTimeString()                                     /* This function formats the   */
                                                           /* time suitable for display   */
{
  TimeHourPointer = itoa(CurDateTime.hour,TimeHour,Radix); /* Format the hour             */
  if(strlen(TimeHourPointer) == 1){
      TimePointer[0] = 0x30;
      TimePointer[1] = TimeHourPointer[0];
  }
  else{
      TimePointer[0] = TimeHourPointer[0];
      TimePointer[1] = TimeHourPointer[1];
  }

  TimeMinutesPointer = itoa(CurDateTime.minutes,TimeMinutes,Radix); /* Format the minutes  */
  if(strlen(TimeMinutesPointer) == 1){
      TimePointer[3] = 0x30;
      TimePointer[4] = TimeMinutesPointer[0];
  }
  else{
      TimePointer[3] = TimeMinutesPointer[0];
      TimePointer[4] = TimeMinutesPointer[1];
  }

  TimeSecondsPointer = itoa(CurDateTime.seconds,TimeSeconds,Radix); /* Format the seconds  */
  if(strlen(TimeSecondsPointer) == 1){
      TimePointer[6] = 0x30;
      TimePointer[7] = TimeSecondsPointer[0];
  }
  else{
      TimePointer[6] = TimeSecondsPointer[0];
      TimePointer[7] = TimeSecondsPointer[1];
  }
}
/***********************************************************************************************/
```

Figure 24. Multiple Processes: Process 2 (Part 3)—DateTimeProcedure and BuildTimeString

```
void BuildDateString()                                                    /* This function formats the  */
                                                                          /* date suitable for display  */
{
    DateMonthPointer = itoa(CurDateTime.month,DateMonth,Radix);           /* Format the month          */
    if(strlen(DateMonthPointer) == 1){
        DatePointer[0] = 0x30;
        DatePointer[1] = DateMonthPointer[0];
    }
    else{
        DatePointer[0] = DateMonthPointer[0];
        DatePointer[1] = DateMonthPointer[1];
    }

    DateDayPointer = itoa(CurDateTime.day,DateDay,Radix);                 /* Format the day            */
    if(strlen(DateDayPointer) == 1){
        DatePointer[3] = 0x30;
        DatePointer[4] = DateDayPointer[0];
    }
    else{
        DatePointer[3] = DateDayPointer[0];
        DatePointer[4] = DateDayPointer[1];
    }

    DateYearPointer = itoa(CurDateTime.year,DateYear,Radix);              /* Format the year           */
    DatePointer[6] = DateYearPointer[2];
    DatePointer[7] = DateYearPointer[3];
}
/*******************************************************************************************************/
```

Figure 25. Multiple Processes: Process 2 (Part 4)—BuildDateString

DosRead

This is the file system function call to read data from a file. This function also applies to pipes and devices that support the file system interface (e.g., DosRead from COM1, where COM1 is the reserved name for serial port number 1). The function moves the specified number of bytes from the file/pipe/device to the input buffer and then returns to the caller.

There are four parameters with this function call.

FileHandle Is a word value containing either the file or device handle obtained on the DosOpen, or the pipe's read handle returned on the DosMakePipe function call.

BufferArea Is a far pointer to the caller's input buffer.

BufferLength Is a word containing the number of bytes to be read into the buffer.

BytesRead Is a far pointer to the address of a word where the number of bytes actually read will be returned.

It is not guaranteed that the number of bytes requested will actually be read. The program should always compare BufferLength with BytesRead upon return from this call.

DosExecPgm

This function allows a program to execute another program as a child process. The two programs can execute synchronously or independently of one another. If the two processes are to run independently, then the new process can run in the same session or run detached.

There are seven parameters with this function call.

ObjNameBuf Is a far pointer to the address of a buffer where information is returned if the DosExecPgm call fails. The name of the object that contributed to the failure of the call is placed in the buffer.

ObjNameBufL Is a word containing the length in bytes of the ObjNameBuf.

ExecFlags Is a word indicating one of several execution scenarios. This flag indicates if the process is to run (1) synchronous or asynchronous to the parent; (2) with or without saving the termination result code; (3) under conditions for tracing, as is used with a debugger; (4) as a detached background process; or (5) only loaded into memory awaiting action by the session manager.

ArgPointer Is a far pointer to the beginning of two argument strings which are passed to the new process. These strings are used as command parameters. The OS/2 command line interpreter uses the convention that the first of these strings is the program name, and the second contains any additional characters entered on the command line.

EnvPointer Is a far pointer to a set of strings passed to the program that contains configuration information.

ReturnCodes Is a far pointer to the address of a double word for information returned from the call. For asynchronous processes, the first word contains the process identifier of the child process. For synchronous processes, the first word contains a system termination code, and the second word contains the ResultCode specified by the last thread in the child process that issued a DosExit.

PgmPointer Is a far pointer to a character string containing the file name of the program to be executed.

When the two processes execute synchronously, it means that the thread issuing the DosExecPgm is placed in a wait state until the child process completes. A child process that runs detached is intended to run in the background without any keyboard or screen I/O. The only exception to this is the use of the VioPopUp function call to handle error conditions. A child process that runs asynchronously must do so within the restrictions of two processes sharing the same session. This includes sharing the keyboard and screen resources for that session.

The operating system builds a Local Descriptor Table (LDT) to provide the new process with its own address space. Inheritable resources that have been opened by the parent process, such as certain file handles and pipes, are made accessible to the child process. In our example, the child process inherits the pipe's read handle.

DosSleep

This function yields the CPU for the remainder of the current time slice and keeps the thread in a wait state for a specified period of time.

There is one parameter with this function call.

TimeInterval Is a double word value indicating the amount of time in milliseconds until the thread should resume execution.

Time values are rounded up to multiples of the scheduler clock interval, and they may be off by one or two clock ticks depending on the execution of other threads in the system.

Description of the Multiple Process Sample Program

As you can see from the high level logic for this example shown in Figure 15, the parent process (Process 1) is very similar to the process in the previous example. We have added a significant amount of video I/O to this example to enhance the visual nature of the program. This includes the use of color, and the program assumes the display is in a mode compatible with the 80 by 25 color text mode of the IBM Color Graphics Adapter. You can see in the high level logic that each of the four threads writes to some area of the display. Therefore, quite a few lines of the program listings are dedicated to declarations and logic that help organize the screen.

As in the previous example, Thread 1 of Process 1 is primarily responsible for starting everything else and then executing the Display Procedure. In the main procedure of Process 1 we create a pipe before we start Process 2. This is so that Process 2 can inherit the pipe. After starting Thread 2 to execute the Keyboard Procedure, Thread 1 calls the Display Procedure. We have enhanced the Display Procedure in this example. Thread 1 executing the Display Procedure has a long window through which it scrolls the most recently received keystroke characters. With each new character, the display thread calculates a new display attribute. This character/attribute pair composes the event message that we want logged. To log the event message, Thread 1 writes the character/attribute pair to the pipe that was inherited by Process 2. Thread 1 continues looping, waiting on the semaphore and then displaying the new characters that come in until the "q" character is received. It then returns from the Display Procedure. The final job of Thread 1 is to properly terminate Process 1 so that Thread 2 is also terminated.

The remainder of Process 1, the Keyboard Procedure, is executed by Thread 2 and is very similar to the previous multiple threads example. The main difference, as we mentioned before, is that both threads output some data to the screen to provide a visual indication of the multitasking that is taking place. Thread 2 executing the keyboard procedure of Process 1 simply toggles between normal and reverse video as it is displaying characters to provide some feedback as to its activity.

Moving down Figure 15, we see that Thread 1 of Process 2 stays in the C main procedure. After it initializes the display, it enters a loop that reads messages from the pipe, concatenates the message with the time and date, and simulates logging the message by writing it to the display. This continues until the "q" character is read from the pipe indicating that the process should terminate.

Thread 2 of Process 2 is responsible for maintaining a current date and time string. In addition to using this string to build the log message, we also display the date and time string about once a second to indicate this thread's execution.

In Figures 16 and 17, we have included the declarations for Process 1. The first executable statement of the main function in Figure 18 is a call to the OS/2 VioScrollUp routine to clear the display. Subsequent VioWrtCharStr and VioWrtCharStrAtt calls are used to label the screen and draw the color-coded "thread windows." The windows for Process 1 use the light red color attribute (octal 034), and the windows for Process 2 (logging process) use the light green color attribute. We use arrays of string constants to draw the window boxes and "for" loops to output the arrays to the display. The VioSetCurPos is used to position the cursor in the window displaying the activity of the thread executing the keyboard procedure.

Once the screen is initialized for Process 1, the program prepares to spawn the child process shown in Figure 19. The first step in our preparation is to allocate a pipe using DosMakePipe. The child process will inherit access to this pipe, and we pass the pipe's read handle to the child process using an argument string. You will recall from the previous API descriptions that the parent process passes an argument string to the child process using a pointer parameter on the DosExecPgm. By convention, the first string in the argument string is the program name. Therefore, the program name is the first string copied into the argument string. After using the itoa (integer to ASCII) function to convert the read handle to a read handle string, we add the read handle string to the argument string. We are now ready to spawn Process 2 using DosExecPgm. The ExecFlags on the DosExecPgm call indicate that we want Process 2 to execute asynchronously of Process 1, so control returns to Process 1 as soon as Process 2 begins executing. The remainder of Process 1 is very similar to the multiple threads example program. Process 1 creates Thread 2 to execute the Keyboard Procedure and calls the Display Procedure with Thread 1.

Figure 20 contains the Display Procedure and the Keyboard Procedure. Their basic logic has remained unchanged from the previous example. We have added the DosWrite call to write each character cell (ASCII character and display attribute) to the pipe. Both procedures have had Video calls added to them so that the execution of the two threads is observable at the display.

Figures 21 and 22 contain the declarations for Process 2. In Figure 23, Process 2 (our logging process) begins by initializing its area of the screen using the same techniques as Process 1. This process creates a second thread that executes the DateTime Procedure. Upon return from the DosCreateThread function call, Thread

1 obtains the pipe's read handle from the argument string passed from Process 1. This thread then enters the loop that reads a character cell from the pipe, scrolls up its window on the display, and outputs the new log string. Thread 1 is also responsible for watching for a "q" character to come through the pipe indicating that the process and all its threads should be terminated.

Figure 24 shows the DateTime procedure executed by Thread 2, which is responsible for maintaining a date and time string, and displaying the date and time at the top of the Process 2 display window. The DateTime Procedure calls the OS/2 function DosGetDateTime, and then calls to other functions to format the date and time as character strings that can be output to the display. This thread also uses the DosSleep function to suspend its execution and go into a wait state for about a second. Thread 2 is terminated when Thread 1 issues the DosExit with the ActionCode set to one.

The BuildTimeString function shown in Figure 24 and the BuildDateString shown in Figure 25 are mainly just string manipulation functions that format the date and time according to the normally accepted format for the United States. We will see in the Advanced Programming chapter of this book (Chapter 7) how these two functions can be built into a dynamic link library, allowing us to support different implementations of them without changing the application program that uses the functions.

Figure 26 outlines the format of the display when the multiple process sample program is executing.

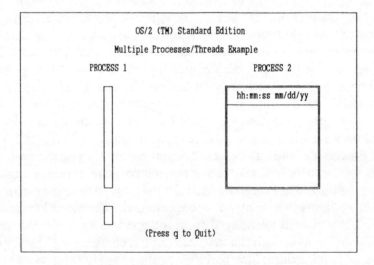

Figure 26. Multiple Processes: Display Outline

MEMORY OVERCOMMITMENT

Before we leave this chapter, let's look at one more programming example that illustrates the OS/2 memory overcommitment capability. Our hypothetical application in this scenario could be a very large spreadsheet. We allow you to specify the amount of memory required by this spreadsheet application. You can even specify more memory than you have in your system. The program simulates the spreadsheet application accessing data in every one of its data segments.

When you invoke this example program from the command line, you also enter the number of 64 KB segments that you would like it to allocate. Once the data segments are allocated, we start referencing each segment in succession, thereby simulating the recalculation of a large spreadsheet. If you have caused the program to overcommit memory, you will observe the indicator light on your fixed disk lighting up. This is a sign that the OS/2 memory manager is swapping these data segments between memory and disk using the Least Recently Used algorithm discussed earlier in the chapter on OS/2 Memory Capabilities (Chapter 2).

One note of caution. In order for this example to work, you must have swapping enabled on your system. This is the default if your swap path is on fixed disk and was not overridden by the CONFIG.SYS statement MEMMAN = NOSWAP. If you have set your swap path to point to a diskette, the default is for swapping to be disabled. You must set MEMMAN = SWAP in your CONFIG.SYS to enable swapping if you have your swap path pointing to a diskette. Swapping to a diskette is generally not recommended.

Let's move on to the example. Figure 27 contains the high level logic and Figures 28 and 29 contain the source code for our memory overcommitment program.

OS/2 Function Calls

The memory overcommitment example shown in Figures 27 through 29 uses one new OS/2 function call.

DosAllocSeg

DosAllocSeg allocates a segment of memory to the calling process. There are three parameters with this function call.

Size Is a word value indicating the size in bytes of the memory segment to be allocated. The size can be from 0 to 65,536, where 0 means to allocate a 64 KB segment.

```
Get amount of memory to allocate (command line argument)
Allocate the segments
Set up current segment pointer
Do forever
  Touch current segment
  Display the segment number just touched
  Increment segment pointer with wrap around
End do
Exit process
```

Figure 27. Sample Program Logic—Memory Management

```
/*****************************************************************************/
/*  Memory Overcommitment - Sample Program                                 */
/*****************************************************************************/

#include <doscall.h>                              /* OS/2 API dynamic link library*/
#include <stdio.h>                                /* C standard I/O run time lib  */
#include <string.h>                               /* C string library             */

/* General Variables *********************************************************/

    unsigned        ErrorCode = 0;                /* Error code return from OS/2  */
                                                  /* function calls               */

    unsigned far    *SelectorTable[256];          /* Array of far pointers        */

    int             SegmentCount = 0;             /* Loop variables               */
    int             TableIndex = 0;
    int             MaxIndex = 0;

    unsigned long   PointerBuilder;               /* Used to build a far pointer  */

    unsigned        FakeDataValue;                /* Used to touch a new segment  */

/* DosAllocSeg Variables *****************************************************/

    unsigned        Size = 0;                     /* Means size = 64K             */
    unsigned        Selector;                     /* Selector returned            */
    unsigned        AllocFlags = 0;               /* Not sharable or discardable  */

/* DosExit Variables *********************************************************/

    unsigned        ActionCode = 1;               /* Exit all threads in process  */
    unsigned        ResultCode = 0;               /* Result saved for DosCWait     */

/*****************************************************************************/
```

Figure 28. Memory Overcommitment (Part 1)—Declarations

Selector Is a far pointer to a word in which a selector is placed. This selector is valid in the calling process's LDT and provides access to the allocated memory.

Flags Is a word value with bits indicating whether the segment can be shared using DosGiveSeg, DosGetSeg, and whether the segment is discardable during low memory situations.

By default, the memory allocated with DosAllocSeg is movable and swappable.

Description of the Memory Overcommitment Sample Program

The first step of our memory overcommitment example requires that we get the amount of memory to allocate. In C, command line parameters are passed to the program in the string array variable identified as "argv." The count of 64 KB segments to allocate is determined by using the atoi (ASCII to integer) function on the first command line argument (argv[1]). The program then displays a status message to give us feedback that the number of segments we think it will allocate is in fact correct.

We then enter a loop to allocate the 64 KB segments. The DosAllocSeg function call is made, specifying a size of 0 to indicate 64 KB, and a status message is displayed upon successful exit from the function. Next, we want to use the returned segment

```
main(argc, argv, envp)                                  /* Start of C main routine    */
int argc;                                               /* argc is count of argument  */
char *argv[ ];                                          /* strings                    */
char *envp[ ];                                          /* argv array contains argument */
                                                        /* strings                    */
{                                                       /* envp is environment strings */

  SegmentCount = atoi(argv[1]);                         /* Get # of segments to allocate*/
                                                        /* entered on command line and */
  printf("Number of 64K segments to allocate is %d\n",SegmentCount); /* output to the display */

  do {                                                  /* Loop to allocate segments  */

    ErrorCode = DOSALLOCSEG(Size,                       /* Allocate a 64K segment     */
                   (unsigned far *)&Selector,
                   AllocFlags);
    if (ErrorCode == 0)
       printf("Successfully allocated segment %d\n",TableIndex+1); /* Display status message */
    PointerBuilder = Selector;
    SelectorTable[TableIndex] = PointerBuilder << 16;   /* Put selector in pointer table*/
    ++TableIndex;
    --SegmentCount;
    }
  while (SegmentCount > 0);                             /* End of allocation loop     */

  MaxIndex = TableIndex - 1;
  TableIndex = 0;

  for(;;) {                                             /* Endless loop to touch      */
    FakeDataValue = *SelectorTable[TableIndex];         /* segments                   */
    printf("Just accessed segment %d \n",TableIndex+1);
    ++TableIndex;
    if (TableIndex > MaxIndex)
      TableIndex = 0;
  }

  DOSEXIT(ActionCode,                                   /* Notify OS/2 of termination */
          ResultCode);
}
/****************************************************************************************************/
```

Figure 29. Memory Overcommitment (Part 2)—Main Function

value to add an entry into a table of pointers for each segment. Building a C far pointer with the returned selector can be a bit tricky. There are several valid techniques that can be used; in this example, we use a shifting technique. The 16 bit unsigned integer selector is assigned to a 32 bit unsigned long integer variable called PointerBuilder. PointerBuilder is then shifted left 16 bits and assigned to a 32 bit far pointer. We now have a far pointer to the first byte in the segment. This technique is bound to give you a compiler warning message of "assignment to different types," but it accomplishes the desired result.

After we have allocated the requested number of segments and built an array of pointers addressing them, we enter into an infinite loop that successively accesses each segment. If you specify to this program to allocate few enough segments so that they fit into your available memory, you will see the program execute relatively quickly with no disk activity. If on the other hand you specify to overcommit memory, you will observe a great deal of disk activity, and the program will run noticeably more slowly.

If you compile and link this program giving the executable file the name "allocmem.exe" as we did, and you wanted to run the program specifying that it allocate over 2 megabytes of storage, you would invoke the program from the command line in the following way.

allocmem 32

Based upon the amount of memory in your system, you should run this program at least twice so that one time there is enough real memory to support the requested memory allocations. You should then run it a second time requesting that enough segments be allocated so that the system has to overcommit memory by using swapping.

5

Application Input/Output Capabilities

WITH TECHNOLOGY IN COMPUTER HARDWARE advancing by leaps and bounds, it is important to be able to use the technology. Of course, utilization of the computer and optional devices is limited by how your applications use the hardware. To give an application the ability to use different devices and to provide a platform for future growth, OS/2 provides a wide range of application programming interfaces (API) and a variety of architected mechanisms for input and output.

What makes the OS/2 methods so much better for applications and subsystems? The benefits are more apparent with a comparison to DOS. As you recall, DOS is a single tasking operating environment. A DOS application can assume it owns all system devices and is unrestricted in what it can do. Figure 30 illustrates the interfaces and mechanisms available to a DOS application for dealing with devices. A DOS application can directly control a device through IN and OUT instructions to the device's I/O ports. Using direct I/O, however, makes the application dependent on the device's characteristics. This means that the application may not work

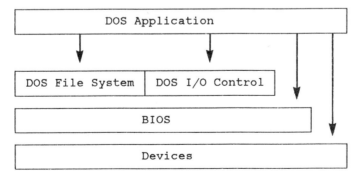

Figure 30. Application Interfaces for Device I/O in DOS

119

if the device is replaced. In addition, you may have problems in the DOS system when the DOS application's control of a device interferes with a Terminate-And-Stay-Resident (TSR) program. To avoid these problems, a DOS application can use other I/O interfaces in the DOS system: the DOS File System, the DOS I/O Control (IOCtl), and the BIOS. While these interfaces provide the benefit of device independence, they are still subject to interference when TSR programs intercept them. When a problem occurs with an interface that is intercepted by TSR programs, it often is impossible to determine which program is the source of the trouble.

The I/O capabilities in OS/2, on the other hand, provide an OS/2 application with both flexibility and discipline. Flexibility is a direct benefit of the freedom of choice. An application developer can choose from the following:

- OS/2 File System interfaces.
- OS/2 I/O Control (IOCtl) interfaces.
- OS/2 subsystem interfaces for video, keyboard, and mouse.
- OS/2 character device monitor mechanism.
- OS/2 IOPL code segment mechanism.

The file system supports I/O to a variety of objects, from files to character devices to pipes. The IOCtl supports device-specific control functions over a large number of devices. The subsystem interfaces enhance the ability of an application to deal with the console devices (screen, keyboard, mouse). The monitor mechanism is a general purpose method for dealing with device data. The IOPL code segment is a method to perform direct I/O to a device's I/O ports. Together, these facilities represent a great improvement over the I/O capabilities in a DOS system. Figure 31 shows the methods available to an OS/2 application for performing I/O.

Discipline for doing I/O is a direct result of the multitasking environment, where system resources are shared among several applications. I/O requires rules to allow concurrent users of devices to coexist peacefully with each other. The OS/2 interfaces and mechanisms enforce these access rules wherever possible. In some cases, the application itself has a measure of control over how other applications may

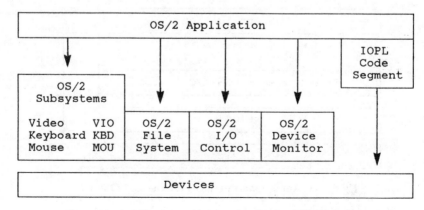

Figure 31. Application Interfaces for Device I/O in OS/2

Commonly Used Devices	I/O Interfaces/Mechanisms				
	File System	Subsystem	I/O Control	Monitor	IOPL
Disk	yes	File System	yes	no	no
Diskette	yes	File System	yes	no	no
Screen	yes	VIO	no	no	yes
Keyboard	yes	KBD	yes	yes	no
Mouse	yes	MOU	yes	yes	no
Printer	yes	Spooler	yes	yes	no
Async Comm	yes	no	yes	no	no
Speaker	no	(DosBeep)	no	no	yes
Clock	yes	Timer Services	no	no	no

Figure 32. Performing I/O in OS/2

access a device that it is already using. For example, the file system allows the application to specify how a file can be shared with other users. In the case of a device where the applications access the device's I/O ports directly, an OS/2 application must follow the conventions that allow it to manipulate the device even though the device is shared with other applications. For a device like the screen, where direct I/O is frequently done, OS/2 has architected an I/O protocol with a number of interfaces in the video subsystem. These interfaces allow an application to directly manipulate the display adapter yet still allow the screen to be shared.

The I/O capabilities in OS/2 establish a basic level of function for a number of devices, with the help of device drivers that come with the operating system. Figure 32 illustrates the usefulness of the different I/O interfaces and mechanisms in OS/2 with respect to a set of commonly used devices supported by OS/2 and its device drivers. Application and subsystem developers can, of course, customize functions for device I/O through system extensions.

FILE SYSTEM I/O

Functionally, the OS/2 File System is an important component for I/O. It allows an application to do the following:

- □ Access many types of devices.
- □ Share or restrict access to these devices.
- □ Redirect I/O from one device to another.

In addition, there are the following benefits that go beyond the functional capabilities of the OS/2 File System interfaces:

□ Media Compatibility with DOS.

Accessing and using files with the OS/2 File System is similar to handling files with the DOS File System. In fact, the two file systems are media compatible. *Media compatibility means that you can create a file with DOS and still use the file with OS/2. Likewise, you can create a file with OS/2 and still use the file with DOS.* This is a critical vehicle for compatibility and for the transition from DOS-based applications to OS/2-based applications.

□ Resident Sharing Mechanism.

One major difference between the OS/2 File System and the DOS File System is the availability of the sharing mechanism. In OS/2, file sharing is automatically performed by the file system. In other words, *file sharing is a resident function of the OS/2 File System.* In DOS, you must first run the SHARE.EXE program before the file system can perform file sharing. This means that for the OS/2 File System, the ability to control how a file is accessed by applications is *always* available. For the DOS File System, the sharing of files may or may not take effect depending on whether the end user ran the SHARE.EXE utility.

□ Volume Management for Removable Media.

Another major difference between the OS/2 File System and the DOS File System is the ability to manage removable media. *The OS/2 File System keeps track of the identity of removable media in order to ensure the integrity of file data.* For example, if the end user removes a diskette before an application is finished, OS/2 can prompt the user to return the specific diskette to the diskette drive. In a multitasking operating environment, the likelihood of having a lot of file I/O occurring is high. The volume management keeps track of which volumes (removable media) are being used.

Usually, you think of the file system as a mechanism for I/O on files. However, the file system can also be used for I/O on other devices. For example, the file system can be used to do I/O to a character device, like a printer or an asynchronous communications line. In fact, the file system recognizes automatically a special class of character devices. These devices are referred to as Standard Devices. The file system is also used for I/O on a pipe, which is a pseudo-file device for interprocess communication. The list of devices that the file system can handle even includes a special type of file device, a logical disk/diskette drive. We discuss the different uses of the file system with respect to these different types of devices.

File Devices

A file device is a storage device for data, usually a diskette or a fixed disk. The file system, in fact, is a subsystem that manages file devices. The file system controls what kind of data is placed where on a file device. As such, the file system dictates how a file device is prepared to hold data, that is, formatted. Both the OS/2 File System and the DOS File System use a File Allocation Table (FAT) algorithm to manage data on a file device. You must format a file device before it can be used to hold data. For a diskette, this means you run a FORMAT utility. For a fixed disk, this means you first partition the disk (with a utility like FDISK), then format the partition.

The file system assigns one or more drive letters to a file device. The drive letter acts as a device name to identify a logical file device. In the case of a diskette drive, the file system may assign it up to two drive letters. If the system contains only one diskette drive, then the file system assigns two drive letters, "a:" and "b:," to represent two logical drives. This allows you to handle data between two diskettes even though you have only one physical diskette drive. If the system contains two diskette drives, then the file system assigns each drive a single drive letter. A file device, such as a fixed disk, can be divided into several partitions. Each partition appears as an individual file device called a logical disk.

Typically, the extent that an application must concern itself with a file device is no further than using a drive letter. Instead of file devices, an application deals primarily with files. A file delimits a specific set of data that is stored on a file device. So, an application uses a drive letter to select a logical file device and a file name to identify some data. The file system uses this information to locate the data on the file device.

The compatibility between the OS/2 and DOS File Systems prescribes consistency in their naming conventions for files. An OS/2 file name is a primary name character string optionally followed by a dot and an extension with the following characteristics:

- The primary name string is 1 to 8 bytes (characters).
- The optional extension is 1 to 3 bytes (characters).
- The characters are ASCII characters, except
    leading blanks are not allowed.
    characters of ASCII value less than 20h are not allowed.
    the specific characters < > + = : | ; , . " \ / [ ] are not allowed.

In the OS/2 environment, any file name formats longer than the 8.3 format are not truncated but instead generate an error. In the DOS environment, however, the name is truncated to 8.3 for compatibility with DOS. Also, the characters ? and * are used for global character indicators, just as in DOS, where the ? is a wildcard for a single character and the * is a wildcard for a group of characters.

The protocol for file I/O with OS/2 is handle-based I/O, which is the same as handle-based I/O with DOS. A handle is a 16 bit value that the file system uses as a special identifier to information about the file. So, an application must do the following:

1. Establish a connection to an existing file (OPEN) or to a new file (CREATE) in order to get a file handle.
2. Read data from or write data to the file using the file handle.
3. Terminate the connection to the file (CLOSE) to release the file handle.

To open or create a file with the OS/2 File System, you need input parameters similar to those required with the DOS File System. Refer to Figure 33 for a summary of the input parameters as they apply to the actions of opening or creating a file. An OS/2 application process supplies a pointer to an ASCII character string that specifies the drive (optional) and directory path (optional), the file name, and a byte of 00h. This string is called a "fully qualified" file name when all parts are present. If the file is being opened, the application process specifies the access mode, which informs the file system of the type of operations that the application process intends to perform on the file (read-only, write-only, read/write). The application process also specifies the sharing mode. The sharing mode informs the file system of the type of concurrent operations that the application process will permit other processes to perform on the file (no concurrent access allowed, concurrent read access allowed, concurrent write access allowed, all concurrent access allowed). Refer to Figure 34 for a summary of the effects of sharing a file. If the file is being created, then the file attribute must be specified, indicating if the file is read-only, hidden, system, archived, or if the name is for a subdirectory.

Once the file has been opened or created, the resulting file handle is the key for I/O. As you recall, the application process is the entity that owns resources, and

Parameter	Description				
Name	File Name				
Open FLAG	Exists			Not Exists	
	Open	Replace	Fail	Create	Fail
Open MODE	Inheritance Write-Through Fail Errors R, W, R/W DR, DW, DRW, DN			Inheritance Write-Through Fail Errors R, W, R/W DR, DW, DRW, DN	
File size		Size		Size	
File ATTRIBUTE		ReadOnly Hidden System Archive Directory		ReadOnly Hidden System Archive Directory	

Access MODE
R   = Read
W   = Write
R/W = Read/Write

Sharing MODE
DR = Deny Readers
DW = Deny Writers
DRW = Deny All
DN = Deny None

Figure 33. DosOpen Parameters Applicable for Files

Type of Sharing Granted	Type of Access Intended		
	Read	Write	Read/Write
Deny Read	Single reader Many writers	No readers Many writers	Single reader Many writers
Deny Write	Many readers No writers	Many readers Single writer	Many readers Single writer
Deny R/W	Single reader No writers	No readers Single writer	Single reader Single writer
Deny None	Many readers Many writers	Many readers Many writers	Many readers Many writers

Figure 34. The Effects of Access versus Sharing

this includes any file handles. This means that all threads in the process can use the same handle to perform I/O to the file. Because all threads of the process have the authority to use the same file handle, the threads must coordinate among themselves to prevent conflicts with their I/O.

I/O to the file is then performed using the file handle. The file system maintains a read/write pointer or I/O pointer to the file and initially sets this pointer to the first byte in the file when the file is opened or created. An application can perform file I/O to bytes in sequential order automatically, since the file system moves the current I/O pointer to the position in the file where the last I/O request ended. An application can perform I/O to bytes in random order by changing the position of the current I/O pointer in the file (this is sometimes referred to as a "logical seek"). Asynchronous I/O can be performed by the application process with two techniques: using the asynchronous read or asynchronous write function calls in the file system, or using a thread to perform the file I/O while other threads in the process perform other activities.

Because of multitasking and the steps involved in performing a requested I/O operation, the file system will not guarantee the order in which multiple outstanding I/O requests issued by the application process are completed. For example, if the application buffer is located in a segment that has been swapped out, then other threads of the application process could execute and issue I/O requests that the file system may be able to satisfy. In addition, the disk device driver performs some optimization for device performance by sorting the requests it receives in terms of starting sector number. It sorts this way in an attempt to reduce the time the device spends in locating the data. If an application process depends on critical data being updated in the file in a certain order, it therefore should not start multiple file I/O requests at the same time. In this case, an application process could choose to dedicate only one thread to issue file I/O requests, as opposed to having several threads issuing file I/O requests.

When an application process no longer needs to perform I/O to a file, it closes the file handle. This action terminates the process's connection to the file and causes the file system to update directory information and clear any internal buffers holding data relating to the file. In the event that an application terminates abnormally, the operating system closes any file handles that the process owned.

In addition, the application process can specify, when it opens or creates a file, if any child processes it starts can inherit the file handle. So, when the parent process starts a child process, the child process will receive a duplicate file handle corresponding to each inheritable file handle owned by the parent process. This means that I/O performed by the child process with an inherited file handle will affect the parent process (and vice versa), because the I/O pointer in the file will be updated as a result of I/O from either of the two existing file handles. However, the two file handles can be closed independently of each other. The child process can close its file handle, and the parent process can continue to use its file handle, and vice versa.

Inheritance of file handles is a key element for redirecting I/O. The parent process controls what the handle actually deals with, whether it be a file or some other object. The parent process can open a new handle or force an existing handle to correspond to a particular object, then start a child process to use the inherited handle for I/O. The child process is oblivious to the identity of the object.

There is a systemwide limit on the number of file handles of 255. An application process is initially allocated 20 handles. An application process can increase the number of handles for its use with a system call, depending on the number of other application processes that exist and their allocations of file handles.

Character Devices

Like the DOS File System, the OS/2 File System can be used to perform I/O to character devices. However, a character device is not like a file device. Once data has been sent to or obtained from a character device, it cannot be altered. Resending data to a character device does not change the data already sent; rereading data from a character device does not obtain the same data. An application must therefore manipulate the data bytes in a certain order. Character devices also have distinct characteristics. Others devices are only input devices (like a keyboard), which means you can only read data from them. Others are only output devices (like a printer), so you can only write data to them. And still other character devices are both input and output devices (like a serial communications device), so you can both read and write to them.

The steps to access and use a character device with the OS/2 File System are similar to those required by the DOS File System. The protocol for I/O using the file system is based on handle I/O. The device handle is like a file handle; it is a 16 bit value that the file system uses as a special identifier to information about the device. An application must do the following:

1. Open the device using the character device name to obtain a device handle.
2. Read or write to the device using the device handle.
3. Close the device using the device handle.

As expected, the naming conventions for character devices are consistent between OS/2 and DOS, with the character device driver providing the name. A character device name is an ASCII string that follows rules similar to file names.

- □ The string is 1 to 8 bytes (characters).
- □ The characters are ASCII characters, except
  leading blanks are not allowed.
  characters of ASCII value less than 20h are not allowed.
  the specific characters < > + = : | ; , . " \ / [ ] are not allowed.

OS/2 automatically installs device drivers for certain character devices. These character devices are guaranteed to be available to applications for I/O. These character devices and their names include:

CON	console device (screen and keyboard)
KBD$	keyboard
LPT1, LPT2, LPT3	first, second, and third parallel printers
NUL	mock device
PRN	another name for the first parallel printer
SCREEN$	screen

While the console, screen, and keyboard devices can be accessed with the OS/2 File System, they are typically utilized through the OS/2 character device subsystems for video and keyboard.

To access and use other character devices with the file system, the appropriate character device drivers must be installed through the DEVICE= command in the CONFIG.SYS configuration file.

To open a character device, the application simply specifies the device name in place of a file name, with no drive and no directory path. An application cannot create a character device. A character device is defined by the installation of a character device driver. In the OPEN system call (in both OS/2 and DOS), a character device name takes precedence over a file name. This means that a file cannot have the same name as a character device. In addition, the application process specifies the access mode; that is, it specifies the type of operations that the application process intends to perform on the character device (read-only, write-only, or read/write). The application process also specifies the sharing mode; that is, it specifies the type of concurrent operations that the application process will permit other processes to perform on the character device (no concurrent access allowed, concurrent read access allowed, concurrent write access allowed, or all concurrent access allowed). Refer back to Figure 34 for a summary of the effects of sharing a device.

The broadening of the file sharing to encompass character devices is an *enhancement* in the OS/2 File System over the DOS File System. Moreover, the character device driver can configure this sharing capability.

The OPEN system call returns a handle that identifies the device to the file system. Refer to Figure 35 for a summary of parameters on the system call to open a character device. Like a file handle, the device handle is owned by a process. All threads in the process can therefore use the handle to perform I/O to the device and must coordinate among themselves to prevent conflicts with their I/O. As with file handles, the application process can specify, when it opens a character device, if any of its child processes can inherit the device handle. In other words, a child process can receive a duplicate device handle corresponding to each inheritable device handle owned by the parent process. The child process can then do I/O to the character device without having to open the device, but the child process and the parent process must coordinate their I/O to the device, because character device data is of the nature of write-once and/or read-once. However, the two device handles can be closed independently of each other. The child process can close its device handle and the parent process can continue to use its device handle, or vice versa.

The device handle can be used in the read and write calls to perform I/O to the device. An application can request a number of bytes to be transferred, and the OS/2 File System will tell the character device driver to perform I/O for that number of bytes. This procedure is different from the DOS File System, where a multiple byte request is sent to the character device driver as several single byte requests. As with files, asynchronous I/O can be performed by the application process with two techniques. The application process can either use the asynchronous read or asynchronous write function calls provided by the file system, or it can use a thread to perform the device I/O while other threads in the process perform other activities.

The device handle can also be used in the other handle-based function calls, where

Parameter	Description
Name	Character Device Name
Open FLAG	Exists
	Open
Open MODE	Inheritance Fail Errors R, W, R/W DR, DW, DRW, DN

Access MODE		Sharing MODE	
R	= Read	DR	= Deny Readers
W	= Write	DW	= Deny Writers
R/W	= Read/Write	DRW	= Deny All
		DN	= Deny None

Figure 35. DosOpen Parameters Applicable for Character Devices

applicable. An application cannot perform I/O to bytes in random order merely by changing the position of the current I/O pointer, because the I/O pointer applies only to files. However, an application can duplicate a device handle.

As with file I/O, the file system will not guarantee the order in which multiple outstanding device I/O requests issued by the application process are completed. For example, if the application buffer is located in a segment that has been swapped out, then other threads of the application process could execute and issue device I/O requests that the device may be able to satisfy. If an application process depends on data being sent to or obtained from the character device in a certain order, then it should not start several device I/O requests at the same time. In this case, an application process could choose to dedicate a thread to read data from the device and/or a thread to write data to the device, as opposed to having several threads performing read/write operations on the device.

When an application process no longer needs to perform I/O to the character device, it closes the device handle. This action terminates the process's connection to the device. In the event that an application terminates abnormally, the operating system closes any device handles owned by the process.

The systemwide limit on the number of file handles includes device handles. The initial allocation of 20 handles to an application process therefore applies to both file handles and device handles. An application process can increase the number of handles for its use with a system call, depending on the number of other application processes that exist and their allocations of file handles.

Standard Devices

Some character devices are automatically recognized by the file system. They are referred to as Standard INPUT Device, Standard OUTPUT Device, and Standard ERROR Device. Standard Devices have predefined device handles that are available to all application processes. These handles are essentially duplicate character device handles for the console device. An application process can read from the keyboard using the Standard INPUT handle or write to the screen with either the Standard OUTPUT handle or Standard ERROR handle. The difference between the Standard OUTPUT Device and the Standard ERROR Device is that the Standard ERROR Device cannot be redirected. Both the Standard INPUT handle and the Standard OUTPUT handle can be redirected, even by the end user from the command line. If an application process needs to display a message to the end user that requires some action (and therefore should not be redirected, for instance, to a file), then the application writes the message to the screen using the Standard ERROR handle.

Like other character devices, the handles for the Standard Devices can be used in a subset of the handle-based I/O function calls. These calls include DosRead, DosWrite, DosReadAsync, DosWriteAsync, DosClose, and DosDupHandle system calls.

The OS/2 File System does not support the Standard AUXILIARY Device or Standard PRINTER Device, which are additional Standard Devices that the DOS File System recognizes.

Pipe Devices

A pipe device is a pseudo-file device that allows related processes to communicate as if they were doing file I/O (refer to the section on interprocess communication in Chapter 3). A pipe, however, is not a storage device; it exists as a data structure in memory.

The steps for pipe I/O involve the handle-based calls. To review, an application process first creates the pipe using a special system call (DosMakePipe) which returns two pipe handles, one for reading the pipe and one for writing to the pipe. When the parent process starts a child process, the child process inherits the pipe handles for writing to the pipe. The pipe handles can then be used to perform I/O to the pipe in the read and write file system calls. When a process is finished using the pipe, it terminates its connection to the pipe by closing the pipe handle.

Since pipe handles are handles that the file system uses, they are allocated out of the same handle pool as file handles and device handles. The number of pipes, files, and character devices in use by other applications will therefore determine how many handles an application process can acquire.

Logical Disk/Diskette Devices

A logical disk/diskette device is a device normally known to applications as a drive letter. A logical disk/diskette device is another term for a partition on a fixed disk or a diskette.

Normally, an application accesses a logical disk/diskette device each time it performs file I/O, because a file resides on media identified by a drive letter. However, a logical disk/diskette device is not initially capable of holding data; the device must first be formatted.

To format an uninitialized partition on a fixed disk or diskette, a system application must gain access to the device. It uses the OS/2 File System to open the logical device. The name used to identify the logical device is like a file name, except that it has only the drive specification (drive, colon). The open system call returns a special device handle. This device handle is used in the DosDevIOCtl function call (see the commands for IOCtl Category 8) to perform a special type of I/O to the device in order to initialize it. When the system application has formatted the logical device, it then closes the special device handle. Refer to Figure 36 for a summary of parameters on the system call to open a logical disk/diskette device.

Parameter	Description
Name	Logical Disk/Diskette
Open FLAG	Exists
	Open
Open MODE	DASD direct Open

Figure 36. DosOpen Parameters Applicable for Logical Disk Devices

General-Purpose Interfaces

These interfaces are not just for files but can be used with a variety of objects, from character devices to pipes.

DosClose Closes the specified handle (file, character device, pipe, Standard Device, or logical disk/diskette device) and terminates the application process's connection to the object. For a file, the file system updates the file's directory entry and flushes any buffers used for I/O to the file. For a character device, the file system will notify the device driver of the CLOSE, if appropriate.

DosDupHandle Returns a handle that is duplicated from the specified file handle, pipe handle, character device handle, or Standard Device handle in the manner requested by the application process. For the returned handle, the file system can either create a new handle or use an existing handle owned by the application process. If the application process wants the file system to force an existing handle to be a duplicate handle of the specified object, then the file system will close the existing handle before redefining it to the target object. Any I/O with a duplicated file handle causes the I/O pointer for the file to be updated for all copies of the file handle. However, a CLOSE using a duplicated handle (file, pipe, or device) affects only that handle—other copies of the handle are still active.

DosOpen Returns a handle for a file, character device, or a logical disk/diskette device. If the object is a file, the application supplies the following:
- The file name.
- The action to take (the Open Flag parameter).
  - If the file exists, the application can choose to have the request fail, to have the file opened, or to have the file replaced.
  - If the file does not exist, the application can choose to have the request fail or to have the file created.
- The file size for a CREATE or a REPLACE action.

□ The file attributes for a CREATE or a REPLACE action (read-only, hidden, system, directory, or archive).

The specified attributes must match the attributes in the directory entry for the file in order to replace an existing file, with the exception that a read-only file cannot be replaced.

□ The mode of the action (the Open Mode parameter).

· The use of the file system buffers for file data (the Write-Through Flag).

The file system buffers are used to cache file data as needed on an I/O request, and a file I/O request can return to the caller before all the file data has been written to the media. The application can inform the file system to commit the file data to the drive on every I/O request so that when the I/O request returns to the caller, the file data resides on the media.

· The handling of media errors (the Fail-Errors Flag).

Media errors can either be reported through the operating system's critical error handler for operator intervention or reported directly to the application with an error code for application control.

· The inheritability of the resulting handle (the Inheritance Flag).

Child processes cannot inherit certain characteristics, specifically the Write-Through Flag and the Fail-Errors Flag.

· The type of access the application intends to perform (the Access Mode): read-only, write-only, or read/write.

· The type of sharing the application extends to other applications (the Sharing Mode): deny readers, deny writers, deny all readers and/or writers, deny none.

If the object is a character device, the application supplies the following:

□ The character device name.

□ The type of action as OPEN the existing device (the Open Flag parameter).

□ The mode of the action (the Open Mode parameter).

· The inheritability of the resulting handle (the Inheritance Flag).

· The handling of media errors (the Fail-Errors Flag).

Media errors can be reported either through the operating system's critical error handler for operator intervention or directly to the application with an error code for application control.

· The type of access the application intends to perform (the Access Mode): read-only, write-only, or read/write.

· The type of sharing the application extends to other applications (the Sharing Mode): deny readers, deny writers, deny all readers and/or writers, deny none.

The file system enforces the sharing access as configured by the character device driver. If the character device driver indicates sharing is not to be enforced by the file system, then the sharing modes are ignored.

If the object is a logical disk/diskette device, the application passes the following:

- □ The drive specification.
- □ The type of action as OPEN the existing device (the Open Flag parameter).
- □ The mode of the action (the Open Mode parameter).
  - • The device type as a media device (the DASD Open Flag).

DosQFHandState Returns the state information for the handle (file, character device, Standard Device, logical disk/diskette device, or pipe). The application process can thus determine the following:

- □ If the handle represents a logical disk/diskette device.
- □ If the handle is inheritable or not.
- □ If the return of a file write request indicates that data has been committed to media or may/may not be in file system buffers.
- □ If critical errors on file I/O are handled by the operating system or reported directly to the application process.
- □ What type of access can be performed on the object.
- □ What type of sharing is allowed on the object.

DosQHandType Returns the type of the specified handle as a file handle, pipe handle, or character device handle. If the handle is a character device handle, the device will be identified as keyboard, screen, or other device. If the handle is a logical disk/diskette device, the handle will be identified as a file handle.

DosRead Reads the specified number of bytes from a file, pipe, or device identified by the handle. If the access to the file does not include read access, then the data is not read from the device. If the data can be obtained, the application process must check the number of bytes actually returned, because the requested number of bytes will not necessarily be available. For example, if the number of bytes actually returned for a file I/O request is zero, then the application process has tried to read beyond the end of the file. The I/O pointer for file I/O is moved to the next position for I/O; that is, its ending location is equal to its position before the request plus the length of the data returned.

DosReadAsync Asynchronously reads the specified number of bytes from a file, pipe, or device identified by the handle. The application process passes a RAM semaphore and a return code buffer in addition to the regular DosRead parameters. The application process must initialize the RAM semaphore (DosSemSet) before calling DosReadAsync. After the file system completes the operation and updates the I/O pointer, it will clear the RAM semaphore. At some point, the application process waits for the RAM semaphore (DosSemWait) to become available. Only after the RAM semaphore becomes available may the application process look at the return code and the number of bytes returned.

DosSetFHandState Sets the state information for the handle (file, character device, Standard Device, logical disk/diskette device, or pipe). The application process can thus set the following:

- □ The handle to be inherited.
- □ A file write request to commit data to media before returning to the requester.
- □ Critical errors on file I/O to be handled by the operating system or reported directly to the application process.

DosSetMaxFH Sets the maximum number of handles available for the application process. All open handles that the application process owns are unaffected by this operation.

DosWrite Writes the specified number of bytes to a file, pipe, or device identified by the handle. If the file is read-only, or if the access to the file does not include write access, then the data is not sent to the device. The application process must check the number of bytes actually written to the device. For file I/O, if the number of bytes written differs from the requested number to write, then there may be insufficient space on the media for the data. The I/O pointer for file I/O is also moved to the next position for I/O; that is, its ending location is equal to its position before the request plus the length of the data. For a write request of data that spans several sectors (where the current definition of a sector is 512 bytes), the file system does not guarantee the order in which the sectors are written to the media. If the application requires that a large quantity of data be written in a specific order, then it should issue separate I/O requests with the Write-Through Flag set so that data is committed to the media before the write request returns to the application process.

DosWriteAsync Asynchronously writes the specified number of bytes to a file, pipe, or device identified by the handle. The application process passes a RAM semaphore and a return code buffer in addition to the regular DosWrite parameters. The application process must initialize the RAM semaphore (DosSemSet) before calling DosWriteAsync. After the file system completes the operation and updates the I/O pointer, it will clear the RAM semaphore. At some point, the application process waits for the RAM semaphore (DosSemWait) to become available. Only after the RAM semaphore becomes available may the application process look at the return code and the number of bytes written.

File-Based Interfaces

We summarize the file system interfaces designed specifically for files in two categories: name-based interfaces and handle-based interfaces. The name-based interfaces require an ASCII character string terminated with a byte of 00h (also called an ASCIIZ string). The handle-based interfaces require a file handle.

File Name-Based Interfaces

The name-based interfaces can be used on files whether or not they are open. However, some actions require that the file not be in use.

DosDelete Deletes the specified file from the specified directory path. If no directory path is specified, it deletes the file from the current directory. Files that have an attribute of read-only cannot be deleted (you must first change the file attribute before deleting a read-only file). In addition, files that have already been opened by other application processes cannot be deleted, because the DELETE function acts as an exclusive user of the file.

DosFindClose Closes a directory search key in order to terminate a search through a directory for a file name or a set of file names. The DosFindFirst call initiates the search through a directory.

DosFindFirst Finds the first file that matches the specified file name in the specified directory. If no directory is specified, it finds the file in the current directory and returns a directory search key to allow DosFindNext to continue the search for this directory. The application process may specify a default directory key (0001h), which is always available for searches, or request that a directory key be returned. If an application process specifies a directory key already associated with a directory search, then the directory key is first closed and then reassociated with the current request. The application process specifies a file name, which may contain global characters, and the file attributes (normal, hidden, system, and so forth). The results of the search are returned in a buffer specified by the application.

DosFindNext Finds the next matching file that matches the target file name in the target directory identified by the directory search key, which was returned by the DosFindFirst call. An application process uses DosFindNext for the directory search key until no more matching files are found. Information on a matching file is returned in a buffer specified by the application.

DosMove Moves a file to another directory and/or file. The application process specifies the current path name/file name and the target path name/file name. If a drive letter is identified, then the drive must be the same for both the source and destination files. This means that a file can be moved to another directory on the drive and renamed but cannot be moved to another drive.

DosQFileMode Returns the setting of the attributes of the file identified by the file name. The file attributes are read-only, hidden, system, subdirectory, and archive.

DosSearchPath Searches the specified directory paths for the specified file name. The application process identifies the search route by one of the following:

- An ASCII string containing a number of directory paths separated by a semicolon and terminated by a byte of 00h.
- An ASCII string containing the name of a variable, which contains the search path, located in the environment of the application process.

The directory paths are searched in the order in which they appear in the search route. If a file name matching the specified file name is found, then the directory, including the drive, is returned in a buffer specified by the application. The file name that is specified by the application is then appended to this directory path, even if the file name contains global characters. This allows the application to locate a directory containing one or more matches for the specified file name and to feed the resulting directory/file string without modification to DosFindFirst.

DosSetFileMode Sets the attributes of the file identified by the file name. The changeable file attributes are read-only, hidden, system, and archive.

File Handle-Based Interfaces

The handle-based interfaces require that the input file be opened.

DosBufReset Flushes the buffers used by the file system for the specified file handle. The file system updates the directory entry for the file with the same information as if the file were being closed. However, the file remains open.

The application process can also specify a "global" file handle (FFFFh) that flushes file system buffers associated with *all* of the process's open files.

DosChgFilePtr Moves the file I/O pointer for the specified file handle. The application process indicates both the manner and the distance for the movement. Specifically, the I/O pointer may be moved as follows:

- From the beginning of the file plus a specified distance.
- From the current location of the I/O pointer plus a specified distance.
- From the end-of-file plus a specified distance.

DosFileLocks Exclusively locks/unlocks a range of bytes in the open file identified by a file handle. The application process specifies the target region as an offset from the beginning of the file and the length of the affected area. The application process can identify both a locked region and an unlocked region as parameters to a single invocation of the system call. Where both functions are requested, the file system does the unlock before the lock. A locked region extending beyond the end of the file is considered valid and does not generate an error.

Range locking/unlocking is a mechanism temporarily to restrict other processes from accessing areas in the open file. Typically, an application process would use locks if it needs temporarily to prohibit other application processes from concurrently writing to the region in the file, or if it needs to temporarily prevent other processes from reading the region in the file while it writes to the affected region.

If a file is closed with locks outstanding, the file system will release the locks. However, the order in which the locks are released is not defined. If a file handle having access to a locked region is duplicated, then the resulting copy of the file handle also has access to the locked region. However, if a child process inherits a file handle with access to a locked region, the inherited file handle will *not* have access to the locked region.

DosNewSize Changes the size of a file identified by the file handle. An application process specifies the new total size of the file, indicating a growth or a shrinkage. This change is not reflected in the directory entry until the file is closed. An extension to the file is allocated out of a contiguous space on the drive, if possible (as opposed to being fragmented), and the value of the data in the new portion is undefined. Whether the file is extended or truncated, it is not actually copied to a new location. A new size cannot be defined for a read-only file.

DosQFileInfo Returns information about the file identified by the file handle. The application process can obtain the following information about the file:

- □ Date and time of creation.
- □ Date and time of last access.
- □ Date and time of last write.
- □ Amount of data (bytes).
- □ Amount of total allocation (bytes).
- □ Attribute.

DosSetFileInfo Sets certain information about the file identified by the file handle, where the file has been opened for write access. The application process can change the following information about the file:

- □ Date and time of creation.
- □ Date and time of last access.
- □ Date and time of last write.

Directory-Based Interfaces

These interfaces permit the application to manipulate directories.

DosChDir Changes the current directory path for the application process to the directory path specified. The directory path is not changed if any portion of the specified path does not exist.

DosMkDir Creates the specified subdirectory. The subdirectory is not created if any portion of the specified path does not exist.

DosQCurDir Returns the application process's current directory path name for the specified drive number.

DosQCurDisk Returns the current default drive for the application process as well as a bit map indicating which of the 26 possible drive letters correspond to logical disk/diskette devices at the time of the system call.

DosRmDir Removes a subdirectory identified by the specified directory path. As in DOS, a subdirectory cannot be removed if it contains any files, including hidden files, or if it is the current or root directory. The last directory in the path name is the directory that is removed.

File Device Interfaces

These interfaces are used to manipulate information about the file devices.

DosQFsInfo Returns the specified level of file system information about a logical disk/diskette device identified by a drive number. The first level of file system information concerns the logical device:

- Number of sectors per allocation unit.
- Number of allocation units.
- Available allocation units.
- Bytes per sector.

The second level of file system information concerns the volume label:

- Creation date and time.
- Length of volume name string.
- ASCII string containing volume label.

DosQVerify Returns the setting of the Write-With-Verify mode for the file and device I/O performed by the process. The application process uses this mode to guarantee that critical data is written to the device without error.

DosSelectDisk Selects the specified drive as the default drive for the application process.

DosSetFsInfo Sets the specified level of file system information about a logical disk/diskette device identified by a drive number. The first level of file system information concerns the logical device and cannot be changed by the application. The second level of file system information concerns the volume label, and the application may change only the volume label string and string length and only if the volume has been opened for write access.

DosSet Verify Sets the Write-With-Verify mode for all file and device I/O performed by the application process. The application process uses this mode to guarantee that critical data is written to the device without error.

CHARACTER DEVICE I/O SUBSYSTEMS

A subsystem in OS/2 is a set of services oriented to a specific device or feature. An I/O subsystem can take many forms, but there are three basic designs:

- □ A **device driver**, which supports application I/O to its device through regular operating system interfaces.
- □ A **dynamic link library**, which supports application I/O with its own customized interfaces.
- □ A **process**, which supports I/O of other application processes through an interface based on interprocess communication (IPC).

Of course, an I/O subsystem can be created as a mixture of the three basic alternatives.

OS/2 Standard Edition has three I/O subsystems serving the console devices: screen, keyboard, and mouse. Each of these I/O subsystems consists of a dynamic link library of application interfaces and a device driver. These I/O subsystems are identified as follows:

- □ VIO, the video I/O subsystem.
- □ KBD, the keyboard I/O subsystem.
- □ MOU, the mouse I/O subsystem.

VIO: Video I/O

The VIO subsystem consists of a dynamic link library, easily distinguishable by the interfaces prefaced by "VIO," and a screen device driver, which is automatically installed by the operating system. The VIO interfaces supply text-oriented functions that represent a superset of the text-oriented functions provided by the BIOS Int 10h video interfaces in the DOS environment. The VIO subsystem provides two basic methods for video I/O: through a logical video buffer (LVB), or through the physical video buffer (PVB).

As you recall, whenever a session is started, a logical video buffer is created and is shared by all the application processes executing within the session. Each session has a unique logical video buffer. The logical video buffer of a session is tied to the physical video buffer (the screen), whenever the session becomes the foreground session (see Figure 37). A session becomes the foreground session whenever the end user switches to it. Whenever the end user switches from one session to another, the VIO subsystem saves the screen of the previous session and displays the screen

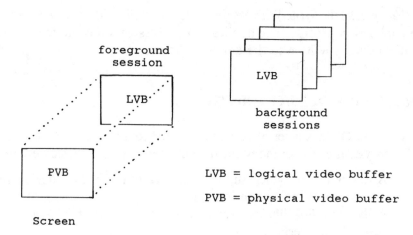

Figure 37. Foreground versus Background Video

of the new session. The logical video buffer of a background session allows any application process in the background session to continue video I/O; however, the logical video buffer will not be displayed until the session is placed in the foreground. There is only one exception for video I/O that permits a background process to temporarily display foreground information: a background process may use a temporary foreground "session" called a pop-up to display information about critical events and interact with the end user.

An application process does not have to use the logical video buffer for video I/O. It can use the VIO subsystem to obtain access to the physical video buffer. However, because the physical video buffer must be shared across sessions, the application process directly manipulating the physical video buffer must adhere to some rules. The application process must lock and unlock the physical video buffer, so that its I/O can be coordinated with other sessions as its session is made foreground or background. The application process must also register for asynchronous notification of a session switch: when the end user switches away from the session in which the application process resides, the application process is told to save its screen; when the user switches back to the session, the application process is told to restore its screen.

The choice of which video buffer to use for I/O is dependent on the type of video I/O desired. Most of the VIO interfaces are oriented to the text modes. If an application is geared to text, it can use the logical video buffer and even manipulate the logical video buffer directly. However, if an application needs to use graphics modes, then the application must manipulate the physical video buffer directly. Here, speed of the I/O is not the critical question. The VIO interfaces are designed to be very responsive in order to encourage applications to avoid direct contact with the hardware in a multitasking environment. Moreover, using the logical video buffer is a migration path to the windowing and graphics services of the Presentation Manager that is provided in the OS/2 Standard Edition Version 1.1 release.

The VIO interfaces are described in terms of some general categories:

- Character I/O.
- Cursor control.
- Scroll management.
- Video device control.
- Pop-up management.
- Logical video buffer management.
- Physical video buffer management.
- Function replacement.

VIO Character I/O

An application can perform I/O to the screen in terms of characters and their attributes (color, intensity, etc.). A character combined with its attribute is called a character cell.

VioReadCellStr Reads a string of character/attribute pairs from the video buffer starting at the specified location. If the end of a line is encountered and the string is not complete, then the READ continues from the next line. If the end of the screen is encountered and the string is not complete, then the READ terminates and the length is set to the number of bytes used in the application's buffer.

VioReadCharStr Reads a string of characters from the video buffer starting at the specified location. If the end of a line is encountered and the string is not complete, then the READ continues from the next line. If the end of the screen is encountered and the string is not complete, then the READ terminates and the length is set to the number of bytes used in the application's buffer.

VioWrtCellStr Writes a string of character/attribute pairs to the video buffer starting at the specified location. If the end of a line is encountered before the WRITE completes, the WRITE continues to the next line. If the end of the screen is encountered, the WRITE terminates.

VioWrtCharStr Writes a string of characters to the video buffer starting at the specified location using the existing attributes. If the end of a line is encountered before the WRITE completes, the WRITE continues to the next line. If the end of the screen is encountered, the WRITE terminates.

VioWrtCharStrAtt Writes a string of characters to the video buffer starting at the specified location using the specified attribute for all the characters. If the end of a line is encountered before the WRITE completes, the WRITE continues to the next line. If the end of the screen is encountered, the WRITE terminates.

VioWrtNAttr Writes an attribute to the video buffer the specified number of times starting at the specified location. If the end of a line is encountered before the WRITE completes, the WRITE continues to the next line. If the end of the screen is encountered, the WRITE terminates.

VioWrtNCell Writes a character/attribute pair to the video buffer the specified number of times starting at the specified location. If the end of a line is encountered before the WRITE completes, the WRITE continues to the next line. If the end of the screen is encountered, the WRITE terminates.

VioWrtNChar Writes a character to the video buffer the specified number of times starting at the specified location. If the end of a line is encountered before the WRITE completes, the WRITE continues to the next line. If the end of the screen is encountered, the WRITE terminates.

VioWrtTTy Writes a character string to the video buffer starting at the current cursor position and moving the cursor to the position after the end of the string (the end of the string plus 1). If the end of a line is encountered before the WRITE completes, the WRITE continues to the next line. If the end of the screen is encountered, the screen is scrolled and the WRITE continues. Certain characters are treated as commands, including the CarriageReturn character, LineFeed character, Backspace character, Tab character, and Bell character. The handling of characters is also affected by ANSI, if ANSI has been activated. This method of handling video characters is known as TTY mode.

VIO Cursor Control

An application can control the position and shape of the cursor, which is generally used to position characters typed from the keyboard.

VioGetCurPos Returns the current row and column position of the keyboard cursor.

VioGetCurType Returns the current height, width, and attribute of the keyboard cursor.

VioSetCurPos Sets the keyboard cursor position to the specified row and column.

VioSetCurType Sets the height, width, and attribute of the keyboard cursor.

VIO Scroll Management

An application can manipulate rectangular areas of the screen image or video buffer through scrolling.

VioScrollDn Scrolls text within a rectangular area down the specified number of rows. It also inserts the scroll number of lines, using the specified cell (character and attribute), at the top of the scroll area.

VioScrollLf Scrolls text within a rectangular area the specified number of columns to the left. It also inserts the scroll number of columns, using the specified cell (character and attribute), at the right of the scroll area.

VioScrollRt Scrolls text within a rectangular area the specified number of columns to the right. It also inserts the scroll number of columns, using the specified cell (character and attribute), at the left of the scroll area.

VioScrollUp Scrolls text within a rectangular area up the specified number of rows. It also inserts the scroll number of lines, using the specified cell (character and attribute), at the bottom of the scroll area.

VIO Video Device Control

An application can utilize the different displays and adapters through a variety of interfaces to get and set display modes, device information, and character code pages (or video character fonts). In addition, an application can activate the ANSI extended screen and keyboard mode, which is part of the VIO Subsystem. (In DOS, the ANSI extended screen and keyboard mode requires the device driver ANSI.SYS to be selected through the CONFIG.SYS configuration file.) ANSI mode defines special control character sequences to position the cursor, erase text from the screen, set the mode of the screen I/O, and redefine the meaning of keyboard characters.

VioGetAnsi Returns the current state of the ANSI extended screen and keyboard mode.

VioGetConfig Returns the type of display, the type of display adapter, and the amount of memory on the display adapter. Identification of the display and display adapter is based on a number of tests performed by the VIO Subsystem to determine the video configuration. While it is not possible to completely identify the video configuration because the video switch settings may not correspond to the actual setup and a display may not actually be attached to the display adapter, the information returned reflects the working assumptions of the VIO Subsystem.

VioGetCp Returns code page ID (font) of the current code page.

VioGetFont Returns the current font (code page) or a specific font in the display adapter ROM (if the adapter maintains fonts).

VioGetMode Returns the display mode in terms of type, number of colors, textual rows/columns, and vertical/horizontal resolutions. The types of modes include monochrome-compatible mode, text mode, and graphics mode, with color burst enabled or disabled. The number of colors is in the power of 2; for example, 1 indictates two colors and 2 indicates four colors. Textual rows and columns indicate the resolution for text mode characters. Vertical and horizontal resolutions indicate the number of pels available on the display.

VioGetState Returns the current settings of the palette registers, border colors, and blink and background intensity.

VioSetAnsi Activates or deactivates the ANSI extended screen and keyboard mode.

VioSetCp Sets the code page, or font, to the code page identified by the code page ID.

VioSetFont Loads a character font, or code page, into the display adapter as supplied by the application process. The character font must be compatible with the current video mode and can be utilized only on those display adapters that support changeable fonts.

VioSetMode Sets the display mode. The mode is set in terms of type, colors, textual rows/columns, and vertical/horizontal resolutions. The types of modes include monochrome-compatible mode, text mode, and graphics mode, with color burst enabled or disabled. The colors must be specified as a number in the power of 2; that is, 1 indicates two colors and 2 indicates four colors. Textual rows and columns indicate the resolution for text mode characters. Vertical and horizontal resolutions indicate the number of pels available on the display. Setting the mode initializes the keyboard cursor position and type.

VioSetState Sets the palette registers, border colors, and blink and background intensity.

VIO Pop-up Management

An application process running in the background can put a temporary window or "pop-up" over the screen image of the foreground session. This allows the background application process to notify the user of an important event and interact if necessary.

VioEndPopUp Releases the ownership of the temporary foreground video buffer.

VioPopUp Requests a temporary foreground video buffer and, if one is not available, either returns an error code or waits for one to become available, depending on the action specified by the application process. If the return code from the VioPopUp function call is successful, the application process can perform I/O to the console (screen, keyboard, mouse). Any VIO services used by the process at this time are directed to the temporary foreground video buffer until the process issues the VioEndPopUp function call. As there can be only one application pop-up in use at a time, the application may need to wait for one to become available. While a pop-up is in effect, the operator is temporarily not permitted to switch sessions, and all video calls from processes in the foreground session are temporarily blocked. However, if the application process owning the pop-up is in the foreground session, then only video calls from other processes in the session are temporarily blocked. In addition, while a pop-up is in effect, the pop-up owner may not access the physical video buffer.

VIO Logical Video Buffer Management

An application can manipulate the logical video buffer directly, without affecting the displayed screen image, and have the physical video buffer updated from the logical video buffer.

VioGetBuf Gets LDT addressability (selector and offset) to a logical video buffer, as well as the length of the logical video buffer, which is dependent on the mode of the display.

VioShowBuf Updates the physical video buffer from the logical video buffer if the application process is in the foreground session. If the application process is in a background session, then this interface has no effect.

VIO Physical Video Buffer Management

Since OS/2 Standard Edition Version 1.0 does not directly provide functions to support display graphics modes, a set of video services enables an application to implement its own video graphics and peacefully coexist with applications executing in other sessions.

The essential protocol for graphics I/O is as follows:

1. Obtain addressability to the physical video buffer.
2. Set the mode to graphics (with VIOSetMode).
3. Lock the physical video buffer for I/O.
4. Perform I/O to the physical video buffer.
5. Unlock the physical video buffer.

A graphics application also needs to dedicate a thread to saving and restoring its screen, because the operator can switch sessions. If the application directly manipulates the registers on the display adapter, the application needs to dedicate an additional thread to restoring the video mode and display adapter registers.

VioGetPhysBuf Gets LDT addressability to the physical video buffer. The application process identifies the physical video buffer by specifying the buffer's address as a 32 bit physical address and the buffer's length. Legal addresses fall into the range of A0000h to BFFFFh. The application process then receives one or more selectors for accessing the physical video buffer. Each selector accesses up to 64 KB of the buffer. So, depending on the length of the target physical video buffer, the application process needs one or more selectors to access the entire buffer. If the length of the buffer is greater than 64 KB, then the first selector accesses the first 64 KB, the second selector accesses the next 64 KB, and so on, with the last selector accessing the remaining space. The application process may manipulate the physical video buffer *only* when it is in the foreground session. To help in coordinating its video I/O, the application process must use VioScrLock and VioScrUnLock.

VioModeUndo Cancels the VioModeWait service issued by another thread in the application process. This is done in one of two ways: either by having the VioModeWait return an error code to the other thread, or by terminating the other thread. The application process can optionally preserve its ownership of the VioModeWait service, even though it has cancelled the current VioModeWait service. See VioModeWait for more details.

VioModeWait Waits for notification to restore the video mode, video state, and display adapter registers. The graphics application process must dedicate a thread for the VioModeWait function call *only* if it writes directly to the display adapter registers in order to restore the video characteristics after a temporary pop-up (from either a critical error or an application in a background session) has ended. The graphics application will *not* need to restore the physical video buffer, because the VIO Subsystem preserves the area used by the pop-up. Once a thread in the application process has issued the VioModeWait function call, it waits until the VioModeWait service returns. When the VioModeWait service returns, the calling thread must check the return code. If the return code is not an error code, then the thread must restore the video mode, video state, and display adapter registers. The VioModeWait thread should avoid making other system calls or causing a critical error because of the potential for system deadlock. When the thread has completed the restoration of the video characteristics, it can then reissue the VioModeWait system call to wait for the next time it needs to restore the display. Obviously, there is only one process in a session that may issue VioModeWait, since the caller is expected to change the state of the display as needed, and VioModeUndo allows that process to cancel its VioModeWait request.

VioSavRedrawUndo Cancels the VioSavRedrawWait service issued by another thread in the application process. This is done in one of two ways: either by having the VioSavRedrawWait return an error code to the other thread, or by terminating the other thread. The application process can optionally preserve its ownership of the VioSavRedrawWait service, even though it has cancelled the current VioSavRedrawWait service. See VioSavRedrawWait for more details.

VioSavRedrawWait Waits for notification to save or restore the physical video buffer. The graphics application process must dedicate a thread for the VioSavRedrawWait function call in order to save or restore the screen image for a session switch. Once a thread in the application process has issued the VioSavRedrawWait function call, it waits until the VioSavRedrawWait service returns. When the VioSavRedrawWait service returns, the calling thread must check the return code. If the return code is not an error code, then the thread checks the notification type and either saves or restores the physical video buffer, video mode, and/or any other information the application requires to complete its screen image. The VioSavRedrawWait thread should avoid making other system calls or causing a critical error because of the potential for system deadlock. Also, when accessing the physical video buffer, the VioSavRedrawWait thread does not lock the physical video buffer (VioScrLock) because it has already been granted ownership through the OS/2 session manager. When the thread has completed the save/restore of the screen image, it can then reissue the VioSavRedrawWait system call to wait for the next time it needs to perform these operations. Obviously, there is only one process in a session that may issue VioSavRedrawWait, since the caller is expected to change the state of the display as needed, and VioSavRedrawUndo allows that process to cancel its VioSavRedrawWait request.

VioScrLock Requests ownership of the physical video buffer. The application process indicates whether it wants to wait until the physical video buffer is available or to have the VioScrLock service return immediately if the physical video buffer is not available. The application process must check the outcome of the function call to determine if the application may use the physical video buffer. There are two reasons why an application process is *not* given ownership of the physical video buffer: if its session is in the background, or if the physical video buffer is owned by another process. Once the application process owns the physical video buffer, it may perform I/O. However, the process must yield ownership of the physical video buffer as soon as possible with VioScrUnLock to allow the operator to switch among the different sessions. Session switching is temporarily disabled while the physical video buffer is locked. However, if the operator attempts to switch to another session during the lock, the operating system places a time limit on the lock of the physical video buffer. If the time limit expires and the owner of the physical video buffer has not released the lock, then the operating system suspends the owning process in the background and proceeds with the session switch. The suspended process will not execute until the operator switches back to the process's session.

VioScrUnLock Releases ownership of the physical video buffer.

VIO Function Replacement

An application or another video subsystem can selectively intercept the VIO Subsystem interfaces to replace or extend the function provided by the base video subsystem. Of course, as with any subsystem, another video subsystem can also extend the video interfaces by adding other interfaces.

VioDeRegister Removes a video subsystem previously registered within a session. Only the application process that issued the VioRegister in the session may issue the VioDeRegister.

VioRegister Registers a video subsystem within the current session. Only one video subsystem can be registered at a time for a session. The registered video subsystem must indicate which of the VIO Subsystem services it will intercept at its registration time. Then, when an application process in the same session as the registered video subsystem invokes a VIO service that is intercepted, the VIO Subsystem calls the registered video subsystem. For an intercepted VIO service, the registered video subsystem can choose to have the base VIO service invoked by returning the special error code of −1 (FFFFh). The VIO Subsystem will then call the base VIO service.

KBD: Keyboard I/O

The KBD subsystem consists of a dynamic link library, easily distinguishable by the interfaces prefaced by "KBD," and a keyboard device driver, which is automatically installed by the operating system. The KBD interfaces have many features that are similar in nature to the services provided the BIOS Int 16h keyboard interfaces to the DOS environment. The KBD subsystem allows an application to receive both the scan code of a keystroke sequence and the ASCII character corresponding to the scan code through a character data record, or to receive a string of ASCII characters. The character data record is described in Figure 38.

Input from the physical keyboard device is placed in a buffer maintained by the KBD I/O Subsystem. As in DOS, when the operator types enough keystrokes to fill the keyboard buffer, additional keystrokes are disallowed. In other words, the input buffer has a fixed length and, when a buffer overrun occurs, a character that won't fit is discarded (and, as in DOS, a tone is sounded through the speaker). Since the keyboard device is part of the console, only applications in the foreground session can receive keystrokes.

As you recall, whenever a session is started, a logical keyboard buffer is created and is shared by all the application processes executing within the session. Each session has a unique logical keyboard buffer. The logical keyboard buffer is tied to the keyboard device whenever the session becomes the foreground session, that is, whenever the operator switches to the session. Whenever the operator switches from one session to another, the KBD subsystem switches the keyboard device to

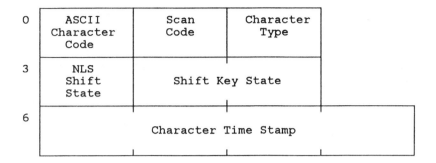

ASCII Character Code from the translated scan code.

Scan Code for the keystroke(s) pressed.

Character Type defines the type of character:

      * Final character
      * Interim character (NLS support)
      * No character, shift key(s) only

NLS Shift State is Reserved (00h).

Shift Key State tells the state of the following:

SysReq Key	Right Alt Key	Insert Key
CapsLock Key	Left Alt Key	Right Shift Key
NumLock Key	Right Ctrl Key	Left Shift Key
ScrollLock Key	Left Ctrl Key	

Character Time Stamp is in milliseconds since IPL.

Figure 38. Keyboard Data Record

the logical keyboard buffer of the new session. The logical keyboard buffer of a background session allows any application process in the background session to continue keyboard I/O. However, keystrokes will not be placed in the logical keyboard buffer of the background session until the session is placed in the foreground. There is only one exception for keyboard I/O that permits a background process to temporarily use the foreground keyboard device: a background process may use a temporary foreground "session" called a pop-up to interact with the operator.

Although each session has a default keyboard buffer, an application process has the choice of using the default logical keyboard or obtaining another logical keyboard. When using the default logical keyboard, the application employs the KBD default keyboard handle (0000h) in the KBD function calls. However, an application process would use a different logical keyboard from the default if a number of processes execute within the session and use the console (screen, keyboard, and/or mouse). The secondary logical keyboard enables a process to isolate its I/O from the other processes in the session. To use a secondary logical keyboard, the application process uses KbdOpen to initialize the logical keyboard and obtain a KBD keyboard handle. Then the application process uses KbdGetFocus to temporarily connect its logical keyboard to the physical keyboard for I/O. I/O can then be performed with the KBD keyboard handle. KbdFreeFocus disconnects the logical keyboard from the physical keyboard and permits other processes to obtain the focus. KbdClose terminates the application process's connection to the logical keyboard.

The KBD keyboard handles are *not* inheritable the way handles allocated by the file system are.

The KBD interfaces are described in terms of some general categories:

□ Character I/O.
□ Device control.
□ Logical keyboard management.
□ Function replacement.

KBD Character I/O

An application performs I/O from a keyboard device by using either the default KBD device handle or a KBD device handle to another logical keyboard and by reading either a character record or a string of characters from the keyboard's FIFO input buffer.

KbdCharIn Reads a keyboard data record from the logical keyboard (default or other) identified by the KBD keyboard handle into the buffer specified by the application process. The application process must also indicate if it wants to wait for a character to become available or to have the KbdCharIn service return immediately if no character is available. A keyboard data record will be returned only if the logical keyboard has the focus, that is, if the logical keyboard is currently tied to the physical keyboard. Typically, the default logical keyboard for the session will have the focus unless another logical keyboard is being used.

KbdFlushBuffer Clears the logical keyboard buffer (default or other) identified by the KBD keyboard handle. The flush occurs when the logical keyboard has the focus, that is, when it is currently tied to the physical keyboard. Typically, the default logical keyboard for the session will have the focus unless another logical keyboard is being used.

KbdPeek Returns a keyboard data record from the logical keyboard identified by the KBD keyboard handle without removing it from the buffer. A keyboard data record will be returned only if the logical keyboard has the focus, that is, if it is currently tied to the physical keyboard. Typically, the default logical keyboard for the session will have the focus unless another logical keyboard is being used.

KbdStringIn Returns the specified number of ASCII characters (character codes only) from the logical keyboard identified by the KBD keyboard handle. The maximum number of characters (bytes) is 255. The application process must indicate whether it wishes to wait or not:

WAIT   In Binary Input Mode, the application process waits until the number of characters can be obtained. In ASCII Input Mode, the application process waits until the NewLine (CarriageReturn) character is pressed.

NO WAIT   In Binary Input Mode, the application process receives as many characters as are available, up to the number requested. If no characters are available, then the KbdStringIn service returns immediately. In ASCII Input Mode, the NO WAIT option is not supported.

Keyboard characters will be returned only if the logical keyboard has the focus, that is, if the logical keybord is currently tied to the physical keyboard. Typically, the default logical keyboard for the session will have the focus unless another logical keyboard is being used.

KbdXlate Translates the scan code and shift key states found in a keyboard data record into an ASCII character code. The translation is based on the code page for the logical keyboard identified by the KBD keyboard handle. The translated character is returned in a translation data record placed in a buffer specified by the application process. Translation flags will be set when the translation is complete. The translation may actually take several calls, due to certain key combinations.

KBD Device Control

An application has a number of interfaces to get and set information about the keyboard device and about how keystrokes are handled.

KbdGetCP Returns the code page ID of the code page used to translate scan codes to ASCII characters for the logical keyboard identified by the KBD keyboard handle.

KbdGetStatus Returns keyboard characteristics for the logical keyboard identified by the KBD keyboard handle. The device information is placed in a buffer specified by the application process. The information includes the following:

□ The Input Mode.
    The Input Mode may be either ASCII Input Mode or Binary Input Mode. In ASCII Input Mode, characters from the keyboard are interpreted with certain "control" characters causing special processing to occur. In Binary Input Mode, characters from the keyboard are not interpreted.
□ The Interim Character Flag.
    The Interim Character Flag may be set to indicate that the application process wants to receive each intermediate character in a multiple

character sequence used to build the final character. This flag is meaningful for languages where several keystrokes are needed to build a character.

□ The Shift Key State.

The Shift Key State indicates whether any of the shift keys have been used. For example, pressing the CapsLock key sets its state to ON, and pressing the CapsLock key a second time sets its state to OFF. The shift keys include the SysReq key, the CapsLock key, the NumLock key, the ScrollLock key, the Alt keys, the Ctrl keys, and the Shift keys.

□ The Echo Mode.

The Echo Mode indicates whether keyboard characters are to be echoed to the Standard OUTPUT device.

□ The NewLine Character Definition.

The NewLine Character Definition identifies which character, ASCII or Extended ASCII, specifies the "turnaround" or CarriageReturn character.

KbdSetCP Sets the code page, identified by the code page ID, used to translate scan codes to ASCII characters for the logical keyboard identified by the KBD keyboard handle. The logical keyboard buffer is flushed to clear characters translated with the previous code page.

KbdSetCustXt Sets the code page to the translate table provided by the application process for the logical keyboard identified by the KBD keyboard handle. The application process must maintain the translate table in memory that it owns. The logical keyboard buffer is flushed to clear characters translated with the previous code page.

KbdSetStatus Sets the keyboard characteristics for the logical keyboard identified by the KBD keyboard handle. The device information is passed in a buffer specified by the application process. The device information includes the Input Mode, the Interim Character Flag, the Shift Key State, the Echo Mode, and the NewLine Character Definition, as described in KbdGetStatus.

KBD Logical Keyboard Management

An application can manipulate a logical keyboard that is separate from the default logical keyboard of the session.

KbdClose CLOSEs the logical keyboard (default or other) identified by a KBD keyboard handle. The default logical keyboard may be CLOSEd by the process but will still exist for the session. A secondary logical keyboard is disconnected, if necessary, from the physical keyboard and flushed before being terminated.

KbdFreeFocus Disconnects the logical keyboard identified by a KBD keyboard handle from the physical keyboard. If no requests for the focus are waiting for the focus, then the focus reverts to the default logical keyboard.

KbdGetFocus Connects the logical keyboard identified by a KBD keyboard handle to the physical keyboard. The application process must specify if it wishes to wait for the physical keyboard to become available or to have the KbdGetFocus service return immediately if the focus of the physical keyboard is already owned by another logical keyboard.

KbdOpen Returns a KBD keyboard handle to a secondary logical keyboard. The logical keyboard is initialized to the default code page.

KBD Function Replacement

An application or another keyboard subsystem can intercept the KBD interfaces in order to replace or extend the service provided. Of course, as with any subsystem, another keyboard subsystem can also extend the keyboard interfaces by adding other interfaces.

KbdDeRegister Removes a keyboard subsystem previously registered within a session. Only the application process that issued the KbdRegister in the session may issue the KbdDeRegister.

KbdRegister Registers a keyboard subsystem within the current session. Only one keyboard subsystem can be registered at a time for a session. The registered keyboard subsystem must indicate which of the KBD I/O subsystem services it will intercept at its registration time. Then, when an application process in the same session as the registered keyboard subsystem invokes a KBD service that is intercepted, the KBD I/O Subsystem calls the registered keyboard subsystem. For an intercepted KBD service, the registered keyboard subsystem can choose to have the base KBD service invoked by returning the special error code of −1 (FFFFh). The KBD I/O Subsystem will then call the base KBD service.

KbdSynch Permits a registered keyboard subsystem to synchronize its access to the physical keyboard device. This function helps keyboard subsystems coordinate actions with the keyboard device driver.

MOU: Mouse I/O

The MOU subsystem consists of a dynamic link library, easily distinguishable by the interfaces prefaced by "MOU," and two device drivers, a mouse device driver and pointer draw device driver, that must be selected by the operator with DEVICE= commands in the CONFIG.SYS configuration file. The MOU subsystem allows an application to control the way the mouse cursor is handled, which type of mouse events are included as data in the input buffer, and otherwise manage the mouse device. The mouse data record is described in Figure 39.

Input from the physical mouse device is placed in a buffer maintained by the MOU I/O Subsystem. Mouse data comes in the form of an event, which consists of one or more buttons being pressed combined with some or no movement of the mouse. Movement of the mouse device is tracked with the mouse cursor (also called a mouse pointer) on the screen. Mouse movement is reported either in terms of coordinates (row, column) or mickeys. A mickey is a term for a relative unit of mouse movement. An application process may select the type of units for mouse movement. Coordinates are the default method for indicating mouse movement and are in character or pixel offsets, depending on the mode of the screen. Coordinate values are relative to the top left corner of the screen, the 0,0 point for the x- and y-directions. If mickeys are selected, then the x,y values are relative to the current position of the mouse. Negative mickey values indicate movement toward the upper and left portions of the screen. When the end user moves the mouse and causes the buffer to fill with mouse data, additional mouse movement and/or button presses is not lost but instead overwrites the "oldest" data in the buffer. In other words, although the input buffer has a fixed length, it is a circular buffer that maintains the most recent mouse events. Since the mouse device is part of the console, only applications in the foreground session can receive mouse data.

As you recall, whenever a session is started, a logical mouse buffer is created

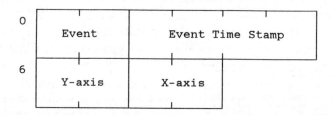

```
Event describes the type of event(s) recorded.

        Button (1,2,or 3) down / no mouse motion
        Button (1,2,or 3) down / mouse motion
        No button down / mouse motion
        No button down / no mouse motion

Event Time Stamp is in milliseconds since IPL.

Y-axis is the vertical position of the mouse cursor.

X-axis is the horizontal position of the mouse
cursor.
```

Figure 39. Mouse Data Record

and is shared by all the application processes executing within the session. Each session has a unique logical mouse buffer. The logical mouse buffer of a session is tied to the mouse device whenever the session becomes the foreground session. Whenever the operator switches from one session to another, the MOU subsystem switches the mouse device to the logical mouse buffer of the new session. The logical mouse buffer of a background session allows any application process in the background session to continue mouse I/O; however, mouse data will not be placed in the logical mouse buffer of the background session until the session is placed in the foreground. There is only one exception for mouse I/O that permits a background process to temporarily use the foreground mouse device: a background process may use a temporary foreground "session" called a pop-up to interact with the operator.

The protocol for mouse I/O is similar to that of other character devices. The application process opens the mouse device with MouOpen, which initializes the logical mouse. Then the application process performs mouse I/O using the MOU mouse handle returned by MouOpen. Finally, the application process issues MouClose to terminate its connection to the logical mouse. To handle mouse events, the application process must follow the transition of the types of events reported. For example, suppose the application process used MouSetEventMask to indicate it wished to have *only* events concerning button 1 reported. Then only those events involving button 1 are reported. For this example, the table in Figure 40 relates the events, which are reported in the mouse input buffer, to the actions performed by the operator.

Operator Action	Mouse Event Type
Button 1 pressed.	Button 1 pressed. No motion.
Button 1 still pressed. Mouse moved.	Button 1 pressed. Motion.
Button 1 released. Mouse stopped.	No button pressed. No motion.
Button 2 pressed.	No event.
Button 2 still pressed. Mouse moved.	No event.
Button 2 still pressed. Mouse still moved. Button 1 pressed.	Button 1 pressed. Button 2 pressed. Motion.
Button 1 released. Button 2 released. Mouse still moved.	No button pressed. Motion.
Mouse stopped.	No event. (no transition with button 1)

Figure 40. Sample Mouse Events Based on Operator Actions

The MOU interfaces are described in terms of some general categories:

- Data I/O.
- Cursor control.
- Device control.
- Function replacement.

MOU Data I/O

An application performs I/O from a mouse device by getting an MOU device handle to the mouse device and READing data records from the mouse FIFO input buffer.

MouClose Closes the mouse device identified by the MOU device handle.

MouFlushQue Clears the mouse event buffer for the mouse device identified by the MOU device handle.

MouGetNumQueEl Returns the number of mouse data records currently in the mouse input buffer and the maximum number of data records that can be held in the mouse input buffer for the mouse device identified by the MOU device handle.

MouOpen Opens the mouse device for the application process and returns a MOU device handle.

MouReadEventQue Reads a mouse data record from the mouse input buffer for the mouse device identified by the MOU device handle. The application process must also indicate if it wants to wait for a mouse data record to become available or to have the MouReadEventQue service return immediately if no data record is available. See Figure 39 for the layout of a mouse data record.

MOU Cursor Control

An application can control the shape and the position of the mouse cursor as well as what areas on the screen the mouse cursor can be displayed.

MouDrawPtr Resets the screen area available to the mouse cursor for the mouse device identified by the MOU device handle. This action causes the mouse cursor to be drawn if its position is in the area previously restricted. MouRemovePtr sets the area restricted to the mouse cursor.

MouGetPtrPos Returns the vertical and horizontal positions of the mouse cursor for the mouse device identified by the MOU device handle..

MouGetPtrShape Returns a copy of the shape used for the mouse cursor for the mouse device identified by the MOU device handle. The default shape for screen text modes is a reverse video block that allows a character already on the screen to remain visible. The default shape for screen graphics modes is an arrow. The application process can change the shape of the mouse cursor with MouSetPtrShape.

MouRemovePtr Sets the screen area available to the mouse cursor for the mouse device identified by the MOU device handle. The application process defines a rectangle in which the mouse cursor cannot appear. If the mouse cursor is located within the restricted area, it is removed. MouDrawPtr releases the restrictions on where the mouse cursor may appear.

MouSetPtrPos Sets the vertical and horizontal positions of the mouse cursor for the mouse device identified by the MOU device handle.

MouSetPtrShape Sets the shape used for the mouse cursor for the mouse device identified by the MOU device handle. The application process must specify the AND and XOR bit masks for the cursor shape, the width and height of the cursor shape, and the starting point.

MOU Device Control

An application has a number of interfaces to get and set information about the mouse device and the mouse input buffer. The application can control which events are reported and who displays the mouse cursor.

MouGetDevStatus Returns the mouse device state at the time of the call of the mouse device identified by the MOU device handle. The state information includes the following:

- If the position of the mouse cursor is in coordinates or mickeys.
- If the application process has the responsibility of maintaining the mouse cursor on the screen.
- If the mouse cursor can be drawn in the current screen mode.
- If a flush of the mouse event buffer is in progress.
- If a READ of the mouse event buffer is in progress.
- If the mouse event buffer is busy with I/O.

MouGetEventMask Returns the types of events reported in a mouse data record for the mouse device identified by the MOU device handle. Button identification is by a logical number, beginning from left to right. The types of events are the following:

- Report button 1 press/release.
- Report button 1 press/release with mouse motion.

- Report button 2 press/release.
- Report button 2 press/release with mouse motion.
- Report button 3 press/release.
- Report button 3 press/release with mouse motion.
- Report mouse motion with no button press/release events.

MouGetHotKey Identifies the mouse buttons, for the mouse device specified by the MOU device handle, that are equivalent to the keyboard keystroke sequence used as the system attention keys, also known as the system "hot keys." Hot keys are defined systemwide; that is, they are the same across all sessions. They allow the operator to invoke the OS/2 program selector, which shows a list of applications to start and a list of current active sessions, or to switch from one session to another. The mouse hot key may be composed of one or more buttons that must be pressed simultaneously.

MouGetNumButtons Returns the number of buttons for the mouse device identified by the MOU device handle.

MouGetNumMickeys Returns the number of mickeys per centimeter for the mouse device identified by the MOU device handle.

MouGetScaleFact Returns the scaling factors for vertical and horizontal movement for the mouse device identified by the MOU device handle. A scaling factor is a value for the number of mickeys required to move the mouse cursor 8 pixels. The default for the vertical scale is 8 mickeys per 8 pixels. The default for the horizontal is 16 mickeys per 8 pixels.

MouSetDevStatus Sets the state of the mouse device identified by the MOU device handle. The settable information includes the following:

- If the position of the mouse cursor is in coordinates or mickeys.
- If the application process wishes to maintain the mouse cursor on the screen.

MouSetEventMask Sets the types of events reported in a mouse data record for the mouse device identified by the MOU device handle. Button identification is by a logical number, beginning from left to right. The types of events that can be reported include the following:

- Report button 1 press/release.
- Report button 1 press/release with mouse motion.
- Report button 2 press/release.
- Report button 2 press/release with mouse motion.
- Report button 3 press/release.
- Report button 3 press/release with mouse motion.
- Report mouse motion with no button press/release events.

MouSetScaleFact Sets the scaling factors for vertical and horizontal movement for the mouse device identified by the MOU device handle. A scaling factor is a value for the number of mickeys required to move the mouse cursor 8 pixels.

MOU Function Replacement

An application or another mouse subsystem can intercept the MOU interfaces in order to replace or extend the service provided. Of course, as with any subsystem, another mouse subsystem can also extend the mouse interfaces by adding other interfaces.

MouDeRegister Removes a mouse subsystem previously registered within a session. Only the application process that issued the MouRegister in the session may issue the MouDeRegister.

MouRegister Registers a mouse subsystem within the current session. Only one mouse subsystem can be registered at a time for a session. The registered mouse subsystem must indicate which of the MOU I/O subsystem services it will intercept at its registration time. Then, when an application process in the same session as the registered mouse subsystem invokes a MOU service that is intercepted, the MOU I/O Subsystem calls the registered mouse subsystem. For an intercepted MOU service, the registered mouse subsystem can choose to have the base MOU service invoked by returning the special error code of −1 (FFFFh). The MOU I/O Subsystem will then call the base MOU service.

MouSynch Permits a registered mouse subsystem to synchronize its access to the physical mouse device.

I/O CONTROL (IOCtl) CAPABILITIES

Besides the file system and other subsystem interfaces for I/O, an application may oversee a device and the device's operations through the I/O Control interface, also known as the IOCtl interface. In general, IOCtls are used to control the settable parameters of a device or device driver. Because the IOCtl interface is closely tied to the type of device, the IOCtl commands are broken into categories by device and into subfunctions within categories. Refer to Figure 41 for a list of device categories currently defined by OS/2.

An OS/2 application makes an IOCtl request through the DosDevIOCtl function call. The prerequisite for the IOCtl request is a handle to the device. This means that the application must first open the device to obtain a file system device handle. In the case of character devices, the application simply uses the character device name in the file system OPEN function call. In the case of block devices, the application must use the drive letter as the device name in the file system OPEN call,

Hex	Device Category
01	Serial Device Control
03	Pointer Draw Control
04	Keyboard Control
05	Printer Control
07	Mouse Control
08	Logical Disk/Diskette Control
09	Physical Disk Control
0A	Device Monitor Control
0B	General Control

Figure 41. IOCtl Categories

flagging the OPEN as a "DASD Open." Once the application obtains a device handle, it can issue an IOCtl command to the device specified by the handle. The operating system takes the IOCtl request and passes it to the device driver of the target device.

An OS/2 application does not necessarily need to send IOCtl commands to the devices it uses. Of the different categories currently defined, an application really needs to consider only the Serial Device IOCtls or the Printer IOCtls, if the application uses those kinds of devices. As for the Keyboard, Mouse, and Pointer Draw IOCtls, an OS/2 application can control the keyboard and the mouse (and the mouse's pointer draw facility) through the KBD and MOU I/O Subsystems, respectively. However, a keyboard subsystem or a mouse subsystem should consider the IOCtls, for those devices. A systems application that formats or partitions the media of block devices must use the Logical Disk/Diskette IOCtls and the Physical Disk IOCtls, respectively. The Device Monitor IOCtls and General Control IOCtls are generally used by the operating system or other system components, although an application or a subsystem may also need to use them.

Additional IOCtl categories and subfunctions within categories can be defined by an application that supplies a device driver or by a subsystem that supplies a device driver. The IOCtl category is a byte-sized field where the highest-order bit (bit 7) is significant. If set, it indicates that an application has defined the category. If clear, it indicates that the operating system has defined the category. Refer to the diagram in Figure 42 for the definition of a category code. The IOCtl subfunction is also a byte-sized field where the three high-order bits are significant, although one of those bits is optional. Bit 7 indicates how the request should be handled if the device or device driver does not support the specific subfunction. Bit 6 indicates if the subfunction is sent to the device driver for processing. Bit 5 is optional and simply organizes the subfunction codes. Refer to the diagram in Figure 42 for the definition of a subfunction number.

```
CATEGORY CODE                          SUBFUNCTION

7   6   5   4   3   2   1   0      7   6   5   4   3   2   1   0

U   *   *   *   *   *   *   *      I   D   G   *   *   *   *   *
```

```
U  =  1    USER-defined
      O    system-defined

I  =  1    IGNORE command if unsupported by device
      O    return error if unsupported by device

D  =  1    send to DEVICE DRIVER
      O    send to operating system

G  =  1    GET data from device (optional)
      O    send data to device  (optional)

*  =  1    Definable
      O
```

Figure 42. The IOCtl Category and Subfunction Definition

In summary, to define a new category, an application or subsystem can set the high-order bit and use any remaining bits as needed to create a category number. And, to define a subfunction, the application or subsystem sets the two highest-order bits according to the desired handling and uses the lower six bits to determine a function number.

USE OF CHARACTER DEVICE MONITORS

A character device monitor is a mechanism that allows an OS/2 application or subsystem to intercept the data stream passing through a device (see Figure 43). The application can modify or consume any or all of the data in one of the following two ways:

- Before the data is put into the device buffer to be read by other applications in the case of an input device.
- Before the data written by other applications is sent to the device in the case of an output device.

A DOS application uses a different technique to accomplish the same operation: a DOS application captures either the device interrupt or the BIOS interrupt in order to know when data is passing through the device.

An application that intercepts a device's data stream is really performing a kind of service to other applications. A character device monitor is an instrument that an application can use *to provide a service transparently to other applications*. Other applications do not need to change to take advantage of these services; they simply perform their I/O as usual.

A character device monitor depends on the device driver for its operations: not

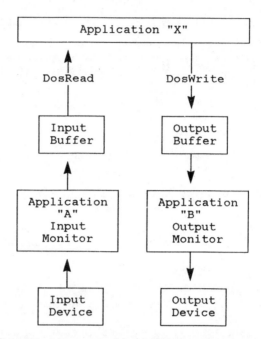

Figure 43. Movement of Device Data Being Monitored

only does the character device driver inherently define the nature of the data stream, but it must also actively redirect the data stream to the monitor. First, the definition of the data stream is important for the relationship of the device (and consequently the monitor) to the system, in other words, how applications do I/O to the device. For example, the data stream may be handled per session as with the keyboard or mouse, or systemwide as with the printer. This means that the scope of a monitor's effects on other applications' I/O is only as large as the scope of the device's data stream. A monitor of a per-session data stream can therefore affect only applications in that session, whereas a monitor of a systemwide data stream can affect applications across all sessions. Second, the device driver's redirection of the data stream to the monitor is important because the monitor cannot personally control the data stream. This means that a monitor can be used only on a device whose device driver supports monitoring.

In OS/2, there are three character device drivers that permit monitoring of their respective data streams: the keyboard, the mouse, and the printer. Both the keyboard device driver and the mouse device driver define a data stream per session. The printer device driver defines a systemwide data stream per device. As an example, an application that monitors keyboard data typically is used to map one keystroke sequence into another. This means that one or more keystrokes can be used as an abbreviation for a longer keystroke sequence. Since there is a keyboard data stream for each session, the operator could actually have different keystroke remappers tailored for the applications in the different sessions: one could be for a spreadsheet session and another for an editor session. As for printers, an application can use a monitor to intercept the print data and redirect it to a different printer or a different device.

Other character device drivers can be written to cooperate with application monitors for their respective devices.

An application monitor is really composed of a high-priority thread that deals with two buffers that can be likened to an IN box and an OUT box. The application must first open the character device for monitor usage. The application then uses the resulting monitor handle to register its monitor with the device. Data from the device is placed in the IN buffer. To process the device data, the application monitor thread reads data from the IN buffer to a private buffer. The monitor can then examine, modify, insert, and/or delete characters in the data. If there is any data to be given back to the device, then the monitor writes the data to the OUT buffer. Data in the OUT buffer is then placed in the device data stream. When the application wishes to terminate its monitor, it closes the monitoring with the monitor device handle.

An application monitor may not be the only monitor of the device's data stream. The existence of other monitors is transparent to an individual monitor. However, when a monitor is being registered, it has the ability to indicate a preference for its position with respect to other monitors (first, last, don't care) on a first-come-first-served basis. In other words, the first monitor registering for the first position is at the head of the list, and the next monitor registering for the first position is second in the list. Similarly, the first monitor registering for the last position is at the tail of the list, and the second monitor registering for the last position is next to last. Any monitors registering with no positional preference are placed before monitors registered for last.

The interfaces that the application requires for monitoring device data are summarized in order of use.

DosMonOpen Opens the character device identified by the character device name and returns a monitor device handle.

DosMonReg Registers the application's monitor according to its positional preference in the list of monitors. It is registered for a specific data stream of the character device identified by the monitor device handle. The application process can register a monitor to each data stream of the device, using the same monitor device handle but identifying a different data stream. In the case of a per-session data stream of a device, the application can register a separate monitor for each session.

DosMonRead Reads a data record from the IN buffer to the private work area specified by the monitor. For the case where no data is immediately available, the monitor must indicate whether it wants to wait for data to become available or to have the READ return immediately.

DosMonWrite Writes a data record from the specified private work area to the OUT buffer.

DosMonClose Closes the device specified by the monitor device handle and severs the connection to the device's data stream.

DIRECT I/O TO HARDWARE

OS/2 defines a mechanism, through IOPL code segments, that allows an OS/2 application or subsystem to perform I/O directly to a device. This means that an application or subsystem has the capability of programming a device adaptor without using a device driver or a control interface such as IOCtls.

There are some instances in which an application or a subsystem needs to control a device directly. Direct control has the advantage of being faster than using some intermediate service. And, for an OS/2 application or subsystem, only the segments that are actually being used need to be resident in system memory, so the segments containing routines for device control do not have to take up space in memory until they are called to execute. In DOS, there are really no restrictions on what an application does with devices it accesses directly, although this freedom can easily lead to conflicts between Terminate-And-Stay-Resident (TSR) programs, all vying to use the same device. In OS/2, an application may access a device directly but only under certain conditions. These conditions exist for two reasons. One is that the protection mechanisms of the 80286 microprocessor place restrictions on what application-level code may do. The other is due to the fact that multitasking environment's direct manipulation of a device that is used by more than one application requires some rules to avoid trouble.

The protection rules of the 80286 prevent application-level code from servicing hardware interrupts. Hardware interrupts must be handled at any privilege level. Since the processor does not permit a privilege level transition from system-level code to application-level code, only system-level code can service a hardware interrupt. As a result, only a **device driver** can service a device interrupt, because it executes at a sufficiently privileged level. This means that a non-interrupt-driven device is the best candidate for direct I/O by an OS/2 application. A good example of such a device is the display adapter, where I/O is mapped from the video buffer and registers on the adapter can be accessed through I/O ports.

To control a device directly, an application must use an I/O instruction like IN, INS, OUT, OUTS, CLI, and STI. IN/INS and OUT/OUTS respectively get and send data to a device's I/O port. CLI and STI respectively disable and enable hardware interrupts. However, the 80286 microprocessor restricts these I/O instructions to code executing at the I/O Privilege Level (IOPL) or at a more privileged level. Since applications execute at the application privilege level (the least privileged level), they cannot normally execute I/O instructions. OS/2 provides the means by which an application or subsystem can execute at a more privileged level in order to perform direct I/O. In order to maintain protection, though, the operating system does not allow all segments of an application or subsystem to exist at the "new" privilege level (IOPL). Instead, only those segments marked as requiring an increased privilege level are allowed to execute at IOPL. For that reason, the application or subsystem must isolate all routines using I/O instructions into one or more code segments and indicate when linking the code segments together which ones require IOPL.

The restriction that system services cannot be made from IOPL code segments effectively safeguards the different privilege levels. However, flagging a segment as an IOPL code segment is not enough. Prior to calling a routine in the IOPL code segment, the application or subsystem must issue a system call to request permission either to use the I/O ports and manipulate the state of hardware interrupts (DosPortAccess), or only to manipulate the state of hardware interrupts (DosCLIAccess).

There is an important additional aspect to IOPL. Since IOPL is a manipulation of the protection mechanism offered by the processor, the end user has control of this option. The user must set the keyword IOPL in the CONFIG.SYS configuration file to allow application and subsystem segments to execute at IOPL. This means that the end user can guarantee the protection and reliability of the system configuration and cannot inadvertently run an application or subsystem (or more than one) that changes the system environment without knowing about it.

6

Interrupt-Driven
Device Management

ONE OF THE MOST IMPORTANT FEATURES of a personal computer is its responsiveness
to actions performed by the end user. At the heart of these actions are the input/out-
put operations that a user and his applications perform in order to manipulate data.
In DOS, I/O operations follow a polled device model in which an I/O operation
must complete before the DOS user can continue an activity. In OS/2, however,
I/O operations are architected to an interrupt-driven device model. This model provides effects that are apparent both to the user and to applications. Interrupt-driven
device management allows I/O operations to take place at the same time as other
operations. Multitasking is therefore more efficient in sharing the processor among
concurrent activities. Better efficiency means increased responsiveness, benefiting
both the operator and the applications that he or she runs.

Why is interrupt-driven device management so important to the system? To understand the magnitude of its effects, we must understand the characteristics of polled
device management.

As you recall, the single tasking feature of DOS means that there is no mechanism
in DOS to notify an application when its I/O request has completed. A DOS application (and consequently the DOS user) must serialize its actions. This requirement dictates the basic tenet of managing I/O under DOS: polling. In other words,
the program that issues the I/O request to the device executes a loop of instructions that test an indicator for a change in state. If the indicator has changed its
state, then the program knows that the I/O operation is done. If the indicator has
not changed state, then the program must perform the loop of instructions again.
The indicator may be the result of a change in value at one of the device's I/O ports
or the result of a device interrupt. In the latter case, the device interrupt invokes
an interrupt handler that changes the state of the indicator that the program is testing
in the loop.

167

Why is it important to know when the I/O is complete? One reason is error handling. If the I/O operation fails, the DOS application may need to retry the operation or inform the operator that the activity had to be aborted. Success of the I/O operation means that the DOS application may proceed to the next action. Another reason is memory utilization. If the I/O operation is complete, the DOS application knows that the memory buffers containing data for the I/O operation are available and can be reused.

Under DOS, an application is not required to manage the polling. In a DOS application that uses system interfaces for I/O, the system interfaces manage the polling for the state of the I/O operation. But a DOS application that directly manipulates devices must manage the polled I/O. In either case, device management under DOS is constrained to be serialized and polled.

Interrupt-driven device management in OS/2, on the other hand, relieves the constraints of polled I/O. Interrupt-driven device management provides a way to notify the I/O requestor of the completion of an I/O operation. Some other activity can then take place at the same time as the I/O operation at the device. In fact, even different kinds of I/O can take place at the same time. Disk I/O, printer I/O, mouse I/O, and screen I/O can all be performed at the same time. System resources can therefore be utilized efficiently across several applications. This is also true of a single application which, with multiple processes or threads, has the ability to overlap its own actions with its I/O requests.

Another benefit of interrupt-driven device management on multitasking is the optimum use of intelligent devices. As work is offloaded from the processor to specialized microprocessors on these intelligent devices, the processor can handle more application-related activities. OS/2 is therefore well suited to future developments in devices.

The basic way interrupt-driven device management works lies in the coupling between the operating system and the program controlling the device, in this case, a device driver. The device driver thread that issues the I/O request to the device yields its remaining timeslice of execution while it waits for the device to complete the operation. Other threads can then execute. When the device is ready, it sends a hardware interrupt to the system. The hardware interrupt breaks into the execution of the currently running thread and causes the device driver's interrupt handler to execute. The interrupt handler resets the interrupt condition at the device and tells the operating system that the device driver thread waiting on the I/O request is ready to run. Once the interrupt handler has completed, the operating system can then schedule the different threads according to their priorities, and the highest priority thread will execute. This ability to schedule high priority threads as they become ready to run is especially important for time-critical application activities that must support the state of a device. One example is in data communications, where certain activities are required to maintain the communications link. When the device driver thread executes, it returns the completion code back to the application that initiated the I/O request.

Interrupt-driven device management thus fully participates with the multitasking of the operating system. Also, it is more responsive to the states of the device, because the device signals its request for attention by sending a hardware interrupt.

Obviously, an application under OS/2 can still perform polled I/O. However, unnecessarily repeating a loop of instructions is an inefficient use of the application's execution time. Instead, the application can use a timer services interface, like DosTimerStart or DosSleep, to pace the frequency with which it checks the device for I/O completion.

THE ROLE OF DEVICE DRIVERS

In OS/2, the interrupt-driven device model is achieved through the use of a device driver. In OS/2, only a device driver may handle device interrupts. Consequently, an application or subsystem that manages an interrupt-driven device must either provide its own device driver or use an existing device driver for that device.

The OS/2 device driver is similar in definition to a DOS device driver. A device driver is a program that manages the flow of data to and from a device. This program is not an independent entity like an application process. Rather, a device driver is more like a subroutine. The operating system calls the device driver to perform some action on behalf of an application I/O request. In fact, a device driver can be viewed as an extension of the operating system.

Application I/O requests in OS/2 appear in two forms. One form comes from the new OS/2 applications executing in the 80286 protected mode. The other form comes from a DOS application executing in the 80286 real mode. Consequently, the operating system calls an OS/2 device driver to perform application I/O requests in either protect mode or real mode, depending on which application environment is active (see Figure 44). Device interrupts also occur regardless of which mode the CPU is running. Therefore, an OS/2 device driver executes bimodally, that is, in both the real mode and protect mode of the 80286.

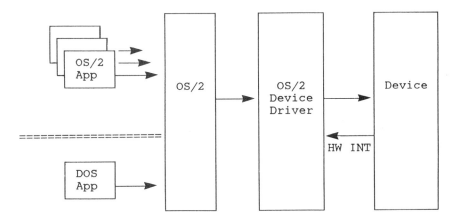

Figure 44. A Device Driver's Place in the System

While in protect mode, an OS/2 device driver executes at the system privilege level, privilege level 0. This automatically confers I/O privilege level (IOPL) on the OS/2 device driver, which gives the device driver the ability to access the device I/O ports with protected I/O instructions like IN and OUT. The device driver may also manipulate the state of the hardware interrupt flag, disabling and enabling device interrupts as necessary. *While an OS/2 application may access device I/O ports from routines isolated within an IOPL code segment, only an OS/2 device driver has the ability to handle device interrupts.*

A device driver is installed in OS/2 in the same fashion as in DOS, through the configuration file CONFIG.SYS with the statement DEVICE=. During operating system initialization, the configuration file is examined, the file specified by DEVICE= is loaded, and the device driver program is called by OS/2 to initialize itself.

There are a number of device drivers provided with OS/2. Some are loaded and configured automatically, specifically the screen, keyboard, printer, disk/diskette, and clock device drivers. Other device drivers must be selected with the DEVICE= statement in the configuration file, including the mouse, asynchronous communications, and virtual disk device drivers. Providing a set of base device drivers gives OS/2 the ability to guarantee a system configuration containing a standard set of devices and a standard set of functions.

The ability to install device drivers is an important way of extending function in the operating system. A new device driver can replace an existing device driver in order to provide additional function for a device. Or, a new device driver can be added to the operating system in order to support a new device.

As in DOS, there are two types of device drivers in OS/2: character device drivers and block device drivers.

A character device typically does I/O on a single character at a time, usually through program I/O (IN and OUT instructions to I/O ports). With character devices, the order of the characters is significant: the character device driver does not randomly access the data. Correspondingly, the order of requests for data is significant: the character device driver satisfies I/O requests in the order it receives them. The primary reason why order is so important to a character device is that a character device typically retains no memory of the data passing through it. Once the data is read or written, it cannot be retrieved. A character device is an identifiable object, referenced by a device name. The identity of a device by name means that an application may treat a character device like a file and use certain file system calls to perform I/O to the device. Examples of character devices and their respective device names are printer (LPT1, LPT2), keyboard (KBD$), and asynchronous communications (COM1, COM2).

A block device typically does I/O on blocks of data at a time, usually through DMA (direct memory access). A data block is normally referred to as a sector, which is defined to be 512 bytes long. With block devices, the block device driver may access any sector at any time. A block device does not require I/O on sectors to be performed in the same order that the sectors are physically located on the device.

This means that the block device driver may reorder I/O requests it receives to optimize device performance. For example, it may sort the requests by relative sector number to minimize time spent waiting for the device to find the sector location. The reason why order of sectors is not critical to a block device is that a block device is a storage device, preserving the data it receives. A block device is also an identifiable object, referenced by a drive letter. However, an application normally does not deal directly with a block device. Instead, the application performs I/O to a file, which is an abstract representation of sector data. The application uses the drive letter to specify on which block device the file is located. Then the file system manages the translation of the application file I/O request to the sector I/O request sent to the block device driver. Examples of block devices are fixed disks, diskette drives, and virtual disks. They have names like a: and b:.

DEVICE DRIVERS AND APPLICATION I/O

Device drivers manage their devices in the context of application I/O. OS/2 applications perform I/O primarily with the file system interfaces, the IOCtl interface, I/O subsystem interfaces, and the character device monitor interface.

Applications use file system interfaces to perform I/O on name-based objects and usually involve only block device drivers. The file system interfaces allow an application to view device data in a logical format. The logical data format for block devices is the file, which can also be thought of as a string of bytes. The application performs I/O on the file by identifying the relative position of the first byte in the file and the number of bytes to transfer. However, the block device driver understands I/O only in terms of sectors. Moreover, the block device driver cannot identify which sectors on the block device contain the application data. The file system therefore maps the byte references of the application I/O request to the sectors on the device that correspond to the file. Then, from the one application I/O request, the file system may send one or more sector-based I/O requests to the block device driver. The block device driver then transfers the sectors as directed.

For example, an application using the file I/O interfaces first OPENs the file, then READs and/or WRITEs to the file, and finally CLOSEs the file. As a result of the application's request to establish the connection to the device (OPEN the file), the file system may ask the block device driver to READ sectors from the device that represent directory and other control information. The file system may also ask the block device driver to WRITE sectors to the device, in order to clear internal file system buffers. See Figure 45 as an example. As a result of the application I/O (READs and WRITEs), the file system tells the block device driver to READ and WRITE sectors. And, as a result of the application's termination of its connection to the device (CLOSE the file), the file system may ask the block device driver to WRITE sectors to the device, representing a final update to directory and other control information stored at the device. The block device driver thus never sees the exact type of request from the application; instead, the block device driver

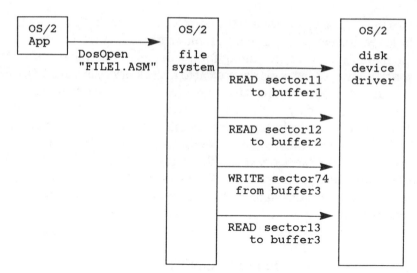

Figure 45. Example of I/O from a Block Device Driver's View

operates within the context of the file system's I/O requests made on behalf of the application I/O requests.

Some file system interfaces may be used for character device I/O since character devices are named objects, specifically the OPEN, CLOSE, READ, and WRITE functions. An application still views character device data in a logical format similar to that for block device data: a string of bytes (or characters). The application performs I/O on the character device by identifying the start of the data string and the number of bytes to transfer. The character device driver can satisfy the application I/O request without the aid of an intermediary. The file system, in this case, may send the application I/O request to the character device driver without any massaging.

For example, an application using the file I/O interfaces first OPENs the device name, then READs and/or WRITEs to the device, and finally CLOSEs the device. As a result of the application's request to establish the connection to the device (OPEN the device), the file system can tell the character device driver to OPEN an application connection to the device. The character device driver can then prepare the device for use, such as setting the device in some initial state. As a result of the application I/O (READs and WRITEs), the file system correspondingly asks the character device driver to READ and WRITE bytes. See Figure 46 as an example. And, as a result of the application's termination of its connection to the device (CLOSE the device), the file system can inform the character device driver to CLOSE the application connection to the device. The character device driver can then shut down the device I/O and reset internal variables. The character device driver can therefore see the type of request from the application; the file system acts primarily to route the application I/O request to the character device driver.

The IOCtl interface, also known as the I/O control interface, is used to send device-specific commands to control a device. The IOCtl interface can interact with either block or character device drivers. When an application issues the IOCtl request, the operating system sends the IOCtl request directly to the target device driver.

For example, an application using the IOCtl interface first OPENs the device name with the file system interface, issues the IOCtl request(s), and finally CLOSEs the device with the file system interface. The OPEN and CLOSE establish the application's connection to the device and are handled by the file system based on the device type. The IOCtl request(s) is then sent to the device driver identified by the application's connection to the device. Both a block device driver and a character device driver will receive an IOCtl command directly generated by the application.

I/O subsystem interfaces are used for I/O services that are tailored to the nature of the device. The I/O subsystems provided with OS/2 are video (VIO), keyboard (KBD), and mouse (MOU), which provide device-specific interfaces for those character devices. The file system can be viewed as an I/O subsystem for block devices. The I/O subsystem interfaces allow the application to view the character device data in a logical format suitable to the nature of the device. For instance, video data can be manipulated in terms of characters and their display attributes, or in terms of a logical video buffer. Keyboard and mouse data can be treated in terms of records, containing information about the device data. When an application makes an I/O request of a subsystem, the subsystem may use IOPL routines, file system interfaces, or IOCtl requests to handle the I/O. In using either file system interfaces or the IOCtl interface, the subsystem will generate requests to the appropriate device driver. In addition, the subsystem may generate one or more requests to the device driver in accomplishing the application's request.

The character device monitor interface is used to control the data stream to or from a character device and applies only to those character device drivers that support monitors. Of the base character device drivers that come with OS/2, the keyboard, printer, and mouse device drivers support monitors for their respective devices. The application monitor does not perform I/O; instead, it acts as a conduit for the device data stream. The application monitor has the opportunity to filter the device data and consume or replace characters in the data stream. The character device driver merely passes any device data it receives to the monitor before sending the device data to the data's ultimate destination.

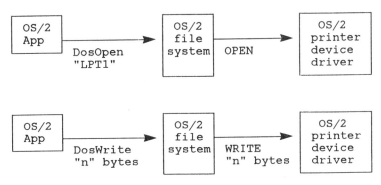

Figure 46. Example of I/O from a Character Device Driver's View

The relationship of the different kinds of application I/O to what device drivers are asked to perform is dependent on the system component responsible for the particular application interface. The system component may make a number of requests of device drivers to carry out the application I/O request. From the viewpoint of the device driver, it may not always be possible to know the exact I/O request made by the application. Only where the device driver is tightly bound to a subsystem or application interface will the device driver be able to identify the exact situation of the calling application. A block device driver has no need of special knowledge of the application I/O request; the file system takes care of connecting an application to the block device for I/O. A character device driver, on the other hand, often needs to manage the application's connection to the character device, especially in the case where there is no subsystem (like the file system) to provide this function. In such a case, the character device driver can ask the file system, via the device header, to tell it when the application establishes or terminates the connection to the character device. In other words, when the application OPENs the device, the file system sends an OPEN command to the device driver. When the application CLOSEs the device, the file system sends a CLOSE command to the device driver. This action allows the character device driver to associate subsequent I/O requests it receives (READs and WRITEs) with a particular application's connection. A character device driver may also need to initialize the state of the device whenever an application first makes the connection to the device (OPEN).

The interface that system components, such as the file system, use to tell a device driver what to do is the request packet interface. The operating system component calls the device driver, passing a pointer to a request packet. The request packet is a data structure. (Figure 47 shows the structure of a request packet.) This struc-

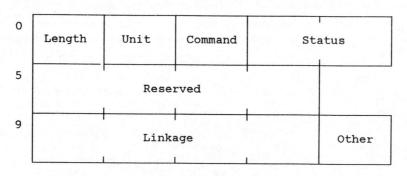

FIELD	WIDTH	MEANING
Length	1 byte	Total length of structure
Unit	1 byte	Which block device
Command	1 byte	Action to perform
Status	2 bytes	Result code of action
Reserved	4 bytes	
Linkage	4 bytes	For linked list of packets
Other	variable	Command-specific information

Figure 47. Request Packet Structure

ture begins with a fixed length header that contains information about the request common to all requests sent to the device driver. The request packet header is followed by a variable length area that contains information tailored to the specific request.

Within the request packet header are five fields of importance: Length, Unit, Command, Status, and Linkage. The **Length** field tells the device driver how big the packet actually is. Because of the variable length portion, the size of the structure is not the same from request to request. The **Unit** field applies only to a block device driver. It identifies which block device owned by the block device driver is the target of the request. The **Command** field informs the device driver of the action to perform. The **Status** field is filled in by the device driver upon completion of the request with a return code. The **Linkage** field can be used by the device driver to maintain a linked list of the request packets. A device driver may need to keep a list of uncompleted requests during those times that the device is already busy and cannot work on another request.

Block Device Commands

The commands that a block device driver can receive are as follows:

- Initialize.
- Media Check.
- Build BIOS Parameter Block.
- Read.
- Write.
- Write With Verify.
- Removable Media Support.
- Generic IOCtl.
- Reset Media.
- Get Logical Drive Map.
- Set Logical Drive Map.
- Query Partitionable Fixed Disks.
- Get Fixed Disk/Logical Units.

In the request packets for these commands, the request packet header Unit field will identify the target block device. The value used in the Unit field is relative to the total number of devices supported by the device driver: it ranges from 0 to $n-1$, where n is the number of logical devices supported by the device driver. For example, a block device driver that supports four devices (two diskette drives and one fixed disk that has two partitions) will see the Unit value range from 0 to 3.

For block devices, the operating system also uses the concept of logical to physical device mapping. In the case where only a single diskette drive exists to handle the two drive letters "a:" and "b:," a physical device is set to only *one* of the two logical devices at a time. In the case where a fixed disk has been partitioned, the physical device is split among several logical devices, which are each referenced by a unique drive letter.

In response to the **Initialize** command, a block device driver is expected to set up its devices and return in the request packet the number of logical devices it supports. For example, in a single diskette drive system, the block device driver would return 2, indicating the support of drives "a:" and "b:." It also must return the kinds of block devices it supports by passing back an array of BIOS Parameter Blocks. A BIOS Parameter Block (BPB) describes the characteristics of the block device, including the number of heads, number of tracks, and sectors per track. This command is issued to the block device driver when the block device driver program file is loaded during processing of the DEVICE= line in the CONFIG.SYS configuration file. If there are any arguments on the DEVICE= line, they are passed to the block device driver.

The file system uses the **Media Check** command primarily to determine if the media in the block device has changed. The block device driver must indicate if the media has changed or not. However, on some block devices, the block device driver cannot detect when the user has changed the media. In this case, the block device driver must respond that it is uncertain of the media in the device. For these block devices, the block device driver must also define the point in time at which it became unsure of the media in the device. Usually, a block device driver that can not detect a media change will keep track of the time interval between I/O requests to the device in question. When the time interval is long enough for someone to replace the media, then the device driver knows that the media *could* have changed. Of course, the media cannot change if the device is a nonremovable fixed disk.

The file system uses the **Build BIOS Parameter Block** command whenever the block device driver says that the media has changed or could have changed. The block device driver, upon receiving this command, must identify the media in the device and return the BIOS Parameter Block and media descriptor for the media.

The **Read, Write,** and **Write With Verify** commands tell the block device driver to transfer a number of sectors, beginning with a particular sector, between a buffer specified by the file system and the media in the device. When the block device driver has carried out the request, it must indicate the number of sectors it actually transferred within the request packet. However, if the block device driver detects that the media has changed or that the media could have changed, it must return the error "Uncertain Media" to the I/O request and to any subsequent I/O requests for that block device until the file system resets the device (see **Reset Media**).

The **Removable Media Support** command is generated by an application's use of the IOCtl to ask whether a block device is a nonremovable or removable media drive (that is, fixed disk versus diskette). The device driver responds by setting an indicator in the request packet.

The **Generic IOCtl** command is sent to the block device driver as a result of an IOCtl request by an application (the DosDevIOCtl call or the Int 21h Generic IOCtl call). The block device driver checks the function category and the subfunction code to determine what action is requested. There are two categories that apply specifically to block devices: Category 8 Logical Disk Control and Category 9 Physical Disk Control. The difference between the two categories is that the Category 8 IOCtl commands refer to a logical device (or a partition on a physical device), whereas the Category 9 IOCtl commands refer to physical, partitionable devices. A brief description of the Generic IOCtl subfunctions that the block device driver can receive follows. There are additional subfunctions that are not passed to the device driver but are intercepted by the operating system, and these will not be discussed here.

CATEGORY	DESCRIPTION
8	Logical Disk Control
43h/63h	Set/Get Device Parameters.
	Tells the device driver to set or get the BIOS Parameter Block for either the block device or for the media in the device.
44h/64h	Write/Read Track.
	Tells the device driver to perform I/O on sectors in a track, using the track table passed in the request packet.
45h/65h	Format and Verify/Verify Track.
	Tells the device driver to set up and/or check the layout of the track, according to the track table passed in the request packet.
9	Physical Disk Control
44h/64h	Write/Read Physical Track.
	Tells the device driver to perform I/O on sectors in a track, using the track table passed in the request packet. The track specified is based from the beginning of the physical drive instead of the logical drive.
63h	Get Physical Device Parameters.
	Tells the device driver to return information about the physical device.
65h	Verify Physical Track.
	Tells the device driver to check the track using the track table supplied in the request packet. The track specified is based from the beginning of the physical drive instead of the logical drive.

The file system uses the **Reset Media** command to acknowledge the error code "Uncertain Media" that the block device driver had returned on previous request(s) to the block device. This command lets the device driver know that it no longer needs to return the error for the media in the block device.

The system uses the **Get Logical Drive Map** and **Set Logical Drive Map** commands to tell the block device driver to select a logical device for a physical device. This pair of commands is used primarily in configurations with only a single diskette drive to support the diskette drive letters "a:" and "b:" —a case where two logical devices are mapped to a single physical device. In particular, these commands allow the device driver and operating system to use a single drive to support media with different format characteristics. For instance, a **Get Logical Drive Map** asks the block device driver to identify which logical device the physical device has been set to. A **Set Logical Drive Map** tells the block device driver to set the physical device to the specified logical drive.

The system uses the **Query Partitionable Fixed Disks** command to identify the number of block devices owned by the block device driver that can be partitioned (that is, how many partitionable fixed disks). The block device driver must return the count in the request packet. This count is of physical devices, not of the number of partitions that exist across the fixed disks.

The system uses the **Get Fixed Disk/Logical Units** command to identify which logical devices (referred to as units) exist on a particular block device or, in other words, how many partitions are on a fixed disk. The block device driver returns a bit map in the request packet. The bit map represents the logical devices that the block device driver owns. The block device driver must set the bit corresponding to the logical device (or unit). For example, a block device driver supports two diskette drives and a fixed disk, where the fixed disk is partitioned into four partitions (or drives). The device driver would set the bit map to indicate that Units 2 to 5 exist on the fixed disk.

Character Device Commands

The commands that a character device driver can receive are as follows:

- Initialize.
- Read.
- Peek (Nondestructive Read No Wait).
- Input Status.
- Input Flush.
- Write.
- Output Status.
- Output Flush.
- Device Open.
- Device Close.
- Generic IOCtl.
- DeInstall.

In the request packet for these commands, there is no field to identify which device the request packet is for. This is because a character device driver uses a different mechanism to differentiate among its devices than a block device driver. A character device driver must define a special data structure, called a Device Header, for each device it owns. Each Device Header must contain a unique entry point into the character device driver. Then, when the character device driver is called with a request packet, it will be called at the entry point associated with the target device.

The **Initialize** command informs the character device driver that is is expected to set up the device as needed for later I/O. This command is issued to the character device driver when the character device driver program file is loaded during processing of the DEVICE= line in the CONFIG.SYS configuration file. If there are any arguments on the DEVICE= line, they are passed to the character device driver.

The **Read** and **Write** commands tell the character device driver to transfer a number of bytes between a buffer specified by the application and the device buffer. When the character device driver has carried out the request, it must set the number of bytes it actually transferred within the request packet.

The **Peek (Nondestructive Read No Wait)** command tells the character device driver to pass a copy of the first byte (character) in the device buffer back to the file system without removing the character from the buffer. If no character exists in the device buffer, then the character device driver simply returns an indicator that the device buffer is empty. This command allows the file system to look ahead one character in the device buffer without having a **Read** request wait in the device driver for data to appear at the device.

The **Input Status** and **Output Status** commands asks the device driver for condition of I/O to the character device. Status on input (read) checks to see if characters exist in the device buffer—if characters are available to be read. Status on output (write) checks to see if the device is busy—if characters are currently being written to the device.

The **Input Flush** and **Output Flush** commands tell the character device driver to discard or terminate all requests it has pending for the device. These commands are commonly used to clear out a queue of requests for a device. They are also used to remove data from any buffers within the device driver.

The **Device Open** and **Device Close** commands tell the character device driver when an application process sets up and takes down a connection to the device. This allows the character device driver to track the application's use of its device. For example, the character device driver may need to serialize access to the device, allowing only one application process to do I/O at a time. Or, the character device driver may maintain a usage count, incrementing it for every **Open** and decrementing it for every **Close**. Then, based on the values of the usage count (e.g., every time it goes to zero), the device driver may place the device into a certain state or flush the device buffers.

The **Generic IOCtl** command is sent to the character device driver as a result of an IOCtl request by an application (the DosDevIOCtl call or the Int 21h Generic

Category Code	Description	Character Device Driver
01h	Asynchronous Device	async comm
04h	Keyboard	keyboard
05h	Printer	printer
07h	Mouse	mouse
03h	Pointer Draw	mouse pointer
0Ah	Character Device Monitor	any

Figure 48. IOCtl Categories for Character Device Drivers

IOCtl call). The character device driver checks the function category and the subfunction code to determine what action is requested. Figure 48 summarizes the categories of IOCtl commands that apply to character device drivers.

Within each category is a number of subfunctions that are oriented for the specific device. The Asynchronous Device Category allows an application to manipulate the line characteristics (e.g., the stop, parity, and data bits), modem control signals, and flow control (transmit immediate, XON, XOFF), among other things. The Keyboard Category allows an application to control parameters of the keyboard, including translate table, shift state, and input mode. The Printer Category includes subfunctions to permit an application to set the frame control (lines and characters per inch) and activate the font. The Mouse Category includes subfunctions to control the mouse pointer and obtain information about the mouse device. The Pointer Draw Category is closely related to the Mouse Category and is primarily used to get information about the mouse pointer as it relates to the screen. The Character Device Monitor Category is used to send specific commands to a device driver which supports monitors for its device.

The **DeInstall** command asks the character device driver to terminate its support of the character device. The character device driver may choose to honor or to refuse this request. If the device driver honors this request, it must release any resources it allocated for the device, such as physical memory and hardware interrupts. This command occurs only during system initialization and indicates that a newly loaded character device driver wants to replace a previously loaded character device driver. In other words, the newly loaded character device driver wants to replace support for a device name already initialized by a previously loaded device driver. The previously loaded character device driver is asked to **DeInstall** its support of the device in question. If the previously loaded device driver performs the **DeInstall**, then the newly loaded device driver is told to **Initialize**. Otherwise, the newly loaded device driver will be discarded, since the previously loaded device driver will not relinquish ownership of the device.

SYSTEM SERVICES FOR DEVICE DRIVERS

Many activities that an OS/2 device driver performs are not solely aimed at controlling the device. As you recall, OS/2 device drivers cooperate with the operating system in handling application I/O from two different execution environments, real mode and protect mode. In addition, device drivers participate in the multitasking support of the operating system. To make it easier for the device driver to cooperate with the operating system, OS/2 provides a number of system services to device drivers. The operating system also provides some system services for functions that are commonly required by device drivers, thereby removing the need to duplicate these functions in each device driver. These system services are collectively known as device driver helper routines, or DevHlp services.

A device driver receives a pointer to the DevHlp interface in the Initialize request packet. The device driver must save this pointer in order to use the DevHlp services. The pointer to the DevHlp interface is a special pointer that is valid regardless of which mode the CPU is in, real mode or protect mode. This means that the device driver can always call the DevHlp interface without special consideration for the mode of the processor. To invoke a specific DevHlp service, the device driver places function arguments into the registers specified by the DevHlp service, loads the function code of the service into the DL register, and does a FAR call through the pointer to the DevHlp interface. While the DevHlp interface can always be called, the availability of individual DevHlp services is dependent on the situation or context in which the device driver is executing. We discuss the different contexts of device driver operations in this chapter's section on Device Driver Components and Their Contexts.

The DevHlp services may be classified into the following groups:

- □ Process management.
- □ Semaphore management
- □ Request Queue managment.
- □ Character Queue management.
- □ Memory management.
- □ Interrupt management.
- □ Timer services.
- □ Character Monitor management.
- □ Advanced BIOS management.

To simplify the following discussions, we use a mnemonic name to refer to a DevHlp service rather than a function code.

Process Management

The Process management DevHlps allow the device driver to obtain process-related information, manipulate its task-time thread of execution, report certain process events to the operating system, and gain access to systemwide information. The Process management DevHlps are **Block** and **Run, Yield** and **TCYield, Done, SendEvent, BIOSCritSection,** and **GetDOSVar.**

Block and **Run** permit the device driver to respectively stop and start a thread of execution. A device driver would typically **Block** the thread of execution when it must wait for some device event to occur before it can finish the task specified by the request packet (which is generated on behalf of an application request). In other words, it releases the CPU while waiting for a timeout or device interrupt. Then, as a result of a timeout or the device interrupt, the device driver can **Run** the thread, in other words, make the thread runnable so that it can get the CPU back to continue execution.

Yield and **TCYield** allow the device driver to stop its thread from executing temporarily, but only under certain circumstances. **Yield** causes the device driver's thread to surrender the CPU only to another thread of equal or higher priority. **TCYield** causes the device driver's thread to surrender the CPU only to a thread having time critical priority. The device driver thread loses the CPU only if some other thread of sufficient priority needs to execute. If the device driver must take an extended amount of time before it can **Block** or return to the operating system (currently defined as over three milliseconds), then the device driver should periodically **Yield** or **TCYield** the CPU.

The device driver can use **Done** at interrupt time to indicate that the action required by a request packet is finished. **Done** need only be used if the device driver does not **Block** the thread of execution when handling the request packet. The device driver uses **SendEvent** to notify the operating system of certain events that affect the system, such as the user pressing the Control-Break keys or the key sequence that is used to switch between sessions. Currently, **SendEvent** is oriented to user-input devices like the keyboard and mouse.

BIOSCritSection helps a device driver to support I/O to its device in the DOS environment. The device driver uses it to flag a critical section of execution in the ROM BIOS, thereby preventing the operator from switching away from the DOS environment. This is important because execution in the DOS environment is suspended whenever the operator switches away from the DOS application. If the DOS application issues an I/O request to BIOS, and BIOS is changing the state of the device, the BIOS must be allowed to finish its operation so that the device can be in a known state for the device driver. The device driver therefore uses **BIOSCritSection** to flag entry and exit from the BIOS and to tell OS/2 when it is safe for the operator to switch away from the DOS application.

GetDOSVar lets the device driver get access to a systemwide information segment and a process-related information segment. The global information segment includes such variables as the system date and time and the drive from which the operating system was loaded (the boot drive). The local information segment includes the process ID, the current priority, and the session number.

Semaphore Management

The Semaphore DevHlps allow the device driver to use both RAM and System semaphores to communicate between components of the device driver and to communicate with applications. The Semaphore management DevHlps are **SemHandle, SemRequest,** and **SemClear.** A semaphore is identified in the DevHlps by a key or semaphore handle. The handle for a RAM semaphore is its address (selector:offset or segment:offset). The handle for a System semaphore must be obtained with **SemHandle,** passing the application-level semaphore handle. Once the device driver has a handle, it can use the **SemRequest** and **SemClear** to manipulate either a RAM semaphore or a System semaphore. **SemRequest** is used to claim a semaphore, and **SemClear** is used to release a semaphore. Typically, a device driver uses RAM semaphores to coordinate activities within itself and System semaphores to communicate events to applications.

Request Queue Management

The Request Queue DevHlps allow the device driver to maintain a linked list of request packets. The Request Queue DevHlps are **Append, Remove, AddSorted, RemoveSpecific, Alloc,** and **Free.** A device driver that can handle multiple outstanding I/O requests to its device usually keeps track of the requests to perform in a work queue. These DevHlps provide some simple linked list management using the linkage field within the request packet to chain requests together. A device driver can therefore easily maintain one or more work queues per device. **Append** (sometimes referred to as PushReqPacket) puts a request packet at the end of the specified work queue. **Remove** (sometimes referred to as PullReqPacket) takes a request packet off the beginning of the specified work queue. **AddSorted** (or SortReqPacket) inserts a request packet to the specified work queue in the order dictated by the starting sector field, giving block device drivers a simplistic means for organizing requests. **RemoveSpecific** (or PullParticular) takes the specified request packet off the work queue, regardless of the position of the request packet in the queue. **Alloc** and **Free** let the device driver obtain and release an empty request packet, which can be filled in by the device driver and used to track I/O requests issued to BIOS by a DOS application or to track multiple stages of an I/O to a multistage device.

Character Queue Management

The Character Queue DevHlps allow the device driver to maintain a simple buffer of characters. The Character Queue DevHlps are **Init, Read, Write,** and **Flush.** Based on the assumption that the character data are one byte wide, these services allow a device driver to keep track of the characters. **Init** sets up the buffer, which must be done prior to calling the other Character Queue DevHlps. **Read** and **Write** add and remove a character from the buffer. **Flush** resets the buffer to its initial empty state.

Memory Management

The Memory management DevHlps allow the device driver to manage addressability across task-time and interrupt-time operations. The Memory management DevHlps are as follows:

- **AllocPhys** and **FreePhys**.
- **PhysToVirt**.
- **Lock** and **Unlock**.
- **VirToPhys**.
- **UnPhysToVirt**.
- **PhysToUVirt**.
- **VerifyAccess**.
- **AllocGDTSelector**.
- **PhysToGDTSelector**.
- **RealToProt** and **ProtToReal**.

AllocPhys and **FreePhys** allow a device driver to allocate and release a fixed (nonswappable, nonmovable) physical chunk of memory. There must be enough physical memory to contain the memory chunk. The device driver can ask for a memory chunk of greater size than 64 KB and can indicate that the memory chunk be located above 1 MB or below 640 KB. The location of the memory chunk can be critical to performance, especially if the device driver plans to access it at interrupt time. Since this memory is physical memory as opposed to virtual segmented memory, the device driver receives a physical 32 bit address for it instead of a selector:offset or segment:offset. This physical memory can never be "unfixed" (made movable and swappable). To access this memory, the device driver must convert the 32 bit physical address to a virtual address with **PhysToVirt**. **PhysToVirt** creates a logical address (selector:offset or segment:offset) based on the current CPU mode and, if the memory address is located above 1 MB and the current CPU mode is real mode, **PhysToVirt** sets up the environment so that the device driver can access the memory with the logical address.

The device driver uses **Lock** and **Unlock** to change an application process's segment, which is movable and swappable, to fixed (not swappable, not movable) and back to unfixed. The device driver would need to fix an application's segment that it expected to access either through DMA or at interrupt-time in order to move data.

The device driver uses **VirToPhys**, after locking the application's segment, to convert the logical address (selector:offset or segment:offset) to a physical 32 bit number. Then, at interrupt-time, the device driver converts the physical 32 bit number to a temporary logical address (selector: offset or segment: offset) with **PhysToVirt** in order to access the segment. When it is done with the converted address, the device driver uses **UnPhysToVirt**. To get addressability to memory provided by an adapter (which is usually located either in the range reserved for BIOS—640 KB to 1 MB—or outside the range of regular system memory), the device driver can use **PhysToUVirt** to create an LDT entry for the memory.

The device driver uses **VerifyAccess** to check the application's authorization to access a segment. **AllocGDTSelector** is issued when the device driver is initializing. This service permits the device driver to allocate a set of GDT selectors for its private use. The device driver uses **PhysToGDTSelector** to set up one of its GDT selectors to a memory location. The memory location is identified as a 32 bit address and a length. The corresponding GDT descriptor is filled in with the appropriate information and remains valid until another **PhysToGDTSelector** call is made for the selector. In order to use these GDT selectors at interrupt-time, the device driver must first check the mode of the processor. If it is real mode, then the device driver uses the **RealToProt** service to change the processor into protect mode. Once in protect mode, the device driver can use the GDT selectors to fetch and process data. If the device driver has to switch processor modes at interrupt-time, then it must restore the processor to real mode with the **ProtToReal** service.

The selectors created by the memory management DevHlp services do not represent normal application-level memory segments. Application-level memory segments are subject to being moved or swapped in the normal course of system activity. Memory segments or selectors that have been fabricated for use by a device driver are managed differently from application-level segments. Because of these characteristics, the device driver-level selectors or segments are for private use by the device driver and cannot be passed on system calls. In other words, the device driver uses these selectors/segments for data.

Interrupt Management

The Interrupt management DevHlps allow the device driver to manage the device interrupts. The Interrupt DevHlps are **SetIRQ** and **UnSetIRQ**, **SetSWVector**, and **EOI**. **SetIRQ** and **UnSetIRQ** allow the device driver to register and deregister an Interrupt Handler for a device interrupt. **SetSWVector** allows the device driver to register a Software Interrupt Handler to intercept a software interrupt in the DOS environment. **EOI** sends the End-Of-Interrupt indication to the hardware interrupt controllers for the device interrupt.

Timer Services

The Timer services DevHlps allow the device driver to manage time processing. The Timer services are **SetTimer**, **ResetTimer**, and **TickCount**. The device driver uses **SetTimer** to register an entry point for a Timer Handler, to be called at every timer tick. **ResetTimer** removes the Timer Handler. **TickCount** is used to set the number of timer ticks to wait before calling the Timer Handler.

Character Monitor Management

The Character Monitor DevHlps let the device driver participate with application-level monitors in processing the device data stream. The Monitor DevHlps are **Create, Register** and **DeRegister, Write,** and **Flush. Create** initializes a monitor list for a device prior to the registration of an application-level monitor. **Register** and **DeRegister** add and remove an application-level monitor to this list of monitors for the device. **Write** sends device data to the application-level monitors in the list for the device. **Flush** sends a flag to the application-level monitors to discard any data and reset internal state information.

Advanced BIOS Management

Finally, the Advanced BIOS DevHlps allow the device driver to utilize Advanced BIOS services when they are provided by the hardware, in this case, the Personal System/2, or PS/2, Models 50, 60, and 80. The Advanced BIOS DevHlps are **GetLIDEntry** and **FreeLIDEntry, ABIOSCall,** and **ABIOSCommonEntry.** The device driver uses **GetLIDEntry** and **FreeLIDEntry** to obtain and release a Logical ID for the device supported by Advanced BIOS. A Logical ID is required before an Advanced BIOS function can be called. **ABIOSCall** and **ABIOSCommonEntry** set up the needed stack frame and call the specified Advanced BIOS function.

DEVICE DRIVER COMPONENTS AND THEIR CONTEXTS

An OS/2 device driver is made up of one or more components that interact with each other to manage I/O to a device. The two major components are the Strategy Routine, which is always present in a device driver, and the Hardware Interrupt Handler, which is required if the device can cause a hardware interrupt. There are two other components that a device driver may need to use: the Timer Handler and the Software Interrupt Handler. Figure 49 shows the relationship between the components of an OS/2 device driver and the system.

The Strategy Routine

The Strategy Routine is the primary component of a device driver. It handles I/O requests generated by applications, so it receives all request packets that the operating system sends to the device driver. The operating system determines the entry point to the Strategy Routine by a field defined in the Device Header of the device driver. This allows the operating system to call the device driver with the INIT request packet, telling the device driver to initialize when it is installed during system initialization.

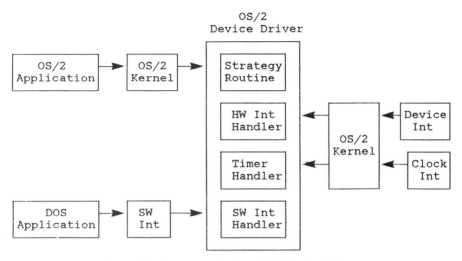

Figure 49. Components of an OS/2 Device Driver

Because the operating system calls the Strategy Routine on behalf of application I/O, the Strategy Routine can receive request packets caused by I/O both from a DOS application running in the DOS environment and from multiple OS/2 applications running in the OS/2 environment. This means that the Strategy Routine can execute in both real mode and protect mode (bimodal). The bimodal nature of the OS/2 device driver affects how the Strategy Routine operates. Refer to the section in this chapter on Bimodal Considerations for a discussion of the implications of bimodality.

In processing a request packet, the Strategy Routine executes at task-time. In other words, the Strategy Routine executes under the thread of the application process that made the I/O request, on the stack of the calling thread. Since the operating system kernel called the Strategy Routine, the term "kernel mode" describes this context of execution. The most important characteristic of running in kernel mode is that a task switch cannot preempt the Strategy Routine thread of execution. In other words, the Strategy Routine thread will not stop executing until it voluntarily **Blocks, Yields,** or tries to access a segment that is not present in system memory. A Not-Present processor exception results in OS/2 swapping the segment back into system memory from disk, during which another thread can be dispatched. This allows the device driver to have the freedom to decide when it may relinquish the CPU, which is especially important because it can change the state of the device. Any state changes must either be atomic or run to completion to keep the device in a known state. The execution of the Strategy Routine, however, can be interrupted by hardware interrupts. Therefore, if the Strategy Routine shares access to data structures with the device driver's Hardware Interrupt Handler (or Timer Handler), it must coordinate its actions with the interrupt-time components.

The Strategy Routine is coded as a FAR CALL, FAR RETURN model. The operating system will make a FAR CALL to the Strategy Routine, which then must do a FAR RET upon completion. And on entry, the Strategy Routine has automatic access to the device driver's data segment (in the DS register) and a stack (in the SS register), regardless of the current CPU mode. By convention, the Strategy Routine will not need to save and restore the contents of registers; the operating system takes care of the register contents for the requesting application thread.

The following example illustrates the operations of the Strategy Routine.

1. The operating system calls the Strategy Routine with a pointer (ES:BX) to a request packet.

    The Strategy Routine executes as a thread under the application process that issued a system call, and it uses a stack provided by the caller. The Strategy Routine has addressability to the device driver data segment (in the DS register). Whenever it is in protect mode, the Strategy Routine executes at privilege level 0, the same as the operating system kernel, with automatic I/O privilege (IOPL).
2. The Strategy Routine validates the request packet.
3. If the desired function
    □ can be handled immediately (like status check), the Strategy Routine performs the function.
    □ must be sent to the device, the Strategy Routine either adds the request packet to a work queue if the device is busy, or sends the request to the device if the device is idle.
4. If the desired function has been completed, the Strategy Routine puts the status in the request packet and returns to its caller, the operating system kernel.
5. If the desired function is still pending (waiting on the device), the Strategy Routine waits by blocking the thread.

    Eventually, the device event will occur and the Hardware Interrupt Handler can wake up the thread in the Strategy Routine.
6. Having blocked the thread, the Strategy Routine has released the CPU. The operating system will dispatch another thread, which could then make a system call. The Strategy Routine can be called again at its entry point.

The Hardware Interrupt Handler

The Hardware Interrupt Handler is a major component of an OS/2 device driver. It is the *only* component in the system that may service a hardware interrupt. A device driver Hardware Interrupt Handler is therefore required if the device generates interrupts. The device driver must register the entry point to the Hardware Interrupt Handler with the DevHlp SetIRQ service. Then, the operating system will call the Hardware Interrupt Handler whenever the hardware interrupt occurs.

Because a device operates asynchronously to the rest of the system, it can generate a hardware interrupt regardless of which application process is executing and regardless of what mode the CPU is in. For example, whenever a DOS application is in the foreground, I/O from an OS/2 application running in the background may complete during the foreground execution. The device signals the completion of the I/O for the protect mode application process by causing a hardware interrupt in real mode. Or, I/O from a DOS application running in foreground may complete during execution of an OS/2 application in background. The device signals the completion of the I/O for the real mode application by causing a hardware interrupt in protect mode. Since device interrupts can occur in either real mode or protect mode, the device driver Hardware Interrupt Handler will execute in both modes, that is, bimodally. The bimodal nature of the OS/2 device driver affects how the Hardware Interrupt Handler operates. Refer to the section on Bimodal Considerations for a discussion of the implications of bimodality.

In processing a device interrupt, the Hardware Interrupt Handler executes at interrupt-time. This means that the Hardware Interrupt Handler executes under an interrupt-time thread, which is different from task-time threads in that it does not belong to any application process. The interrupt-time thread instead executes on a special interrupt-time stack provided by the operating system. The term "interrupt mode" describes this context of execution. The primary characteristic of running in interrupt mode is that interrupt-time execution takes precedence over task-time execution, so a task switch cannot preempt interrupt-time execution. This means that, for performance, it is critical that time spent in the Hardware Interrupt Handler be kept to a minimum. The cost of interrupt-time operations on task-time operations is cumulative: while the interrupt-time thread will be interrupted by those hardware interrupts that have a higher hardware-defined priority level, it can delay the servicing of any lower priority hardware interrupts that *it* interrupted. It is therefore important for the total interrupt-time operation that the time spent within an individual Hardware Interrupt Handler be kept to a minimum. Like the Strategy Routine, the Hardware Interrupt Handler decides when to relinquish the CPU, that is, when to issue the End-Of-Interrupt indicator to the hardware interrupt controller and when to exit the Handler. This allows the Hardware Interrupt Handler to maintain changes to the state of the device in a known state.

Since the operating system kernel call the Hardware Interrupt Handler, it is coded as a FAR CALL, FAR RETURN model. The operating system will make a FAR CALL to the Hardware Interrupt Handler; the Hardware Interrupt Handler must do a FAR RET upon completion. And on entry, the Hardware Interrupt Handler has automatic access to the device driver's data segment (in the DS register) and a stack (in the SS register), regardless of the current CPU mode. By convention, the Hardware Interrupt Handler will not need to save and restore the contents of registers; the operating system takes care of the register contents for the context of the interrupt-time thread.

The following example illustrates the operations of the Hardware Interrupt Handler.

1. The operating system calls the Hardware Interrupt Handler when the device interrupt occurs.

The Hardware Interrupt Handler executes as a special thread that does not belong to any application process. It uses a special interrupt-time stack provided by the operating system. The Hardware Interrupt Handler has addressability to the device driver data segment (in the DS register). Whenever in protect mode, the Hardware Interrupt Handler executes at privilege level 0, the same as the operating system kernel, with automatic I/O privilege (IOPL).

2. The Hardware Interrupt Handler verifies that its device caused a valid interrupt.

The device may generate the interrupt because of either a request sent to it or a spurious event that is not related to a request. In either case, the Hardware Interrupt Handler must reset the interrupting condition at the device.

3. If the interrupt was the result of an earlier command sent to the device, the Hardware Interrupt Handler checks to see if the desired function is completed.

   □ If the desired function has been completed, the Hardware Interrupt Handler puts the status in the request packet and runs the thread waiting in the Strategy Routine.

   □ If the desired function is still pending (for example, being in the middle of a multistage operation), the Hardware Interrupt Handler starts the next stage of the operation.

      Eventually, the last stage will complete and the Hardware Interrupt Handler can wake up the thread in the Strategy Routine.

4. Once the function indicated in the request packet has been satisfied, the Hardware Interrupt Handler can send the next request to the device.

The Hardware Interrupt Handler can go to the work queue established by the Strategy Routine to get the next request.

5. When the Hardware Interrupt Handler has finished its activities for this occurrence of the device interrupt, it returns to its caller, the operating system kernel.

The Hardware Interrupt Handler can be called again at its entry point *at any time after it issues the End-Of-Interrupt (EOI)* to the hardware interrupt controller. The EOI tells the hardware that any device interrupt waiting at the hardware interrupt controller to be sent to the CPU can now be serviced. There could therefore be another interrupt pending at the hardware interrupt controller for the Hardware Interrupt Handler. This means that, during the time between issuing the EOI and returning to the operating system, the Hardware Interrupt Handler can be called at its entry point. This is known as a "nesting" of interrupts.

The Timer Handler

The Time Handler is an optional component of an OS/2 device driver and is used primarily for timing management. The Timer Handler is analogous to the BIOS

Int 1Ch timer in the DOS environment. However, it is actuated by the real-time CMOS clock as opposed to the system timer. Because the Timer Handler is driven by a hardware interrupt, a device driver could use a Timer Handler to know when to poll a noninterrupt-driven device. The device driver must register the entry point to the Timer Handler either with the DevHlp TickCount service, specifying the number of clock ticks to pass before having the Timer Handler invoked, or with the DevHlp SetTimer service, where the time interval is one clock tick. Then, the operating system will call the Timer Handler on each expiration of the time interval.

Because the real-time CMOS clock operates asynchronously to the rest of the system, it will generate hardware interrupts (clock ticks) unmindful of the CPU mode. Since device interrupts can occur in either real mode or protect mode, the device driver Timer Handler will execute in both modes, that is, bimodally. The bimodal nature of the OS/2 device driver affects how the Timer Handler operates. Refer to the section on Bimodal Considerations for a discussion of the implications of bimodality.

Like the Hardware Interrupt Handler, the Timer Handler executes at interrupt-time. The Timer Handler executes under an interrupt-time thread in "interrupt mode." Execution within the Timer Handler therefore must be kept to a minimum, especially since there can be several Timer Handlers in the system. Unlike the Hardware Interrupt Handler, the Timer Handler does *not* issue an End-Of-Interrupt indicator; the operating system manages the clock device. Otherwise, execution within the Timer Handler shares the same considerations as execution within the Hardware Interrupt Handler.

Since the operating system kernel calls it, the Timer Handler is coded as a FAR CALL, FAR RETURN model. The operating system will make a FAR CALL to the Timer Handler; the Timer Handler must do a FAR RET upon completion. And on entry, the Timer Handler has automatic access to the device driver's data segment (in the DS register), and a stack (in the SS register), regardless of the current CPU mode. The Timer Handler will need to save and restore the contents of registers, as the operating system does not perform preservation of register contents for this device driver component.

The following example illustrates the operations of the Timer Handler.

1. The operating system calls the Timer Handler when the clock interrupt occurs.

    The Timer Handler executes as a special thread that does not belong to any application process, and it uses a special interrupt-time stack provided by the operating system. The Timer Handler has addressability to the device driver data segment (in the DS register). Whenever in protect mode, the Timer Handler executes at privilege level 0, the same as the operating system kernel.

2. The Timer Handler can
    □ check for a timeout.
    □ drive I/O for a noninterrupting device.
    If necessary, the Timer Handler can wake up a thread that the Strategy Routine had blocked.

3. When the Timer Handler finishes its activities for this occurrence of the time interval (one or more clock ticks specified when the entry point was registered), it returns to its caller, the operating system kernel.

The Timer Handler does *not* issue an End-Of-Interrupt (EOI) to the hardware interrupt controller; the clock device driver owns the clock device.

The Software Interrupt Handler

The Software Interrupt Handler is an optional component of an OS/2 device driver and is used exclusively to support the DOS environment. The Software Interrupt Handler intercepts a software interrupt issued by a DOS application. The device driver must register the entry point to the Software Interrupt Handler with the DevHlp SetSWVector service (also called SetROMVector), identifying the desired software interrupt. Then, whenever the DOS execution environment is in the foreground, the DOS application can issue the software interrupt which, in turn, directly invokes the device driver Software Interrupt Handler.

Since software interrupts can occur only in the DOS environment, the Software Interrupt Handler executes only in real mode. In fact, the Software Interrupt Handler is the only component of an OS/2 device driver that is *not* bimodal.

Because the Software Interrupt Handler is called immediately by the software interrupt, it executes at task-time as an extension of the application. This context of execution is termed "user mode," and the device driver Software Interrupt Handler is subject to being preempted by task switches. This means that the Software Interrupt Handler is viewed as part of the DOS application, and it is exposed to losing the CPU through the multitasking of background OS/2 application processes. This trait of "user mode" requires consideration if the Software Interrupt Handler must access data structures also used by other components of the device driver. For example, the Software Interrupt Handler could start to update a data structure and then lose the CPU to a background process. This process could make an I/O request that invokes the device driver Strategy Routine, which in turn would update the data structure. In addition to task switches, the Software Interrupt Handler can be interrupted by hardware interrupts. This means that the Software Interrupt Handler must exercise caution in using data structures that the device driver's interrupt-time components (the Hardware Interrupt Handler and the Timer Handler) also use.

An OS/2 device driver typically uses the Software Interrupt Handler to intercept a ROM BIOS software interrupt. A ROM BIOS software interrupt provides a DOS application access to the device managed by the device driver. One motive the device driver has for being aware of what BIOS is trying to do to the device is the need to keep the device in a known state. In this case, the OS/2 device driver, in handling I/O requests generated from the background OS/2 application processes, must coordinate the access to the device between itself and BIOS; that is, it must serialize access to the device. Another motive of the device driver is to protect the BIOS service from being stopped before it completes. Here again, the device driver is interested in keeping the device in a known state. In this situation, the problem is that an operator can choose at any time to switch away (hotkey) from the foreground DOS application and bring a background OS/2 application to the foreground, which suspends execution of the DOS application. If the DOS application had issued a BIOS software interrupt and the operator hotkeys to a different application, the BIOS service will be prevented from completing, which is catastrophic if the BIOS service was in the middle of changing the state of the device. To avoid this, the device driver Software Interrupt Handler can issue the DevHlp BIOSCritSection to flag a critical section of execution in the BIOS and temporarily prevent the operator from switching away from the DOS application.

Since the Software Interrupt Handler is *not* called by the operating system but instead by the software interrupt, the Software Interrupt Handler is coded as an INTERRUPT, INTERRUPT RETURN (IRET) model. The software interrupt will invoke the Software Interrupt Handler in the context of the DOS application with an interrupt stack frame on the DOS application stack; the Software Interrupt Handler must do an IRET upon completion. And on entry, the Software Interrupt Handler must establish access to the device driver's data segment. In addition, the Software Interrupt Handler will need to save and restore the contents of registers on behalf of its caller, the DOS application.

The following example illustrates the operations of the Software Interrupt Handler.

1. The Software Interrupt Handler is called by a DOS application, which issues the software interrupt.

   The Software Interrupt Handler executes as an extension of the DOS application and uses the caller's stack. The Software Interrupt Handler must establish addressability to the device driver data segment by putting a previously saved value into the DS segment register. The Software Interrupt Handler always executes in real mode.
2. The Software Interrupt Handler validates the requested function.
3. If the desired function is permissible
   □ and the device is not busy, the Software Interrupt Handler issues the DevHlp BIOSCritSection to enter a critical section of execution, calls BIOS to perform the function, and reissues the DevHlp BIOSCritSection to exit from the critical section of execution.
   □ and the device is busy, the Software Interrupt Handler sets a flag to indicate BIOS I/O pending and waits on a RAM semaphore with the DevHlp SemRequest. When the semaphore is available (from either the Strategy Routine or the Hardware Interrupt Handler using the DevHlp SemClear), the BIOS I/O may proceed as above.
4. The Software Interrupt Handler returns to the DOS application with an IRET (interrupt return).

   At any time during its execution, the Software Interrupt Handler could be preempted due to timeslicing for background protect mode applications. Also, the Software Interrupt Handler can be suspended if the operator switches the DOS environment to the background, unless the Software Interrupt Handler issues the DevHlp BIOSCritSection to protect a section of execution that must complete. As for re-entrancy, the Software Interrupt Handler will not be invoked at its entry point until after it returns to the DOS application.

BIMODAL CONSIDERATIONS

OS/2 device drivers are intrinsically bimodal, with three of the four components of a device driver executing in both real mode and protect mode. The ability to execute regardless of the CPU mode is termed "bimodal" or "mixed mode" execution, and only the OS/2 device drivers (and the OS/2 kernel) have this ability. (This is different from a Family Application, which is written to the OS/2 API and linked to special "family" libraries that allow the Family Application to execute on either OS/2 or DOS. A Family Application is executed only in the CPU mode in which it was loaded.)

Execution in protect mode means that the device driver's bimodal components must be coded to adhere to certain rules imposed by the 80286 architecture, such as the following:

- Not doing segment arithmetic with the segment registers.
- Not depending on "wraparound" offsets.
- Not accessing beyond the end of a segment.
- Putting only valid selectors values in the segment registers.
- Not writing to a code segment.
- Not putting both code and data in the same segment.
- Not depending on instruction execution speed.

In obeying these rules, the device driver's bimodal components will also be able to execute in real mode, since restrictions on code execution in real mode do not exist.

The major hurdle for the device driver's bimodal components is addressability to memory located above 1 MB while executing in real mode. As you recall, memory addressing in real mode uses only 20 bits, so the highest memory location that can be accessed is FFFFFh or, in segment:offset format, F000:FFFF (which translates to 1 MB). The device driver's bimodal components must take certain actions if they need access to memory located above 1 MB in real mode. These steps are listed as follows:

1. The device driver Strategy Routine, upon receiving an I/O request packet containing an address to a buffer residing in an application's data segment, must make sure that the buffer is fixed in memory (not movable and not swappable). Addresses in the READ and WRITE request packets are already fixed by the file system, so the device driver does not have

to lock the buffers. However, addresses passed with an IOCtl request packet will need to be fixed: the Strategy Routine must use the DevHlp Lock to fix the address in memory. (Memory cannot be fixed at interrupt-time, so only the Strategy Routine can fix memory.)

2. Once the Strategy Routine has determined that the memory is fixed, it must convert the address from logical format, selector:offset or segment:offset, to a physical 32 bit number. It does this by using the DevHlp VirtToPhys. The Strategy Routine then saves the 32 bit number. Addresses in the READ and WRITE request packets have already been converted to the 32 bit number, so conversion need only be done to addresses that the device driver must lock.

3. When the device driver needs to access the memory, it converts the physical 32 bit number to a logical format. The device driver uses the DevHlp PhysToVirt, which returns a selector:offset or segment:offset for the memory location. And, more importantly, if the target location is above 1 MB and the CPU mode is real mode, the DevHlp PhysToVirt sets up the context so that the device driver can access the memory.

4. When the device driver is finished accessing the memory, it must issue the DevHlp UnPhysToVirt, which will return the context to its state before the call to PhysToVirt.

Using these steps, the device driver is *not* required to identify the CPU mode; the device driver can be designed not to care about which CPU mode is active.

OPERATIONAL CONSIDERATIONS

Device driver task-time operations (i.e., in the Strategy Routine and the Software Interrupt Handler) work under the context of the calling application process, although they are affected differently by multitasking. Device driver interrupt-time operations, on the other hand, are special because they run asynchronously to the rest of the system. Being "outside" of multitasking boundaries produces a number of features that affect how the OS/2 device driver interrupt-time components must interact with the task-time components. These features include the following:

- ▫ Memory addressability.
- ▫ Synchronization.
- ▫ Nesting of interrupts.
- ▫ System performance.

Memory Addressability

Memory addressability to application segments at interrupt-time must take into account not only bimodal considerations but also the current application context.

Even in a system configured only for protect mode, multitasking of OS/2 application processes means that an interrupt-time component may execute under the address space of an application different than the one that issued the I/O request. This means that the device driver's interrupt-time components—the Hardware Interrupt Handler and the Timer Handler—must use the memory management DevHlp services to ensure access to application segments at interrupt-time. The task-time component, the Strategy Routine, is responsible for converting any logical addresses received from application processes to physical addresses and storing the resulting 32 bit numbers. The interrupt-time components may then retrieve the 32 bit number, convert it to a temporary logical address, and move data into or out of the application segment.

Memory addressability to the physical memory requires special consideration both at interrupt-time and task-time. Using the DevHlp AllocPhys, the device driver Strategy Routine allocates a physical memory chunk from system memory and receives a physical 32 bit number. This physical chunk is not a segment that can be manipulated directly but rather a block of fixed memory (not movable, not swappable). This is the only mechanism available to a device driver to obtain more memory than what it has in its data segment. To reference this memory chunk, both interrupt-time and task-time components of the device driver must use the DevHlp PhysToVirt to convert the 32 bit number to a temporary logical address. This physical memory is best suited as an intermediate buffer for holding data; it should *not* be used to contain RAM semaphores or other critical data structures.

Memory addressability to nonsystem memory is possible from both interrupt-time and task-time components of the OS/2 device driver. Nonsystem memory refers to memory reserved by BIOS, that is, the range of reserved addresses from 640 KB to 1 MB. The operating system does not use this memory range for holding application or other system segments. In order to get a logical address to reference some location in this reserved memory range, a device driver must first calculate the target location's physical 32 bit address. Then, the device driver uses the DevHlp PhysToVirt to obtain a temporary logical address, which can be used to move data to or from the target area. One example of nonsystem memory is the monochrome display buffer, which starts at B000:0000h (or, as a physical 32 bit number, 000B0000h). Another example of nonsystem memory is memory that resides on an adapter but is addressed within this reserved range, as is typical of devices that use memory-mapped I/O. As an aside, the device driver can also give an application or I/O subsystem addressability to a nonsystem memory block with the DevHlp PhysToUVirt, which creates an LDT selector. However, applications should not use this LDT selector in system calls since it does not point to system memory.

Synchronization

With an OS/2 device driver, synchronization of activities comes in two forms: coordinating activities among the device driver's components, and coordinating activities between the device driver and an application.

Synchronization of the task-time components with the interrupt-time components is a question of if or when a device driver should decide to stop a thread of execution in the Strategy Routine (or Software Interrupt Handler) and when to start it back up. These questions usually depend on the need for the device (and the device driver) to manage multiple outstanding request packets and on how the application is expected to use the interface(s) to the device driver. In general, the following is true:

- □ Only READ and WRITE request packets need to be put on a work queue when the device is busy. As long as the device is busy, the Strategy Routine puts an I/O request packet in a linked list and blocks the thread of execution, waiting for the Hardware Interrupt Handler to process the work queue. The Strategy Routine usually handles other kinds of request packets immediately.

- □ Whenever a request packet requires the status of an I/O to the device, the device driver should block the thread of execution within the Strategy Routine and wait for the Hardware Interrupt Handler to wake the thread when the I/O has completed. The device driver can put the request packet on a work queue (that is, a linked list of request packets) whenever the device is busy. Requests are therefore processed in the order that the device driver wants to process them, whether that be first-come-first-serve or sorted by application process priority. The thread in the Strategy Routine uses the DevHlp Block to stop executing. Whenever the Hardware Interrupt Handler determines that a request is complete, it can use the DevHlp Run to wake the thread in the Strategy Routine. Then, the Hardware Interrupt Handler can take the next request from the work queue and send it to the device.

- □ Whenever the application process passes a buffer address located in the application data segment within a IOCtl request, the device driver should keep a thread of execution within the Strategy Routine until it is done with the buffer. The device driver Strategy Routine must use the DevHlp Lock service to prevent the application segment from being moved or swapped to disk before it gets a physical address. The device driver should keep a thread of execution in the Strategy Routine so that application process segments can be loosened with the DevHlp Unlock. The Hardware Interrupt Handler can then wake this Strategy Routine thread when access to the segment is finished.

- □ If BIOS services the device owned by the device driver, then it may be necessary to serialize access to the device. This is so that if the device is busy, the Software Interrupt Handler can set a flag to indicate that a BIOS I/O is pending and can wait on a semaphore to know when the BIOS I/O is allowable. Either the Strategy Routine or the Hardware Interrupt Handler can clear the semaphore when they see that the BIOS I/O is pending to let the Software Interrupt Handler know that the BIOS may safely access the device.

Semaphores are the primary means to communicate between the device driver and an application. However, there are certain restrictions that dictate how an OS/2 device driver uses semaphores. As you recall, there are two kinds of semaphores, RAM semaphores and System semaphores. A RAM semaphore is a simple, unprotected mechanism for coordinating activities. A System semaphore is a mechanism managed by the operating system and protected from deadlock (such as when the owning process terminates without releasing the semaphore). The particulars of semaphore handling that affect the device driver interactions are summarized as follows:

- A device driver cannot create or own a System semaphore.
- A device driver can manipulate a System semaphore owned by an application process.

  The application process must pass its System semaphore handle to the device driver, as in an IOCtl. The device driver then must convert the process's semaphore handle to a handle usable by the device driver, with the DevHlp SemHandle. Then the device driver can use its handle to the System semaphore in the DevHlp SemRequest and the DevHlp SemClear.

- A device driver can define and own a RAM semaphore located in its data segment, *and* access it at interrupt-time.
- A device driver cannot use a RAM semaphore located in an application process's data segment at interrupt-time.
- A device driver should not give an application addressability to a RAM semaphore located in the device driver's data segment, as the application cannot use the LDT selector in system calls.

What these rules mean is that a device driver must use a RAM semaphore, not a System semaphore, to coordinate activities among the different device driver components. Also, a device driver must use a System semaphore owned and supplied by the application process if there is a need for the device driver to communicate directly with the application.

Nesting of Interrupts

Nesting of interrupts is a consideration for both interrupt-time components of the device driver, although in different ways. Nesting of interrupts means that the interrupt handler has been re-entered at its entry point before it could exit (that is, return) to its caller. Simply put, this means that before the interrupt handler had finished processing one device interrupt, another device interrupt had occurred. Nesting of interrupts may require some special processing. It is dependent on many factors, such as when the Hardware Interrupt Handler issues the End-Of-Interrupt (EOI), what the interrupt rate of the device is, what other device interrupts are active, and what the relative priority of the device interrupt is with respect to the other device interrupts.

The Hardware Interrupt Handler is the most vulnerable to interrupt nesting, as compared to the Timer Handler. The Hardware Interrupt Handler must be careful when allowing interrupt nesting because of the interrupt stack. The interrupt stack will not support an infinite amount of interrupt nesting. Where possible, the Hardware Interrupt Handler should limit the number of times it can be re-entered. This keeps stack usage to a minimum.

The Timer Handler can also experience interrupt nesting, although only indirectly. The Timer Handler effectively operates after the clock device driver sends the End-Of-Interrupt (EOI) to the clock device, so another clock interrupt could occur while the Timer Handler executes. However, the Timer Handler is allowed to complete (return to its caller) before being invoked at its entry point again. This means that the interval that the operating system waits before calling the Timer Handler may expire several times before the operating system has a chance to call the Timer Handler. To check the actual passage of time, the Timer Handler can access the time variables in the global information segment. (Access to the global information segment is obtained through the DevHlp GetDOSVar.)

System Performance

Overall system performance is sensitive to the behavior of the device driver components. By the nature of its activities, a device driver must operate at the level of the operating system, and it thereby affects how the operating system reacts to events. To optimize the effects that a device driver has on the system and maximize the capability of the I/O subsystem/device driver to exist in a multi-application environment, the device driver must operate within certain guidelines:

- □ The device driver should locate critical data structures and data transfer buffers in its own data segment. The device driver data segment is always available immediately for interrupt-time and task-time (kernel mode) access.
- □ When moving large amounts of data to an application data segment, a device driver data segment, or a physical chunk of memory, the device driver must move the data in smaller blocks in order to release the CPU. At task-time, the device driver must use the DevHlp Yield or the DevHlp TCYield periodically (about every three milliseconds) to see if another thread needs to execute. At interrupt-time, the device driver must limit its execution time, so moving large amounts of data is not practical.
- □ The device driver components must limit the time spent executing with hardware interrupts disabled. Disabling hardware interrupts to control access to critical data structures shared between the device driver's task-time and interrupt-time components affects the servicing of *other* device interrupts.
- □ The device driver must minimize the execution time spent during interrupt processing. Both the Hardware Interrupt Handler and the Timer Handler must keep their activities to a minimum, because interrupt-time

operations delay the operating system's response to multitasking events. For example, if the servicing of an interrupt causes a Time Critical class thread to be ready to run, the operating system must get the opportunity to permit the thread to execute, and the thread cannot execute until the servicing of interrupts completes.

In addition, the Hardware Interrupt Handler should issue the End-Of-Interrupt (EOI) to its device as soon as critical processing of the device interrupt is completed. This will allow all other interrupts being held at the hardware interrupt controller to be sent to the CPU for servicing.

INITIALIZATION OF OS/2 DEVICE DRIVERS

The device driver and the devices it supports are made known to OS/2 when the device driver is loaded and initialized during processing of the DEVICE= statements in the CONFIG.SYS configuration file. Each DEVICE= statement is processed in the order in which the statement appears in the configuration file. OS/2 loads the device driver program file identified by the DEVICE= statement and calls the Strategy Routine with an INIT request packet, telling the device driver to initialize itself and its device.

Because device driver initialization occurs under a special operating system "application" process, this context of execution is termed "init mode." Under the special system process, the device driver executes as a thread of the initialization process in protect mode at the application privilege level. This means that the device driver may issue certain dynamic linked system calls, such as the file system interfaces or the message handling facilities. "Init mode" is the only time that a device driver may issue these dynamic linked function calls. The device driver can do file I/O, such as reading in a file containing data fonts or device configuration information, and can use the message handling facilities (DosGetMessage, DosInsMessage, and DosPutMessage) to display messages to the operator on the status of the device driver and device. However, although the device driver initialization occurs at the application privilege level, the device driver has I/O privilege (IOPL) so it can access its device's I/O ports.

Because a device driver occupies memory located below 640 KB, it takes space away from the DOS environment, which is itself limited to memory up to 640 KB. To help relieve the consumption of low memory, a device driver can separate the code and data used only for initialization from the code and data used for regular operations. Then, the initialization-only portions of the code and data segments can be discarded at the end of the device driver's initialization. A device driver can also use this technique to have a maximally sized data segment (64 KB) loaded and then return to the system whatever portion is not needed. Keep in mind, however, that while a device driver is a small model and resides below 640 KB, it can still allocate and use additional memory. This capability is given to the device driver through the memory management DevHlp services.

The following example illustrates the steps that occur during initialization.

1. The operating system calls the Strategy Routine with a pointer (ES:BX) to the INIT request packet. The Strategy Routine executes as a thread under the initialization process and on the process's stack. The Strategy Routine has addressability to the device driver data setgment (in the DS register). It executes at the application privilege level but with I/O privilege (IOPL).
2. The Strategy Routine saves the pointer to the DevHlp interface provided by the INIT request packet for later use.
3. The Strategy Routine obtains arguments for the configuration specified in the DEVICE= statement, if any, from the INIT request packet.
4. The Strategy Routine determines the device configuration, identifying the interrupt level, the I/O ports, and the memory address range used by the device.
5. The Strategy Routine registers additional entry points into the device driver, such as to the Hardware Interrupt Handler, the Timer Handler, and the Software Interrupt Handler.
6. The Strategy Routine initializes the device. If the device initialization fails, the device driver must deregister the entry points it registered and release any memory it allocated.
7. When done, the Strategy Routine puts the status in the INIT request packet, indicates the ending offsets of the code and data segments, and returns to its caller.

ADVANCED BIOS AND INTERRUPT SHARING

The Personal System/2 Models 50, 60, and 80 provide two important features for OS/2 device management not found on the the Personal Computer AT or the Personal Computer XT Model 286. The features are the Advanced BIOS interface and the level sensitive hardware interrupt environment. The Advanced BIOS is important because it provides an OS/2 device driver with an intermediate interface to the device that frees the device driver from depending on specific device characteristics. An OS/2 device driver not written to some intermediate device interface must have intimate knowledge of how the device operates and therefore cannot tolerate changes to that device. The level sensitive hardware interrupt environment is important because it is better suited to hardware interrupt sharing than the edge triggered hardware interrupt environment of the other IBM Personal Computers.

Advanced BIOS

Advanced BIOS (ABIOS) is a device interface layer that has a number of characteristics to distinguish it from BIOS:

- Advanced BIOS is invoked by a FAR CALL rather than a software interrupt.
- Advanced BIOS can execute in both real mode and protect mode.
- Advanced BIOS is told of the actions to perform and parameters to use from a data structure called a request block. The device driver sets up the request block and passes a pointer to the structure when it calls the Advanced BIOS.
- Advanced BIOS identifies a specific device with a device handle called a Logical ID (LID) and a unit number under that LID.
- I/O to the device is accomplished by calling one of the Advanced BIOS entry points: the START entry point to initiate a function, the INTERRUPT entry point to handle an interrupt-time operation, or the TIMEOUT entry point to process a timeout.
- An I/O function can be synchronous or staged. A synchronous I/O request must run to completion before returning to the caller. A staged I/O request requires a series of steps to occur, each of which requires action on the part of the caller to move to the next step.
- Data transfer may be based on a logical address (selector:offset or segment:offset) or a physical address (32 bit number).
- Finally, an OS/2 device driver accesses the Advanced BIOS interface through the DevHlps GetLIDEntry, FreeLIDEntry, ABIOSCall, and ABIOSCommonEntry.

The device driver's first step in using the Advanced BIOS (ABIOS) must be to obtain a device handle—a Logical ID (LID)—in order to identify the device to ABIOS. The device driver uses the DevHlp GetLIDEntry to obtain this ABIOS device handle. Since ABIOS recognizes devices by means of the LIDs and OS/2 recognizes devices by means of the Device Headers, it is the device driver that does the mapping from the way the device is identified by the operating system to the way the device is identified to the ABIOS interface. The device driver must follow some guidelines when mapping the device to the ABIOS device handle (LID) since the LID may identify one device or a group of devices:

- For a character device driver with a single Device Header, the character device is mapped to the first unit of the LID that the device driver obtained. Any other units in this LID are not used and are not available to other device drivers.
- For a character device driver with more than one Device Header, the first character device is mapped to the first unit of the LID that the device driver obtained. The second character device is mapped to the second unit of the LID, and so forth. If the LID does not have enough units to cover all the devices that the character device driver supports, then the device driver must obtain another LID and continue mapping its devices to units in the LID.
- For a block device driver with one or more units specified in its Device

Header, it must map the first unit of the Device Header to the first unit of the LID, and so forth until it has mapped all units its supports. This mapping may require the block device driver to obtain more than one LID.

Any Logical IDs not obtained by the device driver are available for another device driver to claim. When the device driver no longer needs to own a device, it may release the Advanced BIOS device handle with the DevHlp FreeLIDEntry.

Having obtained the LID, the next step for the device driver is to determine what the parameters are for the ABIOS interface for this particular device. To get this information, the device driver must set up a fixed length data structure called a request block, with the LID and a function code to return the LID parameters. The device driver then uses either the DevHlp ABIOSCall or the DevHlp ABIOSCommonEntry to call the START entry point for this LID. ABIOS returns such information as the hardware interrupt level that the device is configured to use, the arbitration level if applicable, the number of units covered by the LID, the length of the request block for the other functions provided by the ABIOS interface, and the characteristics of the data pointers (such as logical versus physical). From this information, the device driver knows for which hardware interrupt to register the Hardware Interrupt Handler, what kind of data pointers the ABIOS interface expects, and how big an area to reserve in the device driver data segment for the ABIOS request blocks.

To invoke a particular ABIOS function, the device driver must first set up a request block with the LID and function code. Then the device driver uses either the DevHlp ABIOSCall or the DevHlp ABIOSCommonEntry to call one of the three Advanced BIOS entry points for the LID. ABIOS performs the requested action and puts the status into the request block. When the DevHlp ABIOSCall or the DevHlp ABIOSCommonEntry return to the device driver, it must examine the request block to determine the outcome of the ABIOS function call.

We use the following example to illustrate how an OS/2 device driver uses ABIOS. The example assumes that the device driver has already performed the necessary initialization to obtain the LIDs, reserve the space for the ABIOS request blocks, identify the hardware interrupt, and register the Hardware Interrupt Handler.

1. The operating system calls the device driver Strategy Routine with a request packet for I/O to the target device.
2. If there is no work active (the device is idle), the Strategy Routine sets up the ABIOS request block with the LID, the function number, and any other parameters required by ABIOS, including initializing the return code field to FFFFh. The Strategy Routine uses either the DevHlp ABIOSCall or the DevHlp ABIOSCommonEntry to invoke the ABIOS entry point to START the function. If the device is busy, the Strategy Routine can place the request packet on a work queue and the Hardware Interrupt Handler may invoke the ABIOS entry point to START the function.
3. On the return from the call to either the DevHlp ABIOSCall or the

DevHlp ABIOSCommonEntry, the Strategy Routine checks the return code field in the request block to determine the outcome of the ABIOS function.

□   If the return code indicates an error, the Strategy Routine sets the status field of the request packet to a device error code and returns to the operating system.

□   If the return code indicates that the function completed successfully, the Strategy Routine sets the status field of the request packet and returns to the operating system.

□   If the return code indicates that the function is ready for the next stage (e.g., it is waiting for the device interrupt to occur), then the Strategy Routine may need to block the thread of execution while waiting for the device interrupt.

The Strategy Routine must check a prearranged flag with the Hardware Interrupt Handler before actually blocking the thread. The reason is that the device interrupt can occur after ABIOS updates the return code field in the request block but before the Strategy Routine interrogates the ABIOS return code. In this case, the Hardware Interrupt Handler is called as a result of the device interrupt, services the request block, and may complete the request. Then, when the Strategy Routine executes, the flag set by the Hardware Interrupt Handler informs the Strategy Routine that the request is already completed and to return the request packet to the operating system instead of blocking the thread of execution.

For a staged request, the START entry point sets the return code of the ABIOS request block to indicate that the operation is incomplete. Several incomplete requests for the LID can be pending at the same time and are usually referred to as outstanding requests for the LID. Once a STARTed request is ready for the next stage, it is considered to be an outstanding request even though the START service has not returned to the caller, as demonstrated in the scenario described previously.

4. The device driver Hardware Interrupt Handler is called as a result of the device interrupt.

5. For each LID associated with this device interrupt (there can be more than one), the Hardware Interrupt Handler must process all outstanding ABIOS request blocks. The Hardware Interrupt Handler must call the ABIOS entry point for INTERRUPT service for every request block that was waiting for the device interrupt in order to service the LID completely. The Hardware Interrupt Handler must also account for the situation where the ABIOS START service had updated the return code in a request block to show it waiting for the interrupt but where the START service had not returned to the caller of the START service. The Hardware Interrupt Handler must check for request blocks in this situation and include them in servicing the device interrupt.

6. If the device interrupt was caused by one of the request blocks for the LID, then the Hardware Interrupt Handler calls the ABIOS INTER-RUPT entry point for the remaining request blocks for the LID. The Hardware Interrupt Handler does not check the remaining LIDs.
7. If a LID has no request blocks pending for the device interrupt, then the Hardware Interrupt Handler calls the ABIOS INTERRUPT entry point for the function to provide the default interrupt service.

The Hardware Interrupt Handler issues the End-Of-Interrupt (EOI) to the hardware interrupt controller only after servicing all outstanding request blocks for the LID that caused the device interrupt.

If the Hardware Interrupt Handler sees that the requested function has completed, the Hardware Interrupt Handler may START the next request block based on the next request packet waiting in the work queue.

When the Hardware Interrupt Handler is done, it returns to the operating system.

Hardware Interrupt Sharing

Sharing a hardware interrupt among several devices is possible only when the devices have been designed for interrupt sharing. Specifically, in order for a device to share a hardware interrupt, it must know if it generated an interrupt. This permits the software interrupt handler to check the device to determine if it requires service. The device can implicitly reset its interrupt pending latch when its interrupt is serviced by the software interrupt handler.

On the Personal System/2 Models 50, 60, and 80, hardware interrupts are level sensitive as opposed to edge triggered. Both terms, level sensitive and edge triggered, refer to the method that the hardware interrupt controller employs to determine if a device has generated an interrupt. When the interrupt controller recognizes an interrupt from a device, it sends the interrupt to the CPU, which uses the interrupt vector table to invoke the software interrupt handler.

For edge triggered interrupts, the hardware interrupt controller recognizes a device interrupt as a specific transition in a signal, like making the signal go from low to high. The signal can remain at a level and can be reset (such as going from high to low) without causing the interrupt controller to think another device interrupt has been generated. It is the specific edge, or transition in value, that informs the hardware interrupt controller of a device interrupt.

For level sensitive interrupts, the hardware interrupt controller recognizes a device interrupt as a specific level or value of the signal. As long as the signal remains at that level, the interrupt controller believes that the interrupt must be serviced. Only when the signal is reset from that level will the interrupt controller stop trying to deal with the interrupt. In other words, for a level sensitive interrupt, the interrupting condition must be reset at the device so it will reset its signal to the interrupt controller. And, the software interrupt handler must issue the End-Of-Interrupt (EOI) *after* the interrupting condition has been removed from the device. If the EOI is issued to the interrupt controller before the interrupt condition has been reset, the signal will still be at the level that defines the device interrupt to the interrupt controller, and the interrupt controller will reissue the interrupt to the CPU. Refer to Figure 50 for a step-by-step explanation of this process.

On the Personal System/2 Models 50, 60, and 80, all hardware interrupts have the potential to be shared among devices. However, there are some circumstances where sharing of an interrupt is not practical. For example, OS/2 does not permit several interrupt handlers to share the system timer interrupt (IRQ O) because it must be available to a DOS application in the DOS environment. Likewise, if an OS/2 device driver uses the BIOS in the DOS environment for interrupt-time processing to support DOS application I/O, then the OS/2 device driver must not share the interrupt since the BIOS assumes it owns the interrupt processing. In addition, the device itself may prevent the hardware interrupt from being shared. For instance, if the device generates interrupts before the Hardware Interrupt Handler can be installed or if it cannot be stopped from generating interrupts, then the interrupt cannot be shared with another device. If the device generates interrupts without having an interrupt handler, then OS/2 is forced to shut off (mask off) that interrupt because there is no way to reset the interrupting condition at the device. If the device will not stop generating interrupts even though its interrupt handler has terminated, then OS/2 must shut off the interrupt because there is no mechanism to reset the device.

To share the hardware interrupt among devices, both the device and the OS/2 device driver must be designed for sharing. When the device driver registers the entry point to the Hardware Interrupt Handler, it must declare both the hardware interrupt and the capability to share the interrupt. If the device driver specifies that

```
1. One or more devices reset the interrupt signal in preparing
   to inform the interrupt controller of an interrupt.

2. One or more devices make the interrupt signal to the level
   that identifies the interrupt to the interrupt controller.

3. The interrupt controller issues the interrupt to the
   CPU.

4. The CPU causes the interrupt handler to execute.

5. The interrupt handler checks the device to determine
   if the device has an interrupt pending.  If so, it
   services the device which resets the device's
   interrupting condition (so this device
   resets the signal to the interrupt controller) and
   issues an EOI.  Upon receiving the EOI, the interrupt
   controller again issues the interrupt to the CPU if the
   interrupt signal still indicates that an interrupt is
   pending.  If another device has an unserviced interrupt
   when the EOI was issued, the device continues to hold
   the signal at the level to identify the interrupt to the
   interrupt controller.
```

Figure 50. Level Sensitive Interrupts

it will not share the interrupt, then OS/2 enforces exclusive rights to the interrupt. If the device driver specifies that it will share the interrupt, then OS/2 allows the registration of other Hardware Interrupt Handlers that also indicate they will share the interrupt. Sharing of hardware interrupts therefore requires some participation on the part of the OS/2 device driver. On the flip side, this means that neither a DOS device driver nor a DOS application can share a device interrupt, especially since execution in the DOS environment is suspended whenever the operator puts the DOS environment in the background.

The different Hardware Interrupt Handlers of the OS/2 device drivers that register to share a device interrupt must follow certain procedures. The Hardware Interrupt Handler is responsible for interrogating its device to check if it caused the interrupt. If its device did not cause the interrupt, the Hardware Interrupt Handler must return to the operating system and indicate that the interrupt does not belong to its device (which is done by setting the Carry Flag before it issues the FAR RET). In addition, the Hardware Interrupt Handler must not issue an End-Of-Interrupt (EOI) since it did not service its device. If its device caused the interrupt, then the Hardware Interrupt Handler must service the device, reset the interrupting condition at the device, issue the EOI as soon as possible, and indicate, when it returns to the operating system, that it owns the interrupt.

OS/2 manages the list of interrupt handlers for a given hardware interrupt. The operating system will call each interrupt handler in the list until it finds one that claims the interrupt. If no interrupt handler claims the interrupt, then, since OS/2 has no mechanism to reset the interrupting condition for a level sensitive interrupt, OS/2 masks off the interrupt and thereby shuts down all devices sharing that interrupt. Without such a drastic measure, the interrupt controller would continue to issue the interrupt to the system.

CREATING AN OS/2 DEVICE DRIVER

The device driver program differs from an application program in several ways:

- A device driver program cannot be a process by itself.
- A device driver program resides at the privilege level of the operating system kernel, not the privilege level of an application.
- A device driver program cannot make dynamically linked function calls.
- A device driver program may have only one code segment and one data segment.
- The device driver segments must be linked so that they appear in a certain order in the EXE file.
- A device driver program does not provide its own stack segment.
- The device driver segments must be linked as a library, not as an application.
- A device driver program may have additional segments only under certain conditions.

- A device driver program must contain at least one Device Header.
- The device driver Device Header must be the first object defined in the data segment.

A device driver can never be a process by itself. Instead, a device driver operates on behalf of an application process. At task-time, when handling a request packet generated by an application I/O request, the device driver executes as a special subroutine to the application. At interrupt-time, when handling a device interrupt, the device driver executes outside the bounds of any application process. A device driver does, however, have some characteristics of a process:

- A device driver has its own addressability to its code and data segments, although this is done through the GDT rather than an LDT.
- A device driver can own memory, although it is physical memory as opposed to segmented memory.
- A device driver can own RAM semaphores, because these objects can be defined in the device driver's data segment.

Beyond these similarities to a process, a device driver appears more like a library module than an application program.

A device driver program operates in the privilege level of the operating system kernel, not of an application. A device driver program is installed as part of the operating system during the system initialization. The operating system then calls the device driver program to perform tasks on behalf of application I/O. The device driver program can really be viewed as an extension to the operating system.

A device driver program cannot issue any dynamically linked system calls. This restriction is imposed because the device driver is not an application process and does not reside on the application privilege level. However, there is a period when the device driver can make dynamically linked system calls, although only to a limited set of the dynamic link system interfaces. This period is during device driver initialization. When the operating system calls with the INIT request packet, the device driver is actually executing in the context of a special system process. In this case, the device driver has been temporarily given a special application status so that it can use dynamically linked APIs (application programming interfaces).

A device driver program may contain only one code segment and one data segment. The size of each of these segments may be defined up to the maximum, 64 KB. The technique of keeping all the code in a single segment (and using a single segment for the data) is known as "small model." In other words, a device driver makes NEAR CALLs from one routine to reference another routine.

The device driver segments must be linked so that they appear in a certain order in the EXE file. The EXE file layout begins with the EXE file header, followed by the segments. The data segment must appear first, followed by the code segment. This arrangement is similar to the rule required of DOS device driver programs, with the only exception being that an OS/2 device driver program is an EXE file. See Figure 51 for an illustration of the EXE file layout of a device driver.

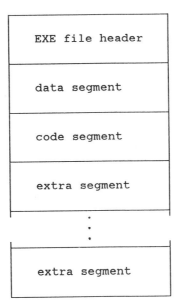

Figure 51. An OS/2 Device Driver EXE File Layout

A device driver program does not have a stack segment. The device driver runs like a subroutine: it uses the stack of its caller. The operating system provides stacks for both task-time and interrupt-time operations. The device driver Software Interrupt Handler runs on the stack of the DOS application. In all cases, the device driver must take care to keep its stack usage to a minimum.

The device driver segments must be linked as a library, not as an application. The device driver program is like a subroutine package, running on behalf of its caller and using its caller's stack. In this respect, the OS/2 device driver program has characteristics similar to a library package. The linker knows of two classes of programs, applications and libraries, and the device driver program is more closely related to a library program than an application program.

A device driver program may include additional segments besides the code and data segments, but only under certain conditions. In those cases, the extra segments must be placed at the end of the EXE file, after the code segment (see Figure 51). The device driver can reference these extra segments *only* during its initialization, that is, only while processing the INIT request packet. After the device driver returns from initializing, the operating system discards extra segments and keeps only the first two, the data segment and the code segment. A device driver typically uses these extra segments as data segments to hold message text bound to the EXE file with the message binder. Then, during initialization, the device driver can use the message handling facilities to display messages to the operator, such as whether the device successfully initialized or failed to initialize.

A device driver program must possess at least one Device Header. The Device Header makes the device known to OS/2 and is structurally similar to the Device

Header in DOS device drivers. There are several fields in the Device Header that the device driver must define. See Figure 52 for a pictorial layout of the OS/2 device driver header.

The **Next Header** must be initialized to a null value (−1 or FFFFh). The *Device Attribute* specifies the traits of the device, including the following:

- ▫ Whether it is a character or block device.
- ▫ If a block device,
  - whether the device driver uses the BIOS Parameter Block (BPB) or the media descriptor byte to identify the media.
  - whether the device driver supports removable media.
- ▫ If a character device,
  - whether the character device name is to protected by the file system sharing rules for file names.
  - whether the device driver wants the file system to pass OPEN and CLOSE requests to the device driver.
- ▫ Whether the device driver owning the device is an OS/2 device driver.
- ▫ Whether the device is a system device, such as clock, null, standard output, or standard input.

The **Strategy Offset** must be set to the offset from the start of the code segment to the entry point of the Strategy Routine. The **Name or Units** is set to the name of the character device or to the number of block devices supported and must be left-justified (start at offset Ah into the structure; refer to the figure). A character device name is like a file name, both are ASCII strings and both are limited to eight letters (not counting the file name extension). However, a character device name takes priority over a file name in the file system interface to open a named object (DosOpen). This means that a file cannot have the same name as a character device, because the file system will open the device first and never try to open the file. To minimize conflicts between character device names and file names, a character device name should include seldom-used ASCII letters, like the "$" sign.

The device driver Device Header must be the first structure in the data segment;

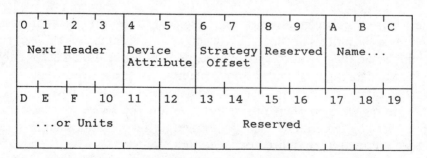

Figure 52. The Device Header

in other words, it must be located starting at offset 0 into the device driver data segment. When the device driver program file is loaded, OS/2 examines the Device Header to understand the device driver. The Device Header is an architected interface to the operating system.

Typically, a single device driver handles only one device. However, a device driver may handle more than one device. A character device driver may support multiple devices through the technique of having multiple Device Headers, one Device Header for each device. A block device driver may support multiple devices by specifying the number of devices in a field within the Device Header. In the case of multiple headers, the device driver must link the headers together, with the last header defining the **Next Header** field as null.

The Device Header allows a character device driver to either add a new character device to the system device list or replace an existing device from a previously loaded character device driver. The key to replace an existing device is provided by the Device Headers from both character device drivers desiring to claim the device. If the device name and device-specific attributes in the Device Header of the newly loaded character device driver match those in the Device Header of a previously loaded character device driver, then the previously loaded character device driver is asked to relinquish or deinstall its device. This means that it must release any resources it allocated on behalf of the device, such as the hardware interrupt. If it does so, the newly loaded character device driver may claim the device. At this point, the newly loaded device driver is asked to initialize its character device.

The technique of replacing existing character devices is particularly useful in enhancing support of standard character devices. OS/2 automatically supports standard character devices, such as the keyboard (KBD$) and the printer (LPT1, LPT2, LPT3). OS/2 supports these devices using a basic set of device drivers that come with the operating system. New or enhanced character device drivers, however, can replace the base device drivers in order to support new or enhanced functions.

A block device driver, on the other hand, may only add devices to the system device list, for there is no mechanism to allow a block device driver to specify which block devices to replace. Instead, the block device driver indicates the number of devices it supports during its initialization, and it will be allocated the corresponding number of drive letters. The order in which block device drivers appear in the configuration file CONFIG.SYS determines the order in which drive letters are assigned.

STANDARD DEVICES ON OS/2

There are a number of device drivers provided with OS/2. They have been categorized into two groups: those that are automatically installed with the operating system, and those that the user selects by putting a DEVICE= statement in the CONFIG.SYS configuration file. These device drivers are listed in Figure 53.

Clock

OS/2 automatically installs the clock device driver during system initialization. The clock device driver is an OS/2 character device driver. It manages the real-time CMOS clock device, which is the device that drives the operating system's time-related functions.

The clock device driver supports application I/O through the timer services of OS/2. Typically, an application uses the DosSetDateTime interface to write to the clock device. An application may query the system time variables, such as date/time and clock rate, in the global information segment. An application can also use the file system interfaces, like DosRead and DosWrite, to do I/O "directly" to the clock device. However, the data read or written to the clock device must be set up in the architected 6 byte format.

Disk/Diskette

OS/2 automatically installs the disk/diskette device driver during system initialization. The disk/diskette device driver is an OS/2 block device driver, and it manages the diskette drives and the fixed disks. The disk/diskette device driver supports any fixed disk of size greater than 32 MB with multiple partitions, each of which can be up to 32 MB and each of which are accessible with a drive letter.

The disk/diskette device driver supports application I/O through the file system interfaces.

Screen

OS/2 automatically installs the screen device driver during system initialization. The screen device driver is an OS/2 character device driver, and it manages the display in conjunction with the VIO subsystem. The screen device driver replaces the output portion of the DOS console device driver.

Base Device Drivers	Installable Device Drivers
Clock Disk/Diskette Screen Keyboard Printer	Mouse Pointer Draw Asynchronous Communications Virtual Disk External Diskette ANSI EGA

Figure 53. Device Drivers Provided with OS/2

The screen device driver supports application I/O through the VIO subsystem interfaces.

Keyboard

OS/2 automatically installs the keyboard device driver during system initialization. The keyboard device driver is an OS/2 character device driver, and it manages the keyboard device. The keyboard device driver replaces the input portion of the DOS console device driver.

The keyboard device driver supports application I/O through the KBD subsystem interfaces. The keyboard device driver also permits character device monitors to examine the keystrokes, so an application may use a keyboard monitor to intercept the keyboard data.

Printer

OS/2 automatically installs the printer device driver during system initialization. The printer device driver is an OS/2 character device driver, and it manages the parallel printer devices, LPT1, LPT2, and LPT3.

The printer device driver supports I/O through the file system interfaces and indirectly through the Print Spool subsystem. The printer device driver also permits character device monitors to examine the output being sent to the printer device, so an application may use a printer monitor to intercept print data.

Mouse

The mouse device driver is installed through the DEVICE= statement in the CONFIG.SYS configuration file.

The mouse device driver is an OS/2 character device driver, and it manages either a parallel mouse or a serial mouse, depending which mouse device driver program file is selected with the configuration file.

The mouse device driver supports application I/O through the MOU subsystem. A DOS application may use the DOS Int 33h mouse interface for I/O. In addition, the mouse device driver supports character device monitors, so an application may use a mouse monitor to intercept mouse data.

Pointer Draw

The pointer draw device driver is installed through the DEVICE= statement in CONFIG.SYS. The pointer draw device driver is an OS/2 character device driver, and it provides the interface to the mouse device driver to have either the default or application-supplied mouse pointer image drawn on the display at interrupt-time.

The pointer draw device driver is not a physical device for I/O, so it does not support application I/O.

Asynchronous Communications

The asynchronous communications device driver is installed through the DEVICE= statement in CONFIG.SYS.

The asynchronous communications device driver is an OS/2 character device driver, and it supports the serial devices COM1 and COM2 on the AT and XT Model 286 and the serial devices COM1, COM2, and COM3 on the PS/2 Models 50, 60, and 80.

The asynchronous communications device driver provides an RS232-C interface through IOCtls to applications, including transmit and receive queues, automatic control modes of the modem control signals, and logical data stream flow control for transmit and receive. An application may also use the file system interface, like DosRead and DosWrite, to do I/O to the serial device. Typically, the asynchronous communications device driver would be used with the OS/2 Print Spool utility if a serial printer were the spooled printer.

Virtual Disk

The virtual disk device driver is installed through the DEVICE= statement in CON-FIG.SYS. The virtual disk device driver is an OS/2 block device driver, and it manages a logical block device that resides in system memory.

The virtual disk device driver supports application I/O through the file system interfaces, like a regular block device.

External Disk

The external disk device driver is installed through the DEVICE= statement in CON-FIG.SYS. The external disk device driver defines a logical disk device. This logical disk device may share an existing block device, like having multiple drive letters refer to the same physical diskette drive, or it may use a disk device that is external to the system, like the 3.5-inch external diskette drive for the AT.

The external disk device driver supports application I/O through the file system interfaces, like a regular block device.

ANSI

The ANSI device driver is installed through the DEVICE= statement in CON-FIG.SYS. The ANSI device driver is a DOS device driver that runs only in the DOS enviroment of OS/2. This device driver provides a mechanism that extends the basic screen and keyboard control through special control sequences that control the position of the cursor, the attributes of the displayed characters, and the definition of keys. For OS/2 applications, the ANSI functions are integrated with the VIO and KBD subsystems.

EGA

The EGA device driver is installed through the DEVICE= statement in CONFIG.SYS. The EGA device driver is a DOS device driver that runs only in the DOS environment of OS/2. It supports the EGA register interface for DOS applications, which is an extension of the BIOS Int 10h video interface. The EGA register interface allows a DOS graphics application to run in the DOS environment in such a way that OS/2 can save and restore the screen whenever the operator switches away from and back to the DOS graphics application. An OS/2 application may also perform its own graphics operations by getting access to the physical video buffer with VIOGetPhysBuf and saving and restoring its screen with VIOSaveRedrawWait.

OS/2 SUPPORT OF DOS DEVICE DRIVERS

As demonstrated in the list of device drivers that come with the operating system, some DOS device drivers may be used in OS/2. There are restrictions imposed by the operating context that limit what a DOS device driver can do. To qualify for execution in the DOS environment of OS/2, a DOS device driver must have the following characteristics:

- □ Be a character device.
- □ Perform only polled I/O.
- □ Have no timing dependencies.
- □ Not issue any DOS Int 21 function calls during its initialization.

The device managed by a DOS device driver may be used only by a DOS application; new OS/2 applications may not perform I/O to this device.

The DOS device driver is installed in OS/2 with the same mechanism as in DOS, through the configuration file CONFIG.SYS with the DEVICE= statement. After the file is loaded, the DOS device driver is initialized in the 80286 real mode.

7

Advanced Programming Concepts

IN THIS CHAPTER, WE TAKE YOU THROUGH some of the more advanced OS/2 programming concepts and considerations. We look in more detail at the **OS/2 Linker** that was introduced in Chapter 4. The discussion begins with how to use the Linker to build application executable modules. Within this discussion, we cover OS/2's capability to define code and data segments as preload or load on demand. In the second section, we look deeper into the mechanism called dynamic linking and how it differs from static link mechanisms. We also describe the concepts of load time and run time dynamic linking for externally defined routines. We then show you how you can use the OS/2 Linker to build your own dynamic link libraries. The third section presents a programming example demonstrating some of the capabilities we discuss in the chapter.

LINKING AN APPLICATION

In Chapter 4, we showed you a sample invocation of the OS/2 Linker. The primary source of input to the Linker is one or more relocatable object modules created by a language compiler or assembler. The Linker uses the object modules to create an application executable module that the operating system can load and execute. OS/2 application executable modules are referred to as **program modules**. Compared with the DOS programming environment, the new OS/2 programming environment offers additional flexibility in the areas of program structure and component distribution. As we describe the functions of the OS/2 Linker, we cover many of the key capabilities and controls that the programmer has for building a program module to make use of this added OS/2 flexibility.

Let's look first at the general syntax for the command line invocation of the Linker

```
LINK object files,[executable file],[map file],

       [library files],[module definition file]

          [/option] [/option] ...
```

Figure 54. Linker—Command Line Syntax

(see Figure 54). We want to introduce some of these additional topics that were not covered in the earlier example.

We have already discussed the object file, executable file, map file, and library files command line parameters for the Link utility. One important point that the previous example did not illustrate is that more than one object file can be listed in this first parameter. This addition to the list permits multiple object modules to be linked into a single executable module. Not only does this mean a program can be developed as separate modules, it also means that different parts of the program can be implemented in different programming languages. For example, some applications are written predominantly in C, with only the performance sensitive routines written in Assembly language.

The module definition file is a feature of the OS/2 Linker that provides information for the link process. It supplies input used by the Linker in addition to the command line input parameters. This file is optional when linking a program module. When it is used, it allows the programmer to override the Linker defaults for certain segment attributes (e.g., the stack segment size). Figure 55 gives an overview of the files used as input by the Linker.

There are primarily two things accomplished by this Linker process. First, the Linker is responsible for resolving the external symbolic references contained in the object modules. Second, the Linker must build the appropriate information into the executable file that allows the loader to load the program into memory. In the upcoming section on Dynamic Linking, we will see that in OS/2 the resolution of external references to dynamic link routines is not completed until the program is loaded. In this case, the Linker just builds data areas in the program module that are filled in later by the loader. But before we begin dynamic linking, let's discuss OS/2's capability to define segments as Preload and Load on Demand.

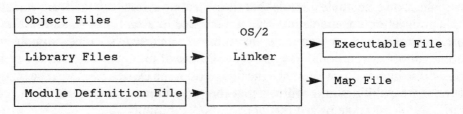

Figure 55. Linker Input and Output Files Overview

Preload Segments

When a DOS program is loaded, all the segments of that program are brought into memory, and all the necessary relocation fields built by the compiler (assembler) and the Linker are filled in by the loader. This process is completed before control is turned over to the main entry point of the program. OS/2 segments that are loaded before the program receives control are called **preload segments**. Three statements that are supported in the module definition file can specify to the Linker that a segment(s) should be preloaded. These statements cause the Linker to build the necessary information into the executable module that directs the loader to preload code and data segments.

The CODE and DATA statements can be used to indicate that all of the CODE or all of the DATA segments, respectively, in an executable module are to be preloaded. For example:

CODE PRELOAD

indicates to preload all code segments in this module.

To specify different load characteristics for different segments in a program module, the SEGMENTS statement is used. For example:

```
SEGMENTS
    CODESEG1    PRELOAD
    CODESEG2    LOADONCALL
```

Now that we understand what a preload segment is, let's discuss what "LOADON-CALL" means.

Load on Demand Segments

As applications become more complex, there is a tendency to include logic that, while necessary under specific circumstances, may not be needed during the normal day-to-day operation of the application. It is highly undesirable in a multitasking system to have the code for this logic, when it is not being used, take up space in either the real or virtual address space of the program. As the system becomes more heavily used, system memory and swap file space cannot afford to be wasted. For this reason OS/2 allows segments to be defined as shown in the previous example. LOADONCALL means that the loader reserves a selector in the application's LDT for this segment, but it does not actually load the segment until the application needs it. The need for the segment is triggered by loading this segment's selector into a segment register. Not until this occurs will the loader load the segment from secondary storage into memory and complete building the segment descriptor.

To conserve system resources in OS/2, the default segment load attribute is LOADONCALL for both data and code segments.

DYNAMIC LINKING

Dynamic Linking is a fundamental capability of OS/2 resulting in many benefits to the operational characteristics of the system. Earlier, we discussed how the Linker is responsible for resolving the symbolic external references in an object module. **Dynamic Linking** is a mechanism that delays the resolution of these external references until after the link process. This mechanism is sometimes referred to as delayed binding. The Linker simply places information about each dynamic link external reference into the program module. This information enables the special OS/2 dynamic linking loader to resolve the external references at a later time.

Let's look at the two types of Dynamic Linking in OS/2.

Load Time Dynamic Linking

As you would expect, the references to load time dynamic linked routines are resolved when the program module is loaded into memory. This is the typical way that external references to libraries of dynamic link routines are resolved. As we mentioned in the introduction, there are several benefits to this type of interface mechanism.

One benefit of the call mechanism is that once the reference is resolved, the caller has a direct entry point into the function. In PC DOS, most of the operating system functions are accessed by placing a function number and all parameters into registers and then issuing the software interrupt 21. This type of mechanism requires that a routing function be executed in between the application request and the initial entry point to the desired function. This routing function is not necessary with the OS/2 dynamic link interface. When an OS/2 executable module is loaded, the external reference pointers point directly at the entry points for the specific OS/2 function. Avoiding the routing function bottleneck is a performance advantage of the dynamic link mechanism.

Another benefit of the dynamic link call interface is that a high level language can implement it directly. A compiler accesses the operating system functions by pushing parameters on the stack and then issuing a FAR call. This is the same convention that languages use to call subroutines within the application. Typically in DOS, language bindings are used to take parameters off the stack, load up registers, and issue software interrupts. These bindings are not needed for OS/2 languages.

It is also easier to extend a programming interface that is based upon the dynamic link mechanism. Adding a function to an interface that has a single entry point and a function router requires a modification to the router. On the other hand, dynamic link functions can be added to the system without affecting previously released functions, and there is no routing function to be updated. Furthermore, the stack is a more consistent and flexible parameter passing mechanism than the varying sets of registers of the microprocessors supported by the operating system.

Dynamic linking also makes it easier to support libraries of routines. Library routines that are dynamically linked can be modified without affecting applications that use the functions. Programs that use a statically linked set of library routines must be relinked when a new version of the routine is required. With dynamic linking, as long as the number of parameters on the function stays the same, an old application can use a new version of a library function without relinking. The version could have a new set of dynamic link routines that support existing applications in a compatible way, and that support new function(s) by interpreting an extended range of values for one or more of the previously defined parameters. This facilitates enhancing library routines over time to accommodate user requirements.

Finally, OS/2's dynamic link API carries with it all of the benefits of an open architecture. The OS/2 open architecture is enhanced because applications can call dynamic link routines added by independent software developers in the same way that they call routines provided with the operating system. As developers come up with innovative functions to add to the system, they can package them as dynamic link modules and distribute them to OS/2 users. Dynamic Linking gives independent software developers the opportunity to extend the operating system.

Run Time Dynamic Linking

Run time dynamic linking is a mechanism for delaying the binding of external references in a program module beyond load time. Examples of the usefulness of this mechanism include any situation where an application wants to perform some processing before specifying the name of a dynamic link module that it wants to use. For example, an application may want to allow a user to choose from a range of performance versus memory characteristics in the implementation of a specific function. Another example would be where a set of routines is chosen based upon some characteristic of the system configuration. In this way, different implementations of the same set of function calls can be utilized within a single application.

A special set of OS/2 functions provides the OS/2 run time dynamic linking support. DosLoadModule loads a dynamic link module. DosFreeModule frees a dynamic link module previously loaded. DosGetProcAddr gets the address of a dynamic link procedure. DosGetModHandle gets a dynamic link module handle. DosGetModName gets a dynamic link module name. With these functions, an application can wait until execution time to find out the name to use to access external code and data. These functions provide mechanisms to dynamically locate, load, and link external modules.

To appreciate the flexibility of these functions, let's look at them in more detail.

DosLoadModule Loads a dynamic link module into memory. A dynamic link module is an executable module (.EXE file) that contains one or more dynamic link procedure entry points. The application passes a pointer to an ASCIIZ string containing the file name of the dynamic link module. The library search path is used to locate the module in the file system. If the function successfully loads the module, a handle for the module is returned. Instead of the module name, the module handle is used with the remaining OS/2 function calls supporting run time dynamic linking. If the module cannot be loaded, two other parameters of the function are used to return the name of the object that caused the failure.

DosFreeModule Indicates to the operating system that the process is through using any external references to procedures within this dynamic link module. If no other processes in the system are using the module, it will be discarded from memory. The module handle is used in this function call to indicate the dynamic link module to be freed.

DosGetProcAddr Returns an address that can be used to call a procedure within a dynamic link module. The caller passes the module handle and a pointer to a procedure name string as parameters on this function call. An alternate mechanism other than the procedure name can be used to specify the procedure within the module to which the caller wants addressability. Instead of passing the name, the caller can pass the number of the procedure in the module. This number is also referred to as the ordinal for that procedure within the dynamic link module.

DosGetModHandle Tests to see if a dynamic link module has already been loaded. The caller passes a pointer to an ASCIIZ string containing a module name. If the module has been loaded, then a handle to that module is returned. If the module has not been loaded, then an error is returned.

DosGetModName Locates a module within the file system. A module handle and a pointer to a buffer are passed to this function. The fully qualified file name, including the drive, path, file name, and extension, is returned in the buffer.

Building a Dynamic Link Library

To review, we have discussed load time and run time dynamic linking. Load time dynamically linked routines are loaded when the application program is loaded. At that time, the OS/2 linking loader fills in all addresses in the program module that provide the linkage to the dynamic link library routines. Run time dynamically linked routines are loaded and linked upon demand by the application using a special set of OS/2 functions. But regardless of their use as load time or run time routines, the dynamic linking mechanisms are essentially the same, and both load time and run time dynamic link libraries are built in the same way.

The OS/2 Linker builds a program module with the data structures necessary to support dynamic linking. The important data structures we discussed are the

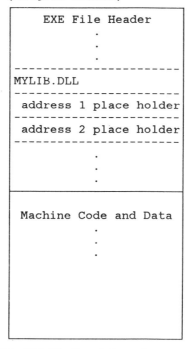

```
MYPROGRAM.EXE
(Program Module)
```

Figure 56. Disk File Containing a Program Module

dynamic link module file name, and the function name (or ordinal) indicating the specific dynamic link function. A pictorial representation of a program module with these data structures is shown in Figure 56.

The OS/2 Linker can also build a dynamic link module that contains the library of routines for which the linking is delayed until load or execution time. One way to picture a dynamic link module is shown in Figure 57.

Now, if we look at these modules after they have been loaded into memory and the linkages between the modules has been established, we arrive at the diagram shown in Figure 58.

We see that the address place holders that the OS/2 Linker built into the program module have been filled in with pointers. These are pointers that can be used to directly call the entry points of the respective dynamic link functions. Now that this dynamic link mechanism has set up the address linkage, the function in the dynamic link library can be called just as efficiently as if it were a subroutine provided with the original application program. Using other terminology, we could say that this application program has effectively imported functions from a dynamic link library and used them as though they were part of the original program.

A utility is provided with OS/2 that builds a special file used by the Linker to build these address place holders in the program module for the imported functions. This special file is called an import library, and the utility that creates it is called the Import Librarian or IMPLIB utility.

```
MYLIBRARY.DLL
(Dynamic Link Module)
```

```
+------------------------------+
|        DLL File Header       |
|               .              |
|               .              |
|               .              |
|------------------------------|
| Function 1 name              |
|------------------------------|
| Function 2 name              |
|------------------------------|
| Function 3 name              |
|------------------------------|
|               .              |
|               .              |
|------------------------------|
| Function 1 Entry Point       |
|                              |
|                              |
|------------------------------|
| Function 2 Entry Point       |
|                              |
|                              |
|------------------------------|
| Function 3 Entry Point       |
|                              |
|                              |
|------------------------------|
|               .              |
|               .              |
|               .              |
+------------------------------+
```

Figure 57. Disk File Containing a Dynamic Link Module

Import Librarian

The import librarian is used to create special library files for dynamic link routines. It is a separate step from the Link process. Libraries for statically linked routines contain the actual object code for the routines. These statically linked routines are copied and bound into the program module at link time. To support dynamically linked routines, special library files created by the import librarian enable the Linker to build the appropriate address place holders into the program module.

The import librarian builds an import library by processing the module definition file for a dynamic link module. Figure 59 gives an example of a module definition file used to link a dynamic link module. This same module definition file is also

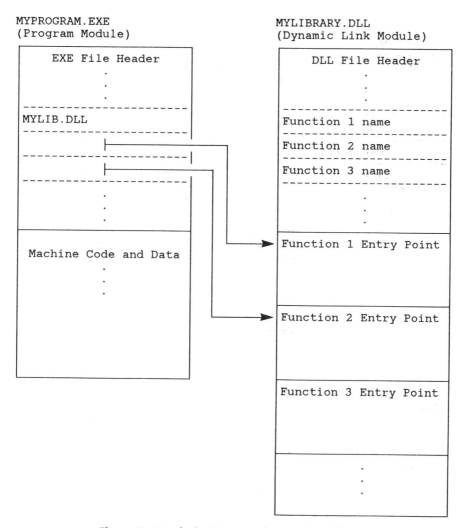

Figure 58. Results in Memory of Dynamic Linking

```
;
; Module Definition File
; MYLIBRARY Dynamic Link Library
; Created by JIK, AMM, and RLW
; 1987
;
LIBRARY
DESCRIPTION ´MYLIBRARY Ver 1.0 Copyright 1987 JIK,AMM,RLW´
EXPORTS
    Function1 @1
    Function2 @2
    Function3 @3
```

Figure 59. Module Definition File for a Dynamic Link Module

used to generate an import library for the dynamic link routines. Although the application programmer can manually specify imported function modules to resolve external references, the Linker can use the import library to resolve these external references automatically. Import libraries permit the programmer to develop programs that use dynamically linked routines just as easily as programs using statically linked routines.

In this example, we see two statements that characterize this as a module definition file for a dynamic link module. The LIBRARY statement specifically declares that this module definition file is for a dynamic link library of routines. The EXPORTS statement allows the module definition file to define the entry point names, entry point ordinals, and some other attributes about the dynamic link routines made available (exported) by this dynamic link module.

We see that the same module definition file that the Linker uses to create the dynamic link module is used by the import librarian to create dynamic link import library files. The dynamic link import library files make it easy for the programmer to link applications that have external references to dynamic link routines.

MODULE DEFINITION FILE STATEMENTS

To get a more complete overview of the options available when you create program modules and dynamic link modules with the OS/2 Linker, let's summarize the statements that are defined for use within a module definition file.

NAME Specifies that the executable module being created is a program module. An optional program module name can be specified with this statement. OS/2 uses the name to identify the program module after it is loaded. If the module name is not specified, then the operating system uses the module file name to identify the module.

LIBRARY Specifies that the executable module being created is a dynamic link library module. As with the NAME statement, an optional library name can be specified to override the default module file name used by OS/2 to identify the dynamic link module after it is loaded into memory.

For dynamic link libraries that require an initialization routine, an additional parameter on the LIBRARY statement characterizes the library's initialization requirements. The LIBRARY statement can specify that this library's initialization routine should be called just once when the library is first loaded, or that it should be called every time a new process gains access to the library.

DESCRIPTION Allows a single line of text to be inserted into a program module. This statement facilitates the correlation of program modules with a version of the program source file. It is also useful for inserting a standard copyright statement into a program module.

CODE Defines the default attributes for all code segments within a module. The load options of "preload" or "load on call" can be specified. The segment access rights of "execute only" or "execute read" can be set. A parameter is also available to indicate if the code segments are to be allowed I/O privilege. This privilege permits routines in the segment to use the 80286 privileged instructions including the IN and OUT instructions.

DATA Defines the default attributes for all data segments within a module. The load options of "preload" or "load on call" can be specified. The segment access rights of "read only" or "read/write" can be set.

A parameter is available to specify the use of the module's automatic data segment. An automatic data segment is allocated for data automatically without specific action by the application. The DATA statement can specify that no automatic data segment exists. Dynamic link modules can use this parameter to specify that an automatic data segment exists and is to be shared by all instances of (processes using) the dynamic link module. This parameter can also specify that a new copy of the automatic data segment should be created for each instance of this module.

A separate parameter specifies the sharing of the other data segments in the module. Specifying the data segments as shared means that all processes accessing the module use one copy of the data segments. Specifying the data segments as nonshared causes a separate copy of all read/write data segments to be created for each process using this module.

As with the CODE statement, the DATA statement has a parameter to indicate if the data segments are to be placed at the I/O privilege priority level.

SEGMENT Allows the specification of attributes for individual code or data segments. It has the same combined parameters available with the CODE and DATA statements, along with a segment name parameter to indicate the specific segment of interest.

STACKSIZE Specifies the number of bytes the system should allocate for the stack associated with a program module. This value overrides any stack specified by the program source code.

IMPORTS Provides an alternative way to resolve external references to dynamic link library routines. Normally these references would be resolved using an import library. If an import library is not available, the programmer can specify the dynamic link entry points with the IMPORTS statement.

Parameters on this statement include a name that is used within the calling program to reference the dynamic link routine, the name of the dynamic link module that contains the routine, and the dynamic link function name or ordinal number within the dynamic link module.

EXPORTS Specifies each entry point into a dynamic link module.

The entry points have a name that can be used to call the function from another module and an optional internal name that can be used instead of the "exported" name when referring to the function from within the module.

An ordinal parameter is available to specify the position of the function in the entry point table for the module. This allows the function to be invoked using either the exported name or the ordinal.

Another parameter is available for functions that are usually called by name even though the ordinal option is available. This parameter directs the system to keep the function's name string in memory for optimal performance when resolving a procedure name reference to this function.

STUB Allows a PC DOS executable file to be placed at the beginning of an OS/2 executable module. The OS/2 loader ignores this stub. The STUB statement makes it very easy to create an OS/2 executable module that displays a warning message if a mistaken attempt is made to execute the module on PC DOS.

HEAPSIZE Specifies the number of bytes the program module needs for its local heap.

PROTMODE Specifies that the module is to execute in protect mode only. This statement sets an indicator in the module and causes the Linker to omit information from the module that could have been used by the BIND utility to build a family application. Specifying PROTMODE conserves space in modules that are not intended to be bound into family applications.

OLD Aids in maintaining consistency in the assignment of function ordinals across updated versions of a dynamic link library. If this statement is used, a search is made for any entry point name in a new module that matches an entry point name of the specified old module. If a match is found, then, when the entry point table for the new dynamic link module is built, this function is given the same ordinal number that it had in the old module.

RUN TIME DYNAMIC LINKING PROGRAMMING EXAMPLE

In this example, we demonstrate the use of some of the linker facilities to build a dynamic link library. We further build upon our multiple processes sample program by making a portion of Process 2 a dynamic link routine. We then use run time dynamic linking to access one of two versions of this dynamic link module.

Process 2 of the multiple processes sample program simulates a process logging an event with the date and time. Suppose we were asked to generalize this logging process so that it could easily be altered to log the date and time using a different date and time format. We can take advantage of the OS/2 dynamic linking facilities to help solve this problem. If we separate the functions that build the date and time strings from the rest of the program, it becomes a straightforward task to provide multiple versions of these functions that format the date and time differently. To keep our example simple, we will build just two versions of these libraries and label them as the "USA Format" and the "European Format."

Let's look now at the specific changes we need to make to Process 1 and Process 2 of the multiple process example. The first step to building our run time dynamic linking example requires us to add a user I/O routine, called SelectLibrary, to Process 1. This routine displays a window asking the user to select the desired time and date format. Since we have only two selections, this SelectLibrary routine displays the available date and time formats and allows the user to make a choice using the cursor keys. Keep in mind that an unlimited number of formats could have been supported by having the user enter the specific dynamic link library name. This is just one illustration of the power and flexibility of run time dynamic linking.

Continuing with our example, we placed the SelectLibrary routine in Process 1, since it is the process responsible for receiving input from the user via the keyboard. Since Process 2 is the routine that will actually use the results of the user's selection to invoke the appropriate dynamic link library, we must pass this information to Process 2 as an argument variable when the process is created.

The changes to Process 2 begin with removing the BuildDateString and BuildTimeString functions from the program, and converting them into a dynamic link library module. One hint to facilitate this conversion is to compile and link these modules using the C large programming model. The large model is used when a program has multiple code and multiple data segments. Therefore, the compiler uses intersegment addressing by default since it is assumes that any pointers, calls, and returns may span segments. Dynamic link routines are in fact loaded into memory in segments different than the calling program and consequently intersegment addressing is very important. When we look more closely at the sample program we will see several examples in which we have taken explicit actions to address the requirements of multiple segment programs.

The remaining changes to Process 2 include the declarations, algorithms, and OS/2 function calls necessary to implement run time dynamic linking.

Allowing the User to Select the Library

To build this run time dynamic linking example, we have four source files and a module definition file for the library modules. The four source files are for Process 1, Process 2, and the two versions of the dynamic link libraries for the date and

```
SelectLibrary function
   Display the user input window
   Highlight the selected library
   Until the Enter key is pressed
      Read the keyboard
      If the up or down arrow is pressed
         Then If library 1 is currently selected
                 Then Select library 2
                      Remove highlight from library 1
                      Highlight library 2
                 Else Select library 1
                      Remove highlight from library 2
                      Highlight library 1
         Else If enter key is pressed
                 Then do nothing
         Else sound beep for invalid key pressed
   Erase the user input window
   Return
```

Figure 60. SelectLibrary High Level Logic

time format functions. Instead of duplicating the description and listing of the entire Process 1 program, we show only the additional declarations and algorithms required to add the SelectLibrary function. Let's look first at the SelectLibrary high level logic in Figure 60.

As in the other examples, we have added the variable declarations to the beginning of the source file. The call to the SelectLibrary function is placed at the beginning of the executable portion of the program so that the user's input can be conveniently

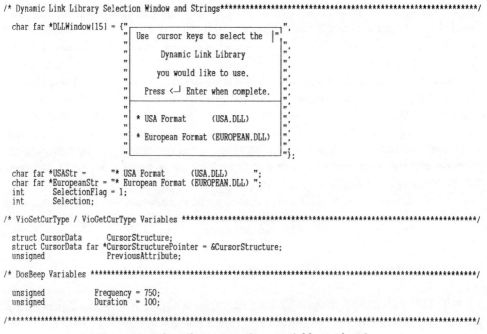

Figure 61. SelectLibrary Function—Variable Declarations

passed to Process 2. Figures 61 through 63 contain the source code for the SelectLibrary function.

We use several new OS/2 function calls in the SelectLibrary function in support of I/O with the user. We use the VioGetCurType and VioSetCurType to control the cursor, and DosBeep to notify the user that an incorrect key has been pressed.

VioGetCurType and VioSetCurType

VioGetCurType and VioSetCurType return and set the current cursor definition, respectively. This cursor definition includes the location, height, width, and display attribute of the cursor within a text mode character cell. There are two parameters with this function call.

CursorData Is a far pointer to a structure containing the specific cursor definition parameters.

VioHandle Is a reserved word of zeros.

The CursorData data structure contains four one-word members (fields). The first two control the size and location of the cursor in the text mode character cell. They are called CursorStartLine and CursorEndLine, and they specify the horizontal scan line within the character cell where the cursor begins and ends, respectively. The third word, called CursorWidth, specifies the cursor width in columns. The OS/2 video subsystem currently supports only a column width of one. The fourth word in the CursorData data structure, called CursorAttribute, specifies the cursor display attribute. In addition to the attribute definitions for the supported display modes, a CursorAttribute value of minus one indicates that the cursor should be hidden.

```
void SelectLibrary()
{
    ErrorCode = VIOGETCURTYPE(CursorStructurePointer,0);        /* Get the current cursor type */
    PreviousAttribute = CursorStructure.cur_attribute;         /* and save it so we can restore*/
    CursorStructure.cur_attribute = -1;                        /* it later                   */
    ErrorCode = VIOSETCURTYPE(CursorStructurePointer,0);       /* Then make the cursor hidden */

    for(RowCounter = 0; RowCounter < DLLWindowLength; RowCounter++)   /* Display the dynamic link   */
                                                               /* library selection window   */
        ErrorCode = VIOWRTCHARSTRATT(DLLWindow[RowCounter],
                            VioLength = strlen(DLLWindow[RowCounter]),
                            Row = 5 + RowCounter,
                            Column = 22,
                            Attribute = "\044",
                            VioHandle);

    ErrorCode = VIOWRTCHARSTRATT(USAStr,                       /* Highlight the current library*/
                            VioLength = strlen(USAStr),        /* selection                  */
                            Row = 15,
                            Column = 24,
                            Attribute = "\137",
                            VioHandle);
```

Figure 62. SelectLibrary Function—Part 1

```
do {                                                              /* Top of loop that responds to */
    ErrorCode = KBDCHARIN(KeyStructurePointer,                    /* user's keyboard input         */
                          IOWait = 0,                             /* IOWait = 0 means block until  */
                          KbdHandle = 0);                         /* character received            */

    if ((KeyStructure.scan_code == 0x48)|(KeyStructure.scan_code == 0x50))   /* Check scan code looking for */
                                                                  /* up or down cursor keys        */
        if (SelectionFlag == 1) {
            SelectionFlag = 2;
            ErrorCode = VIOWRTCHARSTRATT(USAStr,
                                         VioLength = strlen(USAStr),
                                         Row = 15,
                                         Column = 24,
                                         Attribute = "\044",
                                         VioHandle);
            ErrorCode = VIOWRTCHARSTRATT(EuropeanStr,             /* Depending upon the value of   */
                                         VioLength = strlen(EuropeanStr),   /* SelectionFlag, unhighlight */
                                         Row = 17,                /* one selection and highlight   */
                                         Column = 24,             /* the other                     */
                                         Attribute = "\137",
                                         VioHandle);
        }
        else {
            SelectionFlag = 1;
            ErrorCode = VIOWRTCHARSTRATT(EuropeanStr,
                                         VioLength = strlen(EuropeanStr),
                                         Row = 17,
                                         Column = 24,
                                         Attribute = "\044",
                                         VioHandle);
            ErrorCode = VIOWRTCHARSTRATT(USAStr,
                                         VioLength = strlen(USAStr),
                                         Row = 15,
                                         Column = 24,
                                         Attribute = "\137",
                                         VioHandle);
        }
    else if (KeyStructure.char_code == 0x0D) ;                    /* If the Enter key was pressed  */
                                                                  /* don't do anything yet         */
    else
        ErrorCode = DOSBEEP(Frequency,                            /* Sound a beep if any other key */
                            Duration);                            /* was pressed                   */

} while (KeyStructure.char_code != 0x0D);                         /* End loop if Enter key was     */
                                                                  /* pressed                       */
ErrorCode = VIOSCROLLUP(TopRow=5,
                        LeftCol=22,                               /* Selection is complete, erase  */
                        BotRow=20,                                /* the library selection window  */
                        RightCol=60,
                        NumLines=-1,
                        (char far *)FillChar,
                        VioHandle = 0);

CursorStructure.cur_attribute = PreviousAttribute;               /* Restore the cursor            */
ErrorCode = VIOSETCURTYPE(CursorStructurePointer,0);

}
/************************************************************************************************/
```

Figure 63. SelectLibrary Function—Part 2

DosBeep

DosBeep provides a convenient interface for generating sound from from the speaker.
There are two parameters with this function call.

Frequency Is a word value in the range of 37 to 32,767, specifying the tone in cycles
per second (Hertz).

Duration Is a word value specifying how many milliseconds the sound is to be
generated.

This function executes synchronous to the application. Consequently, control returns after the specified number of milliseconds.

Description of SelectLibrary

Figure 62 is the beginning of the SelectLibrary function; it is where we turn off the cursor, display the prompt window, and highlight the currently selected dynamic link library. We use the VioGetCurType to initialize our CursorData data structure with the current cursor definition. Before we change the cursor attribute to minus one indicating to hide the cursor, we save the previous cursor attribute value so that we can restore the cursor at the end of the routine. VioSetCurType is then used to turn off the cursor.

After displaying the library selection window using a "for" loop, we redisplay the line indicating the USA Format library using a different display attribute. This effectively highlights this line and shows the user the library that is currently selected.

Figure 63 is the remainder of the SelectLibrary function. It contains the do-while loop (the Until loop in the high level logic of Figure 60) that responds to the user's keyboard input. First, we issue the KbdCharIn function call specifying to wait for a character. The call returns when a key is pressed, and we check the scan code to see if it was an up or down cursor key. If an up or down cursor key was pressed, we test to see which library is currently selected, as indicated by the SelectionFlag variable. We then update SelectionFlag and switch the highlighting to show that the other library has been selected. If the key pressed was not an up or down cursor key, then we check to see if it was the Enter key. If the Enter key was pressed, we do nothing in the "if" statement since this is the terminating condition for the main do-while loop. The final "else" statement is executed if any other key was pressed, and it calls the DosBeep function to notify the user of an invalid operation.

The SelectLibrary function completes by erasing the library selection window and re-enabling the cursor. Although not shown, we then modified Process 1 to convert SelectionFlag to a character string, and we insert it as the first argument string passed to Process 2 on the DosExecPgm function call.

A New Process 2

We have made several changes to Process 2. We removed the BuildTimeString and BuildDateString functions. We added logic to look for a value in an argument variable in order to determine which run time dynamic link library to use. Finally, we added the declarations and function calls necessary to invoke run time dynamic linking.

At the top of Figure 64, you will notice that we have redeclared some of the C standard run time functions (itoa, atoi, etc.) to use far pointers for the pointer parameters. This is because we are building the program using the C large model.

Next, you see two external reference definitions for the BuildTimeString and Build-

DateString functions. Notice that these external definitions have been turned into comments. They were used with load time dynamic linking in the initial debugging of this program example. Although they are not used with run time dynamic linking, we left them in to show how this can be done. The same module definition file shown in Figure 72 on page 242 can be processed with the import librarian (IMP-LIB) utility to produce an import library. This import library, combined with the external declarations shown in Figure 64, allows you to use load time dynamic linking to access the functions in the dynamic link libraries used in our run time dynamic linking example.

```
/***********************************************************************************************/
/*  Multiple Processes with Dyanamic Linking - Process 2                                       */
/***********************************************************************************************/

#include <doscall.h>                                    /* OS/2 API dynamic link library*/
#include <stdio.h>                                      /* C standard I/O run time lib  */
#include <string.h>                                     /* C string library             */

    char * cdecl itoa(int, char far *, int);            /* These standard library      */
    int cdecl atoi(const char far *);                   /* declarations have been       */
    size_t cdecl strlen(const char far *);              /* modified to take far pointer */
    char * cdecl strcat(char far *, const char far *);  /* parameters for use with large*/
    int cdecl printf(const char far *, ...);            /* model programming            */

/***********************************************************************************************/
/* These external reference declarations are used with load time dynamic linking.             */
/* They have been commented out of the source code but are included as a reference.            */

/*
extern void far pascal BuildTimeString (
    unsigned char,
    unsigned char,
    unsigned char,
    char far *);

extern void far pascal BuildDateString (
    unsigned char,
    unsigned char,
    unsigned,
    char far *);
*/

/* Display window character definitions ****************************************************/

    char far *Proc2Window[12] = {"┌─────────────┐",   /* An array of strings used to */
                                 "│             │",     /* outline the Process 1 display*/
                                 "├─────────────┤",     /* window                       */
                                 "│             │",
                                 "│             │",
                                 "│             │",
                                 "│             │",
                                 "│             │",
                                 "│             │",
                                 "│             │",
                                 "│             │",
                                 "└─────────────┘"};

    int         RowCounter = 0;                         /* Variables used in "for" loop */
    int         WindowLength = 12;

/* General Variables - used throughout the program ****************************************/

    unsigned    ErrorCode;                              /* Error code return from OS/2  */
                                                        /* function calls               */
/* VioWrtCharStrAtt Variables - used to display text prompts and messages ****************/

    char far    *CharStr;                               /* String to be written        */
    unsigned    VioLength;                              /* Length of character string  */
    unsigned    Row;                                    /* Starting position - row     */
    unsigned    Column;                                 /* Starting position - column  */
    char far    *Attribute;                             /* Display attribute           */
    unsigned    VioHandle = 0;                          /* Reserved word of zeros      */
```

Figure 64. Process 2—Variable Declarations (Part 1)

Other changes to the Process 2 variable declarations shown in the following figures include removing some of the declarations used only in the BuildTimeString and BuildDateString functions. These declarations have been moved to the dynamic link library modules.

Figures 64 through 68 contain the C source code for Process 2 of the run time dynamic linking example.

Before we walk through this revised version of Process 2, let's review the new OS/2 function calls used in this example.

```
/* VioScrollUp Variables ******************************************************************/

    unsigned        TopRow;                                    /* Upper left hand corner     */
    unsigned        LeftCol;
    unsigned        BotRow;                                    /* Bottom right hand corner   */
    unsigned        RightCol;
    unsigned        NumLines;                                  /* Number of lines to scroll  */
    char            FillChar[2] = {0x20,0x1F};                 /* Fill character to use      */

/* DosRead Variables **********************************************************************/

    unsigned        ReadHandle;                                /* File handle(pipe read handle)*/
    char            CharacterCell[2];                          /* Input buffer               */
    unsigned        BufferLength = 2;                          /* Input buffer length        */
    unsigned        BytesRead;                                 /* Bytes read - returned      */

/* DosGetDateTime Variables ***************************************************************/

    struct DateTime     CurDateTime;                           /* Date and Time structure    */
    struct DateTime far *CurDateTimePointer = &CurDateTime;    /* Date/Time structure pointer*/

/* DosSleep Variables *********************************************************************/

    unsigned long   TimeInterval;                              /* Sleep time duration        */

/* DosLoadModule Variables ***************************************************************/

    char            ObjNameBuf[32];                            /* Object name buffer         */
    unsigned        ObjNameBufLength;                          /* Object name buffer length  */
    char far        *ModuleName;                               /* DynaLink module name       */
    unsigned        ModuleHandle;                              /* Module handle - returned   */

/* DosGetProcAddr Variables **************************************************************/

    char far        *ProcName;                                 /* DynaLink procedure name    */
    void (far pascal *ProcAddress)();                          /* Procedure address - returned */

    void (far pascal *BuildTimeString)();
    void (far pascal *BuildDateString)();

/* String variables *********************************************************************/

    char            Time[9] = "      \0";                      /* Used to build the time string*/
    char            *TimePointer = Time;

    char            Date[11] = "        \0";                   /* Used to build the date string*/
    char            *DatePointer = Date;

    char            LogString[22];                             /* Used to build the log string */
    char            *LogStringPointer = LogString;

/* DosExit Variables ********************************************************************/

    unsigned        ActionCode=i;                              /* Exit all threads in process */
    unsigned        ResultCode=0;                              /* Result saved for DosCWait  */

/***************************************************************************************/

    void far        DateTimeProcedure();                       /* Function declaration       */

/***************************************************************************************/
```

Figure 65. Process 2—Variable Declarations (Part 2)

```
main(argc, argv, envp)                                              /* Start of C main routine     */
int argc;
char far *argv[ ];
char far *envp[ ];

{

/* DosCreateThread Variables ************************************************************************/

    unsigned            ThreadIDWord;                               /* New thread ID               */
    unsigned char       NewThreadStack[100];                        /* New thread stack            */

/* Start of executable program *********************************************************************/

    ErrorCode = VIOWRTCHARSTRATT(CharStr = "PROCESS 2",             /* Label area of screen used   */
                                 VioLength = strlen(CharStr),       /* for Process 2               */
                                 Row = 5,
                                 Column = 55,
                                 Attribute = "\032",
                                 VioHandle = 0);

    for(RowCounter =0; RowCounter < WindowLength; RowCounter++)      /* Display the Process 2 window */

        ErrorCode = VIOWRTCHARSTRATT(Proc2Window[RowCounter],
                                     VioLength = strlen(Proc2Window[RowCounter]),
                                     Row = 7 + RowCounter,
                                     Column = 48,
                                     Attribute = "\032",
                                     VioHandle);

    if (atoi(argv[0]) == 1) {                                       /* Library selection passed in */
                                                                    /* argv[0]                     */
        ErrorCode = DOSLOADMODULE((char far *)ObjNameBuf,
                                  ObjNameBufLength,                 /* USA format uses library     */
                                  ModuleName = "USA",               /* module the filename USA.DLL */
                                  (unsigned far *)&ModuleHandle);

        ErrorCode = VIOWRTCHARSTRATT(CharStr = "USA Format",
                                     VioLength = strlen(CharStr),
                                     Row = 20,
                                     Column = 54,
                                     Attribute = "\032",
                                     VioHandle);
    }

    else {

        ErrorCode = DOSLOADMODULE((char far *)ObjNameBuf,
                                  ObjNameBufLength,
                                  ModuleName = "EUROPE",            /* European format uses library */
                                  (unsigned far *)&ModuleHandle);   /* module with the filename    */
                                                                    /* EUROPE.DLL                  */
        ErrorCode = VIOWRTCHARSTRATT(CharStr = "European Format",
                                     VioLength = strlen(CharStr),
                                     Row = 20,
                                     Column = 52,
                                     Attribute = "\032",
                                     VioHandle);
    }
```

Figure 66. Process 2—Main Function (Part 1)

DosLoadModule

DosLoadModule loads a dynamic link module into memory and returns a module handle that is used to reference the module in any subsequent run time dynamic linking functions. There are four parameters with this function call.

ObjNameBuf Is a far pointer to a character buffer where the operating system will place the name of the object that may have caused the problem if the function call fails.

```
ErrorCode = DOSGETPROCADDR(ModuleHandle,           /* The dynamic link modules are */
                ProcName = "BUILDTIMESTRING",       /* loaded and we must get the   */
                (unsigned long far *)&BuildTimeString);  /* two procedure addresses that */
                                                    /* are used to call the dynalink*/
ErrorCode = DOSGETPROCADDR(ModuleHandle,           /* procedures                   */
                ProcName = "BUILDDATESTRING",
                (unsigned long far *)&BuildDateString);

ErrorCode = DOSCREATETHREAD(DateTimeProcedure,      /* Create Thread 2 for date and */
                (unsigned far *)&ThreadIDWord,      /* time procedure               */
                (unsigned char far *)&NewThreadStack[981]);

ReadHandle = atoi(argv[1]);                         /* Get the pipe read handle from*/
                                                    /* the second argument string   */
do{                                                 /* Top of loop that continues   */
                                                    /* reading character cells from */
   ErrorCode = DOSREAD(ReadHandle,                  /* the pipe until a "q"          */
                (char far *)CharacterCell,          /* character is received        */
                BufferLength,
                (unsigned far *)&BytesRead);

   ErrorCode = VIOSCROLLUP(TopRow=10,               /* Scroll the window with the   */
                LeftCol=49,                         /* new attribute                */
                BotRow=17,
                RightCol=69,
                NumLines=1,
                (char far *)CharacterCell,
                VioHandle = 0);

   LogString[0] = CharacterCell[0];                 /* Build the log string         */
   LogString[1] = 0x00;
   LogStringPointer = strcat(LogStringPointer," ");
   LogStringPointer = strcat(LogStringPointer,TimePointer);
   LogStringPointer = strcat(LogStringPointer," ");
   LogStringPointer = strcat(LogStringPointer,DatePointer);

   ErrorCode = VIOWRTCHARSTRATT((char far *)LogStringPointer,  /* Display the new log string */
                VioLength = strlen(LogStringPointer),
                Row = 17,
                Column = 49,
                Attribute = &CharacterCell[1],
                VioHandle);

}
while(CharacterCell[0] != 0x71);                     /* Test for a "q" character      */

ErrorCode = DOSFREEMODULE(ModuleHandle);            /* Free module from memory       */

DOSEXIT(ActionCode,                                  /* Notify OS/2 of termination    */
        ResultCode);

}
/*****************************************************************************************/
```

Figure 67. Process 2—Main Function (Part 2)

ObjNamBufL Is a word containing the length of the object name buffer.

ModuleName Is a far pointer to a character string containing the name of the dynamic link module. This string should only be from one to eight characters in length, since a file name extension of .DLL is assumed, and the file must reside in one of the directories in the library search path.

ModuleHandle Is a far pointer to a word in which the operating system will place the module handle.

The handle that is returned is used to specify the module in any subsequent calls to DosGetProcAddr, DosGetModName, or DosFreeModule.

```
void far DateTimeProcedure()
{
  for(;;){                                                       /* Begin endless loop        */
    ErrorCode = DOSGETDATETIME(CurDateTimePointer);              /* Get the date and time     */
    (*BuildTimeString)(CurDateTime.hour,                         /* Call BuildTimeString      */
                       CurDateTime.minutes,
                       CurDateTime.seconds,
                       (char far *)TimePointer);
    ErrorCode = VIOWRTCHARSTRATT(TimePointer,                    /* Display the time string   */
                       VioLength = strlen(TimePointer),
                       Row = 8,
                       Column = 51,
                       Attribute = "\032",
                       VioHandle);
    (*BuildDateString)(CurDateTime.month,                        /* Call BuildDateString      */
                       CurDateTime.day,
                       CurDateTime.year,
                       (char far *)DatePointer);
    ErrorCode = VIOWRTCHARSTRATT(DatePointer,                    /* Display the date string   */
                       VioLength = strlen(DatePointer),
                       Row = 8,
                       Column = 60,
                       Attribute = "\032",
                       VioHandle);
    ErrorCode = DOSSLEEP(TimeInterval);                          /* Sleep for about a second  */
  }                                                              /* This thread terminates when */
                                                                 /* the process terminates      */
}
/*******************************************************************************************/
```

Figure 68. Process 2—DateTimeProcedure

DosGetProcAddr

DosGetProcAddr returns a far address to a specified procedure in a dynamic link module. There are three parameters with this function call.

ModuleHandle Is a word containing the handle returned from the DosLoadModule function call. It identifies the specific dynamic link module previously loaded into memory.

ProcName Is a far pointer to a character string containing the name of a specific procedure within the dynamic link module. If the selector portion of this pointer contains a word of zeros (null), the offset portion is defined to accept an ordinal number indicating the desired procedure. The ordinal number is the entry number of the procedure within the module.

ProcAddress Is a far pointer to a far address (double word) into which the operating system places the address of the requested procedure. This address is then used to call the dynamic link procedure.

Dynamic linking using ordinals instead of procedure names is slightly more efficient, and it is the only mechanism available for accessing the functions supported by the OS/2 DOSCALLS module. The ordinal is an integer number specifying the procedure's position within the sequence of procedures contained in the module. The appropriate ordinal numbers for OS/2 functions are used when an application object module is linked with DOSCALLS.LIB.

DosFreeModule

DosFreeModule indicates to the operating system that this process is through using the specified dynamic link module. There is one parameter with this function call.

ModuleHandle Is a word containing the handle returned from the DosLoadModule function call. It identifies the specific dynamic link module previously loaded into memory.

The ModuleHandle becomes invalid when this call completes. If no other process has a valid handle to this module, obtained via either DosLoadModule or DosGet-ModHandle, the module is removed from system memory.

Description of Process 2

As in the multiple process example, Process 2 begins by labeling its area of the screen and copying the string array to the display that defines its window.

The first piece of new logic determines which dynamic link library should be loaded. As we mentioned earlier, this example is written to support only two different libraries. You will also notice that we used the first of the two argument strings to pass the flag indicating which library the user selected. Normally this argument variable, argv[0], would contain the name used to start the child process, as was demonstrated in the previous example. Multiple arguments would then be concatenated into a single ASCIIZ string, and then the child process would parse the string to extract the individual arguments. We are not using the program name string in Process 2. In the interest of simplicity, we pass the flag that indicates which library should be loaded in the first argument string instead of the program name string.

A string with the character "1" for argv[0] indicates that the USA format library should be used. If argv[0] does not contain the "1' string, it is assumed to contain the "2" string, indicating that the European format library should be used. Depending upon the result of this test of argv[0], the appropriate dynamic link library is loaded using DosLoadModule, and we also display a string to explicitly label the format being used.

The handle returned from the DosLoadModule function call is used in two successive calls to DosGetProcAddr to get the entry point addresses for the two dynamic link functions used in this example.

The remainder of the logic of Process 2 in this run time dynamic linking example is the same as in the multiple process example. The only differences are in the syntax used to call the BuildTimeString and BuildDateString functions, and the call to DosFreeModule to free the dynamic link module when the process terminates. We used the following CL command to compile this program.

cl /c /G2 /Alfu /Fs proc2b1b.c

The command line options are defined as follows.

/c   Performs the compilation step only so that we can specifically invoke the linker.
/G2   Enables for the 80286 instruction set.
/Alfu Uses the C large model format.
/Fs   Creates a source listing.

We used the following Link command to link Process 2.

link proc2,proc2,,llibc5.lib llibc.lib doscalls.lib;

Let's move on now and look at what we did to put the two string functions into a separate dynamic link library module.

The Dynamic Link Library

There are a few key differences between the code in Figures 69 through 71 and the code used to perform these same functions in the previous example.

```
/***********************************************************************************************/
/* USA.DLL - USA format dynamic link library                                                 */
/***********************************************************************************************/

#include <doscall.h>                                    /* OS/2 API dynamic link library*/
#include <stdio.h>                                      /* C standard I/O run time lib  */
#include <string.h>                                     /* C string library             */

    char * cdecl itoa(int, char far *, int);            /* These standard library       */
    int cdecl atoi(const char far *);                   /* declarations have been       */
    size_t cdecl strlen(const char far *);              /* modified to take far pointer */
    char * cdecl strcat(char far *, const char far *);  /* parameters for use with large*/
                                                        /* model programming            */

    int _acrtused = 0;                                  /* Allows for no main function  */

    char          TimeHour[3];                          /* String variables used to     */
    char          *TimeHourPointer = TimeHour;          /* build the time string        */
    char          TimeMinutes[3];
    char          *TimeMinutesPointer = TimeMinutes;
    char          TimeSeconds[3];
    char          *TimeSecondsPointer = TimeSeconds;

    char          DateDay[3];                           /* String variables used to     */
    char          *DateDayPointer = DateDay;            /* build the date string        */
    char          DateMonth[3];
    char          *DateMonthPointer = DateMonth;
    char          DateYear[5];
    char          *DateYearPointer = DateYear;

    int           Radix;

/***********************************************************************************************/
```

Figure 69. USA.DLL—Declarations

```
extern void far pascal BuildTimeString(Hour, Minutes, Seconds, TimePointer)    /* This function formats the  */
unsigned char Hour;                                                             /* time suitable for display  */
unsigned char Minutes;
unsigned char Seconds;
char far *TimePointer;
{

  Radix = 10;

  TimeHourPointer = itoa(Hour,TimeHour,Radix);                                  /* Format the hour            */
  if(strlen(TimeHourPointer) == 1){
      TimePointer[0] = 0x30;
      TimePointer[1] = TimeHourPointer[0];
  }
  else{
      TimePointer[0] = TimeHourPointer[0];
      TimePointer[1] = TimeHourPointer[1];
  }

  TimePointer[2] = 0x3A;                                                        /* Format the minutes         */
  TimeMinutesPointer = itoa(Minutes,TimeMinutes,Radix);
  if(strlen(TimeMinutesPointer) == 1){
      TimePointer[3] = 0x30;
      TimePointer[4] = TimeMinutesPointer[0];
  }
  else{
      TimePointer[3] = TimeMinutesPointer[0];
      TimePointer[4] = TimeMinutesPointer[1];
  }

  TimePointer[5] = 0x3A;                                                        /* Format the seconds         */
  TimeSecondsPointer = itoa(Seconds,TimeSeconds,Radix);
  if(strlen(TimeSecondsPointer) == 1){
      TimePointer[6] = 0x30;
      TimePointer[7] = TimeSecondsPointer[0];
  }
  else{
      TimePointer[6] = TimeSecondsPointer[0];
      TimePointer[7] = TimeSecondsPointer[1];
  }

}
/******************************************************************************************************/
```

Figure 70. USA.DLL—BuildTimeString Function

First, you will notice that there is no C main function in the dynamic link library. The main function defines the initial entry point for a program when the program is loaded. The technique used in this program to allow us to compile and link the dynamic link module without a main function is to define an integer variable, called _acrtused, and assign a value of one to it. This variable is used as part of the IBM C/2 run time support, the details of which are beyond the scope of this book.

You will also notice in Figures 69 through 71 that, as in Process 2, we have redeclared some of the standard library routine's parameters for use with this large model program.

The CL command used to compile this dynamic link library module is:

cl /c /G2 /Gs /Alfu /Fs usa.c

where

>   **/Gs**   is used to remove stack probes.

The Link command is also only slightly different:

link usa.obj,usa.dll,,llibc5.lib llibc.lib doscalls.lib,usa.def

```
extern void far pascal BuildDateString(Month, Day, Year, DatePointer)     /* This function formats the  */
unsigned char Month;                                                      /* date suitable for display  */
unsigned char Day;
unsigned Year;
char far *DatePointer;
{

  Radix = 10;

  DateMonthPointer = itoa(Month,DateMonth,Radix);                         /* Format the month           */
  if(strlen(DateMonthPointer) == 1){
     DatePointer[0] = 0x30;
     DatePointer[1] = DateMonthPointer[0];
  }
  else{
     DatePointer[0] = DateMonthPointer[0];
     DatePointer[1] = DateMonthPointer[1];
  }

  DatePointer[2] = 0x2F;                                                  /* Format the day             */
  DateDayPointer = itoa(Day,DateDay,Radix);
  if(strlen(DateDayPointer) == 1){
     DatePointer[3] = 0x30;
     DatePointer[4] = DateDayPointer[0];
  }
  else{
     DatePointer[3] = DateDayPointer[0];
     DatePointer[4] = DateDayPointer[1];
  }

  DatePointer[5] = 0x2F;                                                  /* Format the year            */
  DateYearPointer = itoa(Year,DateYear,Radix);
  DatePointer[6] = DateYearPointer[2];
  DatePointer[7] = DateYearPointer[3];

}
/*********************************************************************************************************/
```

Figure 71. USA.DLL—BuildDateString Function

The difference in this link command is that we explicitly named the resulting executable module with an extension of .DLL. We also specified a module definition file. The module definition file is shown in Figure 72.

This module definition file specifies that this is a library routine, and that the routine runs in protect mode. It includes a description and defines the two procedure name strings to be exported, BUILDTIMESTRING and BUILD-DATESTRING.

As we discussed earlier, if we wanted to use this dynamic link library with load time dynamic linking, we would use this same module definition file with the im-

```
;
; Module Definition File
; MYLIBRARY Dynamic Link Library
; Created by JIK, AMM, and RLW
; 1987
;
LIBRARY
PROTMODE
DESCRIPTION 'MYLIBRARY Ver 1.0 Copyright 1987 JIK,AMM,RLW'
EXPORTS
   BUILDTIMESTRING
   BUILDDATESTRING
```

Figure 72. Module Definition File

port librarian to create an import library. The implib statement would look something like this:

implib usa.lib usa.def

We would probably even name the library "datetime.lib" or something else equally generic. This import library could be used to dynamically link to any set of date and time string formatting dynamic link routines as long as they had the same parameter passing conventions.

8

Supporting the International Environment

In Chapter 1, we introduced the National Language Support and message handling features of OS/2. It is clear that in releasing this operating system in eleven languages, with initial support for five code pages and keyboard and other country-dependent information for seventeen countries, that OS/2 is intended to address the needs of an international audience. The facilities in OS/2 that provide these functions are the OS/2 National Language Support (**NLS**) services. Also to support the requirements of this audience, OS/2 provides system services for message handling that make it easier to translate software into different languages. In this chapter, we review these various facilities that support the international environment. We begin with a review of the OS/2 language translation plan, and then we look at the message handling API and the National Language Support functions.

OS/2 LANGUAGE SUPPORT

OS/2 is released in eleven different languages. Since OS/2 was initially developed in United States English, this version was the first to become available. Subsequent releases for ten other languages have had all messages that are displayed by the operating system, as well as all the related publications (User's Guide, Technical Reference, etc.), translated into these languages. These languages are all listed in Chapter 1.

To aid the translation process, OS/2 message text is kept separate from the individual components of the operating system. A set of message facilities is used instead to support the system's access of these messages. These message facilities have been generalized and their mechanisms and interfaces published to make it easier for independent software developers to publish OS/2 applications and subsystems in different languages.

MESSAGE FACILITIES

The OS/2 message facilities are comprised of a set of utilities, along with a set of function calls. Some of these utilities are used only during the application development process and are provided only with the OS/2 Toolkit. The remainder of the utilities and all of the message function APIs are standard features of the base operating system.

The message facilities include three utilities. **MKMSGF** is the make message facility, which is a utility that converts a file of messages into a form that can be utilized by the other message utilities and function calls. This utility is part of the OS/2 Toolkit. **MSGBIND** is the message bind utility that adds messages to a program's executable load module (.EXE file). This utility makes these messages resident in memory so that the system does not have to go through the file system to retrieve the message from a file. MSGBIND is also provided with the OS/2 Toolkit. **HELPMSG** is the help message utility. The user executes it to access an extended message for a more detailed description of a short message displayed by the system or an application. This utility allows an application developer to provide two levels of messages. HELPMSG comes as a standard part of the operating system.

There are also three dynamic link functions available to support the general OS/2 messaging facility. DosGetMessage is a dynamic link function call that allows an application to retrieve a message. It is transparent to the application whether the message comes from memory or from a file. The function also inserts any variable message text within the message if applicable. DosInsMessage inserts variable message text for a previously retrieved message. DosPutMessage outputs a message to a specified file or device. The output includes a word wrap feature that formats the message for an 80-column display.

Now, let's look at each of these functions in more detail. We begin with the utilities.

MKMSGF Converts a file of messages into a form that can be utilized by the other message utilities and function calls. It is provided with the OS/2 Toolkit. This utility takes two input parameters: an input file name, and an output file name. The input file contains a set of messages in a particular format that can be interpreted by this utility. The output file contains the messages in a form that can be used by the other message utilities and function calls.

The message file has three parts:

1. A variable number of comment lines that can be used to identify and document the file.
2. A three-character component identifier that identifies the application (or subsystem) or application subcomponent that uses this message file.
3. The individual message entries.

```
;
; This is the message file for the XYZ program
; Created by JIK, AMM, and RLW
; 1987
;
XYZ
XYZ0000W: Warning! Fixed disk %1 is about to be erased!
XYZ0001P: Please enter your name: %0
XYZ0002E: Can't find file %1
XYZ0003E:
XYZ0004E:
XYZ0005H: Name format is Lastname, First MI
XYZ0006H:
XYZ0007I: %1 records created
```

Figure 73. Example of a Message File

Figure 73 gives an example of a message file. Each individual message entry is composed of a message header followed by the message text. The message header includes the component identifier, a four-digit message number, and a message classification character. A single message file can contain a maximum of approximately 6,000 messages. Messages are classified as Error(E), Help(H), Information(I), Prompt(P), or Warning(W). The header is delimited by the two-character sequence of colon and space (:).

Following the header is the text of the message, including up to nine place holders (variable text identifiers) for variable message text. This variable message text capability allows a program to contain a minimum number of generic messages with variables for specific information to be inserted at execution time. The nine variable message text place holders are coded with the character sequences %1, %2, . . . , %9. The character sequence %0 is used at the end-of-message line to suppress the output of a terminating carriage return and line feed. %0 can be used to allow the user to enter data following a prompt. The sample message file in Figure 73 contains messages with place holders for variable message text.

Notice in Figure 73 that the message numbers must be consecutive integers. Although unused numbers must be included as blank entries, the first number does not have to be 0000.

There is a required file naming convention for message files. It uses the three-character component identifier as the file name with the standard extension .MSG. Application developers should attempt to define component identifiers that are mnemonic and unique. Message file name ambiguity between applications that use the same component identifier is not a problem as long as the applications are installed in different file directories, and the fully qualified file name, including the path, is used to retrieve a message from the file. The example in Figure 73 has the component identifier XYZ, and therefore the message file would be named XYZ.MSG.

MSGBIND Adds messages to a program's executable load module (.EXE file) and is provided with the OS/2 Toolkit. There are three files involved in the bind process: a message file (.MSG), an executable file (.EXE), and a specially formatted

```
>c:\codepath\XYZ123A.EXE
<c:\messages\XYZ.MSG
XYZ0000
XYZ0002
>c:\codepath\XYZ123B.EXE
XYZ0000
XYZ0002
```

Figure 74. Example of a Message Bind Input File

ASCII file that contains processing directions for the Message Bind utility. The Message Bind utility reads the ASCII input file to determine which messages from a message file should be bound to which executable load module. See Figure 74 for an example of a Message Bind utility ASCII input file.

In Figure 74, we see that the greater than symbol (>) is used to indicate to the Message Bind utility that this line contains the name of an executable load module to which subsequent messages are to be bound. The less than symbol (<) is used to indicate a line that contains the message file name for the file from which subsequent messages are to be retrieved. The indicated messages are then copied into a message segment and bound (appended) to the .EXE file.

The Message Bind utility in a single invocation can bind messages from more than one message file to an .EXE file and can bind messages to multiple .EXE files. The executable file name entries, message file name entries, and the message identifiers in the ASCII input file all drive this process. As new file names and message numbers appear in the input file, the utility looks for messages in the last message file specified and adds them to a message segment for the last executable load module specified.

HELPMSG Is executed by the user to access an extended message for a more detailed description of a short message displayed by the system or an application. It comes as one of the standard utilities with OS/2. This utility enables the program designer to provide the user with two levels of error and warning messages. A simple example should serve to illustrate the usefulness of this function.

Let's assume the user has just installed the program XYZ123A, which happens to be a desktop publishing application. The user knows that the application requires a second large fixed disk but does not know why. This user's system has had a second large fixed disk for quite some time, so this did not seem to be a problem. Just before saving the first composite document to test out the application, the user gets this message:

XYZ0000: Warning! Fixed disk D: is about to be erased!

If our hypothetical desktop publishing application took advantage of the Help Message facility, then the user could gracefully recover from this situation without having to go to the application's user's manual. Instead, the user could type:

HLPMSG XYZ0000

At this point, the Help Message utility can use the message identifier to retrieve a help message from the application's help message file. The utility displays the original message and then the help message. It might look something like this:

XYZ0000: Warning! Fixed disk %1 is about to be erased!

Explanation: XYZ123A uses a special file system to store its large composite documents with images. XYZ123A is about to initialize drive D: so that it can store these documents.

Action: Copy any existing files on drive D: to another drive before continuing.

Note that the HELP statement can also be used to retrieve a help message. This statement is used to turn on/off a help line on the display. It can also be used to invoke HLPMSG to retrieve help messages.

Help Message files are built in the same way as regular message files. The only differences are that the message classification character for help messages is H, and the last character of the file name is an "h" for Help Message files. For this example, the Help Message file name would be:

XYZH.MSG

The example given above is also intended to show the use of **variable insertion text** in messages. If you refer back to Figure 73, you will see that message XYZ0000 does not actually contain a drive letter. Instead, the message has the variable text identifier %1 that the application replaces with the appropriate driver letter before the message is displayed. This is a simple example of how a minimum number of generic messages defined in a message file can accommodate a wide range of specific messages to the user.

Now, let's look at the three dynamic link function calls available to support the OS/2 message facilities.

DosGetMessage Is used by an application to retrieve a message that was previously processed by the Make Message File utility. The function automatically looks for the message in memory and only goes to the message file if the message is not in a message segment bound to the program. This means that using the message facilities, the programmer can vary which messages are loaded with the program and which ones remain on disk without making any changes to the program source code.

A call to the Get Message function passes the message file name (including the path), message number, a table of text strings to insert for the message variables (variable message identifiers) if any exist, and pointers to a buffer where the function will place the resulting message and its length.

DosInsMessage Performs just the variable insertion part of the previously described Get Message function. This function is useful because it allows the program to retrieve a message from a message file using the Get Message function before the variable insertion text is known. When the variable portion of the message is known, the Insert Message function can be used to build the complete message.

This function provides an alternative to binding a message to an executable module for getting a message into memory. A program designer can avoid allocating the memory to hold this message for the duration of the execution of the program, as would occur if the message were bound to the executable module. The message can be retrieved before the variable insertion text is known but while access to the message file is still assured. This retrieval might be done just before some operation that would jeopardize access to the message file. Insert Message can then be used to add the variable insertion text to the message for display.

The arguments passed to this function are essentially the same as for Get Message, except that they include a pointer to the input message already in memory instead of to the message file name.

DosPutMessage Is used to output a message. The output is handle-based so the application can output the message to an open device such as the console (display) or printer, or it can output the message to a file. Since this function is handle based, message output can be redirected.

The parameters on this function are the output file or device handle, a pointer to the buffer containing the message, and the length of the message.

Message Facility Summary

We can now see that OS/2 has a powerful set of messaging facilities. As we pointed out earlier, although these facilities were motivated by the requirement to provide a system environment in which applications can be readily translated to different languages, the benefits do not stop there. These message facilities have the flexibility that enables them to improve the development and ultimately the usability of an application. Professional communicators can develop the message text without having to deal with the programming of the application. The programmer can easily change the run time location of messages from disk to memory to tune the application for performance and storage and to eliminate potential deadlock situations (e.g., trying to read an error message off a diskette to tell the user that the diskette has become unreadable). Finally, the usability of the application can be improved by providing an additional level of help messages and allowing the messages to be redirected to other devices or files.

CONFIGURING THE SYSTEM FOR DIFFERENT COUNTRIES

An international product like OS/2 has several technical challenges with which it must cope. It has to deal with the fact that in some countries, devices such as keyboards, displays, and printers are different. Various countries also display the same information in dissimilar ways. For example, they may format the date and time differently, and they may use different currency symbols and different decimal separator characters. (The decimal separator is the character placed between the fractional part and the whole part of a decimal number; in the United States we use a period.) To further complicate matters, the languages of some countries require symbols that do not have any meaning in another country's language. And, as if this were not enough, some countries use different 8 bit codes in their computers to represent the same character! A particular definition of all the permutations of eight binary bits is called a **code page.** Finally, some languages require more than 256 symbols (characters), so they cannot all be encoded in an 8 bit binary code.

Earlier versions of DOS introduced facilities to address some of these problems. OS/2 has expanded upon these initial concepts to meet the operating system requirements of an even broader international audience. A broader audience improves the opportunity for an increase in the size of the market for OS/2 applications and subsystems.

The facilities in OS/2 to deal with these challenges are generally referred to as the OS/2 National Language Support, or NLS. The OS/2 NLS capabilities can roughly be categorized into three areas:

1. Profiling on a country by country basis the conventions used for date and time format, currency symbol, etc.
2. Multiple code page support.
3. Double Byte Character Set (DBCS) enabling for the countries whose languages use more than 256 characters.

Country-Dependent Information

As part of the OS/2 NLS architecture, each country is identified by a three-digit country code. OS/2 uses a country-dependent information profile to specify the conventions that that country employs to display certain information. A table listing all of the seventeen countries for which OS/2 has a country-dependent information profile is shown in Figure 75. The language conventions profiled on a country-by-country basis in OS/2 are as follows:

- □ Date format.
- □ Date separator.
- □ Time format.
- □ Time separator.

- Currency indicator.
- Currency format.
- Decimal places in currency indicator.
- Decimal separator.
- Thousands separator.
- Data list separator.
- Primary code page.

As you can see, this country-dependent information deals with certain processing performed by the system that must be done differently for certain languages in certain countries. The processing of this country-dependent information complements the OS/2 language translation plan for the eleven supported languages.

Code Page Switching

A code page is a mapping between the different 256 possible combinations of 8 bits (codes) and the symbol that the code represents (e.g., in the ASCII code page 437, the binary value 01000001 is mapped to the capital letter A). As we mentioned in Chapter 1, OS/2 supports the United States IBM PC extended ASCII code page 437, Portuguese code page 860, Canadian French code page 863, Nordic code page 865, and the multilingual code page 850.

The goal of the definition of the multilingual code page is to omit any nonessential

Country	Country Code	Keyboard	Code Page Primary	Secondary
United States	001	US	437	850
United Kingdom	044	UK	437	850
France	033	FR	437	850
Germany	049	GR	437	850
Italy	039	IT	437	850
Spain	034	SP	437	850
Denmark	045	DK	865	850
Finland	358	SU	437	850
Netherlands	031	NL	437	850
Norway	047	NO	865	850
Portugal	351	PO	860	850
Sweden	046	SV	437	850
Asia	099	--	437	850
Australia	061	--	437	850
Belgium	032	BE	437	850
Canada	002	CF	863	850
Latin-America	003	LA	437	850
Switzerland	041	SF,SG	437	850
Arabic	785	--	864	850
Hebrew	972	--	862	850
Japan	081	--	932	437
Korea	082	--	934	437
Peoples Republic of China	086	--	936	437
Taiwan	088	--	938	437

Figure 75. NLS Support—Country Codes, Keyboards, Code Pages

graphics character codes and to define the most important 256 symbols necessary to encode text in as many languages as possible. Using the multilingual code page, an application can maximize its portability between different countries.

The need for code page support is not limited just to language translation. The more sophisticated of the new generation of character handling devices can support programmable (usually referred to as downloadable) code pages and symbol definitions (also called symbol tables and font tables). Support for these devices levies requirements on the operating system.

OS/2 addresses these requirements by tracking the active code page for every process in the system. Only two different code pages are allowed to be prepared (made available) in the system when it is initialized during CONFIG.SYS processing. The operating system will automatically switch the active code page depending upon the active process. This code page will then be used in support of I/O to devices such as the keyboard, display, and printer.

The primary code page is one of the characteristics included as part of the country-dependent information defined for each country code. Figure 75 lists the countries for which OS/2 tracks country information. The list includes the country code, keyboard layout, and primary and secondary code pages.

Double Byte Character Set (DBCS) Enabling

A Double Byte Character Set is actually a mixture of double byte and single byte characters. The range of 8 bit binary values from 00H to FFH is divided by a Double Byte Character Set into subranges. If a character code lies outside of these subranges, it is defined as a single byte character. If a character lies within one of these subranges, it is defined as the first byte of a double byte character. In OS/2, the range that can be used to define the subranges for the first byte of double byte characters is limited to within 81H to FCH inclusive. DosGetDBCSEv is a dynamic link function call that can be used to get the specified or system default Double Byte Character Set ranges.

The statement that OS/2 is enabled for DBCS means that when components of OS/2 manipulate character strings, DBCS characters will not be split or malformed. Although the OS/2 language translation plan does not include any DBCS languages, enabling the operating system for DBCS characters lays a foundation and indicates a potential area for future enhancement.

OS/2 NLS Facilities

The OS/2 NLS facilities are of three general types:

1. System initialization directives contained in CONFIG.SYS.
2. User commands that can be issued during system operation.
3. Dynamic link function calls that can be issued by applications.

CONFIG.SYS NLS Commands

We describe the processing of the CONFIG.SYS file during OS/2 system initialization in Chapter 9. The three statements defined for the CONFIG.SYS file related to NLS support are COUNTRY, CODEPAGE, and DEVINFO.

COUNTRY=nnn Is used to specify the country code. The system then uses the predefined set of conventions for the country-dependent information associated with the specified country code.

CODEPAGE=xxx,[yyy] Is used to activate one or two code pages in the operating system.

DEVINFO= Is used to cause device specific commands to be sent to a character device that supports code page switching. The information on the DEVINFO= statement and the commands sent are specified on a per device basis.

User NLS Commands

CHCP Is issued by the user from the command line and is used to set (or query) the code page for a session. Any subsequent process (application) started in this session will be tagged as using the code page that the user set with this command. The display, keyboard, and printer subsystems then use this information when performing I/O on behalf of this process.

> *Note: The code page switching support for the printer subsystem is contained in the print spooler. Therefore, to receive the benefit of code page switching for printed output, the print spooler must be active.*

Dynamic Link NLS API

The following NLS function calls are a standard part of the OS/2 application programming interface.

DosSetCp Sets the code page for this process. The only parameters are the code page identifier and a reserved word set to zero. The keyboard and display code page are set. The file system uses this process code page to initialize file system I/O to the printer, but the print spooler must be loaded for this printer code page support to have any effect.

DosGetCp Returns the code page currently assigned to this process and the list of code pages that are available in the system. OS/2 currently allows up to two code pages to be available in the system.

DosGetCtryInfo Gets the specified or system default country-dependent information. This includes the country code, the current process code page, and all the parameters of the country-dependent information discussed previously.

DosCaseMap Performs case mapping on a binary string. Case mapping means mapping a string of mixed upper- and lowercase characters to all uppercase.

DosGetDBCSEv Returns the specified or system default Double Byte Character Set ranges. These are the ranges of characters that are used as the first byte in double byte characters.

9

Beyond System Defaults: A User's Perspective

WHEN YOU POWER ON your IBM personal computer after installing OS/2 on the fixed disk, the hardware ROM code automatically performs a number of tests. If no errors are found in the hardware, then the ROM code starts the Initial Program Load (IPL) of the operating system. The operating system then initializes itself, establishing the environment in which you may run your applications. The setting up of the environment in which to execute applications takes place in three phases:

- The configuration phase.
- The automatic execution phase.
- The program selection phase.

During the configuration phase, OS/2 searches for a special file that contains information about the settable parameters of the system initialization. This special file has the name of **CONFIG.SYS**, an adoption of the familiar name used by DOS for the DOS configuration file. The operating system assigns the values indicated in the configuration file for the specified options. For those parameters not specified or incorrectly specified, or for the case when the configuration file cannot be found, the operating system assigns default values or default actions. The system configuration is important because it determines how applications are handled while the personal computer is powered on. In other words, once established, the system configuration cannot be dynamically altered. The configuration file *can* be modified, but the changes cannot take effect until the system has been reset (using the Ctrl-Alt-Del key sequence to restart the initialization process) or powered off, then powered on (sometimes called the Big Red Switch).

257

Once the configuration has been determined, applications can be executed so that the next phase, automatic execution, proceeds. In this phase, the operating system looks for a special file that contains commands normally used at the command prompt (sometimes called the command line). This file is called **STARTUP.CMD** and is similar to the AUTOEXEC.BAT batch file used by DOS. If the operating system finds a STARTUP.CMD file, then the command processor automatically starts an OS/2 session and handles the commands in the STARTUP.CMD file. In this way, OS/2 applications can be started automatically (in separate sessions from the current command processor session) without any operator intervention. As long as there is no command to exit this session in the STARTUP.CMD file, the command processor session is displayed to the user. If there is an exit command, the command processor terminates and the Program Selector displays its menu.

The Program Selector is the program selection phase and is available until the personal computer is powered off or reset. The Program Selector is a special application that presents a menu-driven interface to you, the computer user, to give you the means to perform and control multiple activities. (See Figure 76 for an illustration of the Program Selector menu as it appears before the operator has added applications or started other sessions.)

With the Program Selector, you can do the following:

- Access the OS/2 command prompt.
- Access the DOS command prompt.
- Start applications.
- Switch between applications.
- Get on-line help.

When you select an OS/2 command prompt, the system checks for a special file named **OS2INIT.CMD,** which also contains commands that are used at the com-

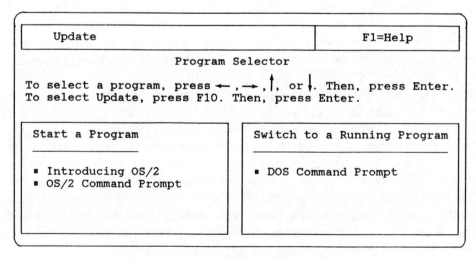

Figure 76. The OS/2 Program Selector Menu

mand prompt just like a batch file. This file permits you to execute commands to set up such application environment items as the directory search paths for applications and the data files for the session just started. Of course, when you select the DOS command prompt for the first time, the operating system executes the familiar DOS file **AUTOEXEC.BAT**, in order to assign parameters for the DOS application environment.

CONFIGURATION OPTIONS

OS/2 provides an installation program to help you set up your personal computer to run OS/2. This installation program creates the configuration file, giving you a choice of using preselected values, using the operating system defaults, or using values you enter for the various options. Then, once OS/2 is installed, you can modify the CONFIG.SYS file directly with a text editor. We discuss the different options controlling how OS/2 handles the system and application environments in terms of their system defaults and what they mean to you. Where they are significant, we also identify the default values chosen by the installation program. If you do *not* want the system or installation default action for a particular option, you must include the option in CONFIG.SYS and specify the value or action.

Interactive Initialization

OS/2 initialization can be interactive (attended initialization) or noninteractive (unattended initialization).

PAUSEONERROR   System Default: Prompt for user response before continuing with system initialization.

As OS/2 configures itself during its initialization, it may encounter a problem with an option specified in the configuration file. When an error occurs, the operating system takes the default value or action for the option in order to complete initialization. Then, after dealing with the configuration options but before handling automatic execution (like STARTUP.CMD or starting the user interface program), OS/2 displays error messages. At this point, if you select attended initialization, the operating system prompts you to press the ENTER key to signify that you are ready to proceed. Otherwise, the operating system automatically goes to the next phase of initialization. If there are no problems with the configuration options, OS/2 simply proceeds with the automatic execution phase without pausing.

Waiting for you to respond to the prompt is the way the operating system ensures you are aware of the problems it encountered with the configuration options. Obviously, the operating system must initialize regardless of problems, whenever possible, so that you can correct the errors by modifying the configuration file or checking the hardware.

There are, however, situations in which you may not always have an operator to attend the computer, such as in the case of a server. In this case, you would want the operating system to IPL without operator intervention.

File System Operations

The options concerning the file system affect the performance of I/O only to files. The performance of I/O to the other objects that the file system can access, such as character devices, is unchanged.

BUFFERS   System Default: Have the file system allocate and use 3 buffers for managing file I/O.

Install Default: Have the file system allocate and use 30 buffers for managing file I/O.

The file system uses internal buffers to manage the movement of file data between the application and the disk/diskette device. The application specifies file data in terms of bytes, and the file system translates the bytes into sector-sized blocks for I/O with the block device. A sector is a fixed length block of data, 512 bytes long. Data for a file typically fills a number of sectors completely, with any remainder using a sector only partially (as at the beginning or end of a file). The file system uses the internal buffers to manage these partial sectors.

Increasing the number of buffers increases the file system's efficiency in handling file I/O. However, there is a point at which increasing the number of buffers does not provide any further benefit for file I/O performance; in fact, it may even degrade performance. The most appropriate number of file system buffers is dependent on a number of factors, such as the amount of memory that is configured in the system and what kinds of applications you run. To determine what that number should be requires some experimentation.

DISKCACHE   System Default: Do not allocate memory for a disk cache.

Install Default: Allocate 64 KB for a disk cache.

The OS/2 disk device driver supports a disk cache for those models of the PS/2 family of computers on which OS/2 can run (Models 50, 60, and 80). The disk cache is a buffer that the disk device driver uses to temporarily store information read from a fixed disk. This technique can improve file I/O performance: if desired information is located in the cache, it saves the time of obtaining the information from the fixed disk.

As with the number of file system buffers, determining the best amount of memory to allocate for a disk cache depends on several factors, such as the amount of memory and the frequency and scope of file I/O. To determine what that amount should be requires some experimentation.

Device Support

To use a device other than the ones the operating system automatically supports, you must have a device driver for that device, especially if the device is interrupt-driven. The device support option allows you to have the operating system install that device driver.

DEVICE System Default: Install only the base OS/2 device drivers.

The operating system automatically installs device drivers for a set of devices that include the screen, keyboard, printer, and disk/diskette. This gives you immediate support for a number of devices. However, you can use other devices by identifying device drivers to the operating system. You can also specify device drivers that replace previously installed device drivers, in order to replace or extend the functions supported for the devices. In fact, you can even install certain DOS device drivers for use in the DOS environment.

Country Support

The way that keyboard, screen, and printer data are treated depend on the culture and the language of the individual using the system. Since OS/2 is an international product, it is important to have the ability to adapt to a country's customs and language. The country-dependent items include date/time format, decimal separator, and currency symbol. Language affects the character set (code page), character case mapping, collating sequences, and double-byte character set (DBCS) environment. Of course, the two factors (country and language) are interrelated: it does not make sense to mix and match country and language.

Refer to the section in Chapter 8 on Country-Dependent Information for more information on these options and how to use them for national language support (NLS). In general, whenever you specify CODEPAGE, you must also specify DEVINFO.

CODEPAGE System Default: Use the native character set of the display and printer, if the font exists in the device, and use the character set for the keyboard as indicated by the country code from the COUNTRY option.

COUNTRY System Default: Handle country-dependent information in the United States format and United States English.

DEVINFO   System Default: Do not prepare a device for code page switching.

Protection Scope

The 80286 processor provides the protection mechanism for protected instructions and privilege levels, but the protection applies only to OS/2 applications.

IOPL System Default: Do not allow OS/2 applications to issue the protected I/O instructions, that is, directly control a device.

An OS/2 application normally executes at the application privilege level. In order for the application to execute I/O instructions, the operating system must grant the application I/O Privilege Level (IOPL). An OS/2 device driver, on the other hand, always has I/O Privilege in order to control its device. The protected I/O instructions include IN and OUT, which move commands and data directly from and to device ports, and CLI and STI, which disable and enable hardware interrupts.

Because an application can jeopardize other applications' ability to use the device, OS/2 requires you to be aware that you are using an application that goes directly to the hardware (the application cannot control the hardware unless you specify this option in the configuration file).

PROTECTONLY System Default: Configure the system for both the DOS environment (real mode operations) and OS/2 application environment (protect mode operations).

A fully protected system is one without a DOS environment; that is, it is a system that executes in protect mode only. In the DOS environment, or real mode, a DOS application can perform any activity without restriction or constraint, including accessing memory in the range from 0 KB to 640 KB and manipulating devices directly. Even if you specify the size of the DOS environment as smaller than the amount of memory below 640 KB, the DOS application still has the potential to access all memory below 640 KB. Likewise, devices that must be shared in the multitasking system are vulnerable to a DOS application's single-minded purpose. Protection is therefore compromised whenever you have real mode operations.

If, instead, you run only OS/2 applications, then you do not need a DOS environment. The benefits are in the increased level of protection and in the increased amount of memory available to OS/2 applications, as the area below 640 KB is no longer dedicated to the DOS environment.

OS/2 Application Environment

To help you manage OS/2 applications, there are many options concerning how the operating system manages dynamic linking and how you specify programs that you wish to run.

LIBPATH System Default: Use the root directory of whichever device was used to start (IPL) the operating system, either the fixed disk (c:\) or diskette (a:\), as the location of dynamic link libraries.

Install Default: Use the directories, as established by the installation program, that contain the system files.

For the dynamically linked interfaces used by OS/2 applications, OS/2 must locate the corresponding libraries in order to load the libraries and resolve the linkages to the applications. The search for the dynamic link libraries is automatically done across all OS/2 sessions and all OS/2 applications.

By specifying different subdirectories to search for libraries, you can organize the libraries in subdirectories according to your own criteria and control the order in which those subdirectories are examined.

PROTSHELL System Default: Use the OS/2 Program Selector as the user interface program and the OS/2 command processor, CMD.EXE.

Install Default: Use the OS/2 Program Selector as the user interface program and the OS/2 command processor, CMD.EXE, with the parameter of OS2INIT.CMD.

The user interface program is started at the end of system initialization. This program is responsible for managing your access to the different sessions or applications. The command processor handles the protect mode command line interface.

You can choose to have your own user interface program and/or your own command processor.

RUN System Default: There is no default system program to start.

Install Default: Start the print spooler.

You can start a noninteractive program to execute in the background during system initialization, before the user interface program is started. This program cannot perform video, keyboard, or mouse I/O except through a pop-up.

Multitasking

You can adjust many factors in multitasking that affect performance to suit your requirements.

MAXWAIT System Default: Use three seconds as the timeout value.

Because of the number of active Regular class threads and their relative priorities, a Regular class thread may end up waiting for some time before executing. This phenomenon is sometimes termed "CPU starvation." To prevent total exclusion in access to the CPU, the operating system limits the time that a Regular class thread waits for a chance to execute. When the time limit expires, the operating system temporarily boosts the priority level of the Regular class thread in order to give it a chance to execute for a minimum time period.

This factor affects the performance of Regular class activities in the system. Determining the most appropriate value depends on the number of applications that you run concurrently, what kind of activities they perform, and the frequency of the activities. In other words, you can experiment with different values against your mix of applications.

PRIORITY System Default: Dynamically adjust the priority of a Regular class thread.

To optimize performance of Regular class threads, the operating system watches over the different kinds of activities, like CPU usage or I/O usage, and dynamically adjusts the priorities of Regular class threads.

In certain application environments, however, you may require the predictability that results from priorities determined strictly by class and level.

THREADS System Default: Set the total number of threads available in the system to 64.

To optimize performance and memory available to applications in different configurations, the number of threads in the system is variable.

As you add system extensions and applications to your system, you may need additional threads. Otherwise, by limiting the number of threads, you may find that performance suffers in a more complex operating environment as the system extensions and applications are forced to serialize activities that would otherwise occur concurrently.

TIMESLICE System Default: Set the maximum timeslice to 248 milliseconds; set the minimum timeslice to 32 milliseconds.

The maximum timeslice is used to limit the time that a thread executes before giving another thread *at the same priority level* a chance to execute. Timeslicing in a round-robin fashion ensures that threads of equal priorities have equal opportunities to execute. The minimum timeslice is used to control special situations.

If you have applications that perform activities that are more timing-dependent, you may need to lower the maximum timeslice to allow the activities to execute more frequently when round-robin scheduling occurs. However, you should avoid very small values because, at some point, the operating system will end up spending more time scheduling and dispatching threads than allowing the threads to execute. You should also avoid very large values because, at some point, a thread at the same priority level as other threads will end up spending an excessive amount of time waiting to execute.

Memory Management

You can control certain effects of memory management on your system.

MEMMAN   System Default: Use swapping and compaction if starting from fixed disk; use only compaction if starting from diskette.

The management of storage allocation has two factors that affect system performance: swapping and compaction. Swapping allows the operating system to temporarily save a data segment on disk in order to free physical memory for other use (a code segment does not need to be swapped; instead, it can be discarded from memory and later brought in from disk). Compaction allows the operating system to move segments in physical memory to consolidate unused fragments that result from the use of different sized segments. Together, swapping and compaction permit applications to overcommit physical memory. By itself, compaction permits a more efficient use of the physical memory.

If you have an application or system extension that depends heavily on timing, you may need to prevent swapping and compaction to ensure the necessary responsiveness. However, you would be trading performance at the cost of memory utilization. In other words, you will not be able to run as many applications as before, and the applications that you do run are limited in the memory they can allocate.

SWAPPATH   System Default: Use the root directory of whichever device was used to start (IPL) the operating system, either the fixed disk (c:\) or diskette (a:\), as the location of the system swap file.

The system swap file is used to temporarily store data segments that must be removed from system memory in order to satisfy a request for memory. You can isolate the swap file in a subdirectory or in a separate partition on a fixed disk, which may be desirable since the swap file can grow quite large given sufficient overcommit of physical memory.

The DOS Environment

You can control the size of the DOS environment on OS/2.

RMSIZE   System Default: Set the highest memory address to the smaller of either the total memory installed minus 512 KB or the highest memory address of memory installed below 640 KB (that is, 512 KB or 640 KB).

In general terms, OS/2 maximizes the amount of memory below 640 KB for the DOS environment, taking into account memory needed for protect mode operations. However, if you don't need that much memory for any DOS application you run, you may want to specify a smaller value. Any memory not used by the DOS environment is utilized for protect mode operations.

OS/2 supports a set of options used by DOS, specifically, BREAK, FCBS, and SHELL. These options affect *only* the DOS environment. The defaults that OS/2 assigns to these options are summarized as follows.

BREAK   System Default: Do not check for the Ctrl-Break key sequence in the DOS environment except during Standard device operations.

FCBS   System Default: Allow sixteen File Control Blocks (FCBs) to be open at the same time and keep the first eight opened FCBs from being reused when more than sixteen opened FCBs are needed.

SHELL   System Default: Use the OS/2 compatibility command processor for the DOS environment, COMMAND.COM.

AUTOMATIC EXECUTION

OS/2 provides an autostart facility in the STARTUP.CMD batch file that is similar in many ways to the AUTOEXEC.BAT file in DOS. If the STARTUP.CMD batch file is found, OS/2 starts the first OS/2 session with the OS/2 command processor to interpret the file. This mechanism means that you do not have to go through the user interface program to get applications running. If the STARTUP.CMD file cannot be found, then the operating system runs the user interface program. Refer to Figure 77 for an example of a STARTUP.CMD file.

```
PATH c:\;c:\os2;c:\batch;
START acomm
START editor
START appoint
EXIT
```

1. Sets up the directory search order to locate programs.

2. Starts another session running the async comm program.

3. Starts another session running the text editor program.

4. Starts another session running the appointments program.

5. Terminates the current session.

Figure 77. Sample STARTUP.CMD Batch File

The key command to use in the STARTUP.CMD batch file is the command START. Although you can use this command at the OS/2 command prompt (command line), the START command is most useful in conjunction with the autostart mechanism. A program or batch file identified by the START command is put into a separate session and executed. There is a similar command that is used in the configuration file, CONFIG.SYS, called RUN. However, the RUN command can only be used to start noninteractive programs, that is, programs that execute primarily in the background.

Specifying environment parameters with such commands as PATH, DPATH, PROMPT, and SET affect only the applications that run in the session in which the STARTUP.CMD file is being processed. However, you can cause another batch file to execute in another session by using the START command. This batch file can then execute commands to set up the environment prior to invoking an application in a fashion familiar to batch files used in DOS.

PROGRAM SELECTION

Program selection is the phase that deals with operator activities until the computer is powered off or reset. OS/2 defaults the user interface program to the Program Selector, which lets you manage the applications running in the system through a menu-driven interface. Of course, you can always select a command prompt, either an OS/2 command line or the DOS command line, and start applications and sessions from there. And, if you do not wish to use the Program Selector menu to select a session to switch to, you can use a key sequence (ALT-ESC) as a "hot key" to cycle through the different active sessions. If at any time you wish to invoke the Program Selector menu, you can use another key sequence (CTRL-ESC) to switch to the Program Selector.

Of course, any OS/2 application that you switch away from continues to execute in the background. However, if you switch away from the DOS environment, it is stopped until you switch back to it.

BATCH FILES AND BATCH LANGUAGE

Batch files in OS/2 serve the same purpose that they do in DOS: they allow you to execute a sequence of commands at the command prompt automatically, without having to type the commands yourself. We have already encountered some special-purpose batch files in the STARTUP.CMD, OS2INIT.CMD, and AUTOEXEC.BAT files.

OS/2 batch files are easily identifiable by the .CMD file extension, as opposed to the .BAT file extension used by DOS batch files. A batch file with a .BAT file extension will not execute at an OS/2 command line; a batch file with a .CMD extension will not execute at a DOS command line. This distinction helps you avoid running a batch file in the wrong environment. This is important because otherwise you might start a batch file that changes the environment "permanently" (e.g., erasing files) only to discover too late that the application that the batch file invoked cannot execute in the current mode, leaving you unable to recover the changes.

As in DOS, a batch file in OS/2 not only handles commands for the command prompt but also provides a number of commands to control how the batch file functions. These batch commands include the capability to call other batch files, replace parameters on commands, control the displaying of batch file commands, branch to other parts of the batch file, loop repeatedly to execute a sequence of commands, and test error conditions. Refer to Figure 78 for a list of the batch commands.

```
Command    OS/2   DOS
--------   ----   ---
CALL        *      *
ECHO        *      *
ENDLOCAL    *
EXTPROC     *
FOR         *      *
GOTO        *      *
IF          *      *
PAUSE       *      *
REM         *      *
SETLOCAL    *
SHIFT       *      *
```

Figure 78. Batch Commands

10

Where to Go from Here

OS/2 STANDARD EDITION PROVIDES the steppingstone for applications to take advantage of the environment made possible by the 80286 microprocessor, both in terms of protection and large physical memory and in terms of the capabilities of multitasking and dynamic linking. Applications are not all that benefit from OS/2: the user of the personal computer gains as well, through the ability to run multiple applications, the interactive installation procedure, the compatibility of the OS/2 prompt commands to DOS prompt commands, and an easy-to-use user interface program. The application developer also profits, both from the open architecture and from the aids in the programmer toolkit. OS/2 Standard Edition is the core of function that serves as a platform for growth. The Standard Edition is staged over two releases (see Figure 79) to complete the operating system core with windowing and graphics interfaces as well as enhancements to the user interface with the Presentation Manager.

The next step of OS/2 is the Extended Edition. The Extended Edition adds solu-

```
                                            Version 1.1
                                       ┌──────────────────────────┐
                                       │ ▪ Windowing              │
                  Version 1.0          │ ▪ Graphics               │
                                       ├──────────────────────────┤
        ┌──────────────────────────┐   │ ▪ Protection             │
        │ ▪ Protection             │   │ ▪ Large Physical Memory  │
        │ ▪ Large Physical Memory  │   │ ▪ Virtual Memory         │
        │ ▪ Virtual Memory         │   │ ▪ Multitasking           │
        │ ▪ Multitasking           │   │ ▪ Multiprogramming       │
        │ ▪ Multiprogramming       │   │ ▪ Dynamic Linking        │
        │ ▪ Dynamic Linking        │   │ ▪ DOS Compatibility      │
        │ ▪ DOS Compatibility      │   └──────────────────────────┘
        └──────────────────────────┘
```

Figure 79. OS/2 Standard Edition

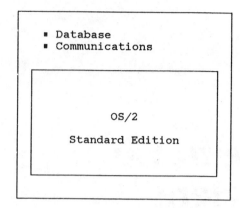

Figure 80. OS/2 Extended Edition

tions for communications and database management (see Figure 80). The Extended Edition is a single solution for those individuals who require either or both communications and database services. The Extended Edition is flexible: you can individually select and install the types of services you need. The communications support covers a wide range of connections and protocols, with emulation of multiple terminal types and file transfer. The database support covers a relational model of data in simple tabular form where the management of the data is served by the Structured Query Language (SQL).

THE PRESENTATION MANAGER

The Presentation Manager supplies the support for windowing and graphics. Windowing permits you to view several applications simultaneously and even permits a single application to have more than one window. You can control the window size and position; an application can create and delete windows. You can extract data out of a window and move it to another window (called a clipboard function); that is, you can move data from one application to another. Graphics allows applications to take advantage of displays that support All Points Addressable (APA) modes. The interfaces support vector operations, raster operations, and multiple font styles and sizes.

THE DATABASE MANAGER

The Database Manager provides a relational model of data similar to IBM Database 2 (DB2) and IBM Structured Query Language/Data System (SQL/DS). The definition, retrieval, modification, and control of the data comes via the Structured Query Language (SQL), which is a high-level data management language that both end users and applications can utilize.

Data is structured in the form of simple tables, with records and fields. You therefore define and operate on data in terms of tables. This means you do not have to be an expert in complex physical data structures to manage your database. SQL allows you to indicate what you want to do, and SQL takes care of how it is done. You can perform arithmetic operations on data, selectively retrieve data, dynamically sort data, and prepare customized reports.

The Database Manager also provides import/export functions to exchange data with other applications based on other PC databases.

THE COMMUNICATIONS MANAGER

The Communications Manager of the Extended Edition serves both the end user and the applications that need communications support. With the Communications Manager, communications between personal computers or between a personal computer and a host system are possible. The Communications Manager supports many types of connections, including SDLC, Distributed Function Terminals (DFT) mode to an IBM 3174 or 3274, IBM Token-Ring Network, IBM PC Network, and asynchronous links. With these different types of connections, the Communications Manager utilizes the appropriate protocol, from LU6.2 to 3270 data stream (LU2) to asynchronous protocols. Of course, concurrent emulation of different terminal types is provided, including the IBM 3270, IBM 3101 and other ASCII terminals, and file transfer is supported. For flexibility, the emulators and connections can be individually selected and installed. The Communications Manager also provides alerts for network management, problem determination functions, and other controls.

The Communications Manager aids application productivity with a number of programming interfaces. The application programming interfaces include the following:

□ Advanced Program-to-Program Communications (APPC).

The LU6.2 architecture specifies the functions that conforming applications can use for APPC over the data links. Both data stream-independent (mapped) and data stream-dependent (basic) functions are available.

□ Server-Requester Programming Interface (SRPI).

Requester applications can obtain services of host server applications using LU2 protocols.

□ Asynchronous Communications Device Interface (ACDI).

Applications can manage data over asychronous links, as well as control characteristics of the communication line with ACDI.

Other interfaces include the 3270 program interface, IBM NetBIOS, and IEEE 802.2.

THE STAGE IS SET

OS/2 Standard Edition 1.0 enables us to embark on the first two stages of the multiple-stage transition to the workstation software of the future. These first two stages can be thought of as follows:

□ Rewriting existing DOS applications so they can run in the OS/2 execution environment. These rewritten existing applications can then run in the multiple session environment that OS/2 provides. Only one DOS environment session is provided by OS/2.

□ Designing new applications or restructuring and redesigning old applications to take advantage of the new functions and features that OS/2 Standard Edition Version 1.0 provides. Large memory support and multitasking are two features that many applications can successfully exploit.

Some of the additional stages would be as follows:

□ Exploiting the graphics and windowing capabilities that the OS/2 Standard Edition Version 1.1 Presentation Manager provides.

□ Incorporating the facilities that the OS/2 Extended Edition Communications Manager and Database Manager provide into applications that can benefit from them.

Index

80286. *See* Microprocessor
80386. *See* Microprocessor
8086. *See* Microprocessor
8088. *See* Microprocessor

ABIOS, 26, 201–5
ABIOS, Logical ID, 202, 203, 204, 205
Advanced BIOS. *See* ABIOS
API. *See* Application programming
    interface
Application environment, 7, 10, 11, 12,
    15, 23, 259, 262–63, 265–66
  DOS. *See* DOS environment
  LIBPATH, 263
  multiple, 5, 9, 10, 12, 14, 15, 16, 23,
    44, 49, 57, 58, 59, 258
  OS/2, 259, 262–63. *See also*
    OS2INIT.CMD
  PROTSHELL, 263
  RUN, 263
Application migration. *See* Migration
Application monitor, 120, 121, 161–64,
    173
Application programming interface
    (API), 5, 11, 24, 49, 61, 65, 67,
    68
  example, 83, 89
  extendability, 18, 220
  library, 89, 263
Argument string, 65, 66
ASCIIZ string, 93
Assembly language, 84
Asynchronous communications device
    driver. *See under* Device driver

Asynchronous execution, 59, 63, 64, 66,
    68
AUTOEXEC.BAT, 258, 259, 266, 267
Automatic execution phase, 258, 266–67

Background session, 11, 59, 60, 61, 140,
    144, 155
Basic Input Output System. *See* BIOS
Batch file, 60, 259, 267–68
  .BAT, 267
  .CMD, 267
  commands, 268
  extension, 267
Batch processing, 1, 268
Bimodal, 11, 169, 194
BIOS, 6, 12, 13, 26, 44, 89, 120
  Advanced. *See* ABIOS
  compatibility. *See* BIOS
Block device. *See under* Device driver
BREAK, 266
BUFFERS, 260
Bus, 25, 28

C language, 83, 84
C, standard run time functions, 83, 86
CC command, 84
Character device, 122, 126–29. *See also*
    under Device driver
  I/O, 122, 126–29, 131–34
  I/O sharing mode, 127
  monitor, 120, 121, 161–64, 173
  names, 127, 170
CHCP, 254
CL command, 86, 241

Clock device driver. *See under* Device driver

CMD.EXE. *See* Command processor

Code page, 22, 143, 144, 151, 152, 252. *See also* Country support
  switching, 22

CODEPAGE. *See* Country support

Command line. *See* Command prompt

Command processor, 60, 62, 66, 258
  CMD.EXE, 60, 61, 258
  COMMAND.COM, 60, 266

Command prompt, 60, 258, 267

COMMAND.COM. *See* Command processor

Communications Manager, 271

Compaction. *See* Segment, motion

Compiler, 83, 84

CONFIG.SYS, 11, 39, 47, 49, 253, 254, 257, 259

Configuration phase, 257. *See also* System configuration

Console, 120, 127, 149

Cooperative processing, 8

COUNTRY. *See* Country support

Country-dependent information, 251

Country support, 11, 21, 245, 261–62
  CODEPAGE, 254, 261
  COUNTRY, 254, 261
  DEVINFO, 254, 262

CPU. *See* Microprocessor

CPU starvation, 263

CRT. *See* Display

Current privilege level (CPL), 38

Cursor
  definition, 231
  position, 104

Database Manager, 270

DBCS. *See* Double byte character set

Delayed binding, 220

Descriptor privilege level (DPL), 38

DevHlp, 180–86
  ABIOS management, 186, 202
  character monitor management, 186
  character queue management, 183
  interrupt management, 185
  memory management, 184–85

process management, 181–82
request queue management, 183
semaphore management, 182–83
timer services, 185

DEVICE, 127, 170, 261

Device attribute. *See under* Device driver

Device driver, 20, 39, 41, 164, 168, 169–215
  ANSI, 143, 214
  application I/O, 171–75
  asynchronous communications, 214
  base, 170, 211–12, 261
  bimodal operation, 169, 194–95
  block, 27, 170, 171, 173, 174, 175–78, 202, 211
  character, 170, 172, 173, 174, 178–80, 202, 211
  clock, 212
  commands, 175–80
    Build BIOS Parameter Block, 176
    DeInstall, 180
    Device Close, 179
    Device Open, 179
    Generic IOCtl, 176, 179
    Get Fixed Disk/Logical Units, 178
    Get Logical Drive Map, 178
    Initialize, 176, 179, 181
    Input Flush, 179
    Input Status, 179
    Media Check, 176
    Output Flush, 179
    Output Status, 179
    Peek, 179
    Query Partitionable Fixed Disks, 178
    Read, 176, 179
    Removable Media Support, 176
    Reset Media, 176, 177
    Set Logical Drive Map, 178
    Write, 176, 179
    Write With Verify, 176
  components, 186–94
  creating, 207–9
  definition, 169
  DevHlp, 180–86
  DEVICE, 127, 261
  device attribute, 210
  Device Header, 174, 209–11

disk, 125, 212
diskette, 125, 212
DOS, 12, 215
EGA, 215
EXE file format, 208–9
external disk, 214
Hardware Interrupt Handler, 28,
    188–90, 196, 197, 198, 199, 200,
    203, 204
initialization, 200–201
installation, 170, 261
IOPL, 170
keyboard, 213
memory addressability, 55, 184–85,
    195–96
mouse, 213
names, 170
pointer draw, 213
printer, 213
privilege level, 170
request packet, 174, 175, 203
screen, 212
Software Interrupt Handler, 192–94,
    195, 197
Strategy Routine, 186–88, 194, 195,
    196, 197, 201, 203, 204, 210
synchronization, 196–98
system performance, 199–200
system services. *See* Device driver,
    DevHlp
Timer Handler, 190–92, 196, 198, 199
virtual disk, 47, 214
Device handle, 126, 128, 131–34
Device Header. *See under* Device driver
DEVINFO. *See* Country support
Direct I/O. *See under* I/O
Direct memory access (DMA), 25, 27,
    55
Disk device driver. *See under* Device
    driver
DISKCACHE, 260
Diskette device driver. *See under* Device
    driver
Display, 2, 6, 13, 25, 26, 127, 139–48
Display. *See also* Video
    cursor definition, 142, 231
    graphics, 6, 140, 144, 145–47
    scroll, 100, 142–43

strings, 91, 102, 141–42
strings with attributes, 102, 141–42
DOS, 4, 6, 21, 23, 28, 40, 44, 50, 57, 89,
    220
DOS application, 5, 12, 119, 120, 122,
    167
DOS environment, 5, 7, 8, 10, 11, 12, 15,
    16, 18, 58, 60, 63, 259, 265–66.
    See also AUTOEXEC.BAT
  BREAK, 266
  FCBS, 266
  RMSIZE, 265
  SHELL, 266
DosAllocHuge, 52, 53, 54
DosAllocSeg, 46, 51, 52, 54, 115
DosAllocShrSeg, 52, 53, 54
DosBeep, 232
DosBufReset, 136
DOSCALLS.H, 89
DosCaseMap, 255
DosChDir, 137
DosChgFilePtr, 136
DosCLIAccess, 165
DosClose, 71, 129, 131
DosCloseQueue, 72, 73
DosCloseSem, 77
DosCreateCSAlias, 52
DosCreateQueue, 72
DosCreateSem, 76
DosCreateThread, 68, 74, 97, 113
DosCwait, 66, 67
DosDelete, 135
DosDevIOCtl, 130, 159, 176, 179
DosDupHandle, 129, 131
DosEnterCritSec, 68
DosExecPgm, 61, 65, 66, 67, 74, 110, 113
DosExit, 67, 92, 114
DosExitCritSec, 68
DosExitList, 67
DosFileLocks, 136
DosFindClose, 135
DosFindFirst, 135
DosFindNext, 135
DosFlagProcess, 75
DosFreeModule, 222, 239
DosFreeSeg, 51
DosGetCp, 254
DosGetCtryInfo, 255

DosGetDateTime, 80, 114
DosGetDBCSEv, 255
DosGetHugeShift, 53, 54
DosGetInfoSeg, 81
DosGetMessage, 200, 249
DosGetModHandle, 222
DosGetModName, 222, 238
DosGetProcAddr, 222
DosGetPrty, 70
DosGetSeg, 51, 52, 54
DosGetShrSeg, 52, 53
DosGiveSeg, 51, 52, 54
DosHoldSignal, 75
DosInsMessage, 200, 250
DosKillProcess, 67, 74
DosLoadModule, 221, 236
DosLockSeg, 51
DosMakePipe, 71, 105, 130
DosMkDir, 137
DosMonClose, 164
DosMonOpen, 163
DosMonRead, 163
DosMonReg, 163
DosMonWrite, 163
DosMove, 135
DosMuxSemWait, 78, 79
DosNewSize, 137
DosOpen, 124, 131–33
DosOpenQueue, 72
DosOpenSem, 76, 77
DosPeekQueue, 72, 73
DosPortAccess, 165
DosPurgeQueue, 73
DosPutMessage, 200, 250
DosQCurDir, 138
DosQCurDisk, 138
DosQFHandState, 133
DosQFileInfo, 137
DosQFileMode, 135
DosQFsInfo, 138
DosQHandType, 133
DosQueryQueue, 73
DosQVerify, 138
DosRead, 71, 110, 129, 133
DosReadAsync, 129, 133
DosReadQueue, 73
DosReallocHuge, 54
DosReallocSeg, 51, 54

DosResumeThread, 68
DosRmDir, 138
DosSearchPath, 135
DosSelectDisk, 138
DosSelectSession, 62
DosSemClear, 78, 79, 96
DosSemRequest, 77, 78, 96
DosSemSet, 78, 79, 95, 133, 134
DosSemSetWait, 78, 79
DosSemWait, 78, 79, 133, 134
DosSendSignal, 74, 75
DosSetCp, 254
DosSetDateTime, 80
DosSetFHandState, 134
DosSetFileInfo, 137
DosSetFileMode, 136
DosSetFsInfo, 138
DosSetMaxFH, 134
DosSetPrty, 69
DosSetSession, 62
DosSetSigHandler, 75
DosSleep, 80, 112, 114, 169
DosStartSession, 61, 62
DosStopSession, 62
DosSubAlloc, 54
DosSubFree, 54
DosSubSet, 54
DosSuspendThread, 68
DosTimerAsync, 80
DosTimerStart, 80, 169
DosTimerStop, 80
DosUnlockSeg, 51
DosVerify, 139
DosWrite, 71, 107, 113, 129, 134
DosWriteAsync, 129, 134
DosWriteQueue, 72
Double byte character set (DBCS), 253
Dynamic link, 5, 8, 10, 17, 18, 23, 217,
    220
  library, 222, 240
  load time, 19, 220
  module, 224
  run time, 19, 20, 221
    example, 228
    freeing a module, 222, 239
    getting module handle, 222
    getting module name, 222
    getting procedure address, 222, 238

loading a dynamic link module, 221, 236
Edge-triggered interrupts. *See* Interrupt
Environment string, 65, 66
Exception, 36, 37, 38, 41, 45, 48
Exitlist, 66, 67
Extended Edition 269–72

Family application 83, 194
Family application programming interface (FAPI), 18
FCBS, 266
File, 62, 122–26
File Allocation Table (FAT), 18, 123
File device, 122–23
File handle, 64, 123, 124, 125, 126, 131–34, 136–37
File I/O, 122, 123–26, 131–39
File name, 66, 123, 124, 135–36
File system, 10, 20, 120, 121–39, 172, 260
    access mode, 124, 125, 127
    BUFFERS, 260
    CLOSE, 123, 126, 127, 128
    handle I/O, 131–34
    I/O pointer, 125, 126, 133, 134
    media compatibility, 122
    OPEN, 123, 124, 127, 128
    READ, 109, 123, 127, 128
    removable media, 122
    sector, 170, 260
    sharing mode, 122, 124, 125, 127
    volume management, 122
    WRITE, 107, 123, 127, 128
Font, 143, 144
Foreground session, 11, 59, 60, 61, 62, 139, 144, 155
Function declarations, 84, 87

Gate, 39, 40, 270
Global descriptor table (GDT), 31, 34, 35, 36, 38
Graphics, 7, 140, 144, 145–47

Handle, 123, 126
    file. *See* File handle
    device. *See* Device handle
    pipe. *See* Pipe, handle
    system limit, 126, 128, 134

Help, on–line, 258
HLPMSG, 248
Hot key, 10, 11

I/O, 25, 27, 119–65
I/O
    asynchronous, 125
    character device, 27, 122, 126–29, 131–34, 172
    direct, 119, 121, 164–65, 262
    file. *See* File I/O
    handle-based, 123, 131–34
    interrupt driven, 10, 20, 167–69
    memory mapped, 6, 13, 26, 44, 55
    polled, 12, 20, 58, 167–68
    random order, 125
    redirection, 126
    sequential order, 125
I/O control. *See* IOCtl
I/O pointer. *See under* File system
I/O privilege level. *See* Privilege
IMPLIB, 224, 242
Import Librarian, 224, 242
Include files, 87
Infoseg, 81
Infoseg, global, 81
Infoseg, local, 81
Inheritance, 65, 66, 71, 77, 126, 128, 132
Initial Program Load. *See* System initialization
Initialization. *See* System configuration; System initialization
Input/Output. *See* I/O
Installation program, 259
International considerations. *See* Country support
Interprocess communication (IPC), 10, 17, 52, 63, 70, 93
Interrupt, 20, 27, 28, 32, 39, 40, 205–7
    edge triggered, 29, 205
    hardware, 12, 28, 40
    level sensitive, 29, 205, 206
    nesting, 198–99
    non-maskable (NMI), 25, 39–40
    sharing, 29, 205–7
    software, 40, 74
Interrupt driven I/O, 10, 20. *See also* Device driver

IOCtl, 120, 121, 159–61, 172–73
IOPL. *See* Privilege
IOPL code segment, 120, 121, 164–65, 262
IPC. *See* Interprocess communication
IPL. *See* System initialization

KBD subsystem, 121, 148–53
KbdCharIn, 97, 150
KbdClose, 152
KbdDeRegister, 153
KbdFlushBuffer, 150
KbdFreeFocus, 150, 153
KbdGetCp, 151
KbdGetFocus, 150, 153
KbdGetStatus, 151
KbdOpen, 149, 153
KbdPeek, 150
KbdRegister, 153
KbdSetCp, 152
KbdSetCustXt, 152
KbdSetStatus, 152
KbdStringIn, 91, 150
KbdSynch, 153
KbdXlate, 150
Keyboard, 127, 148–53, 162
   data record, 148, 149, 150
   example, 89, 92
   input, 91, 97
   logical, 149, 150, 151, 152, 153
   physical, 149, 153
Keyboard device driver. *See under* Device driver

Language bindings, 220
Least recently used (LRU), 14, 37, 45, 115
Level sensitive interrupts. *See* Interrupt
LIBPATH, 263
Library functions, 221
LID. *See* ABIOS
Linker, 84, 85, 217, 223
Linking an OS/2 program, 85, 217
Local descriptor table (LDT), 31, 34, 35, 36, 37, 46, 49, 64, 111
Logical disk/diskette device, 122, 130, 131

Logical ID. *See* ABIOS
Logical keyboard. *See* Keyboard
Logical seek, 125
Logical video buffer, 60, 139, 140, 145
Loosely coupled, 98, 99

MAXWAIT, 263
Media compatibility, 122
MEMMAN, 265
Memory, 2, 6, 23, 25, 26, 43, 49, 265
   640 KB, 4, 5, 6, 8, 11, 13, 15, 26, 44, 46, 47, 200, 262
   address, 26, 30, 32, 37
   allocation, 115
   example, 114
   large, 7, 10, 13, 14, 24, 37, 43, 44, 45
   mapped input/output. *See* I/O
   MEMMAN, 265
   motion. *See under* Segment
   overcommitment, 10, 14, 44, 45, 48, 114, 265
   physical, 6, 13, 14, 24, 30, 32, 34, 35, 36, 43, 44, 45, 47, 49, 50, 51, 55
   protection, 37–39, 43, 46, 262
   random access memory (RAM), 6, 7, 25, 26
   read only memory (ROM), 6, 13, 25, 26, 257
   real. *See* Memory, physical
   RMSIZE, 265
   segment. *See* Segment
   shared, 17, 46, 50, 51, 52, 70, 71. *See also* Segment, named-shared
   SWAPPATH, 265
   virtual, 6, 10, 13, 14, 15, 24, 33, 34, 37, 43
Memory suballocation package, 50, 54
Message facilities, 21, 22
Message, 246
   binding, 246, 247
   displaying, 250
   getting, 249
   help message, 246, 248
   make message file, 246
   variable insertion, 249, 250
Mickey. *See* Mouse
Microprocessor, 25, 29
   80286, 6, 13, 15, 24, 30, 43

80386, 6, 7, 13
8086, 7, 43
8088, 6, 7, 13
Migration, 122, 272
MKMSGF, 246
Module definition file, 48, 218, 225
  statements, 226
Monitor, 120, 121, 161–64, 173
MOU subsystem, 121, 153–59
MouClose, 155, 156
MouDeRegister, 159
MouDrawPtr, 156
MouFlushQue, 156
MouGetDevStatus, 157
MouGetEventMask, 157
MouGetNumButtons, 156, 158
MouGetNumMickeys, 158
MouGetNumQueEl, 156
MouGetPtrPos, 156
MouGetPtrShape, 157
MouGetScaleFact, 158
MouOpen, 155, 156
MouReadEventQue, 156
MouRegister, 159
MouRemovePtr, 157
Mouse, 153–59, 162
  data record, 154
  event, 154, 155
  mickey, 154
Mouse device driver. *See under* Device
  driver
MouSetDevStatus, 158
MouSetEventMask, 155, 158
MouSetPtrPos, 157
MouSetPtrShape, 157
MouSetScaleFact, 158
MouSynch, 159
MSGBIND, 246, 247
Multiple applications environment. *See*
  Application environment
Multitasking, 5, 8, 16, 28, 57, 58, 59,
  120, 125, 263–64
  MAXWAIT, 263
  PRIORITY, 264
  process example, 98
  thread example, 93
  THREADS, 264
  TIMESLICE, 264

National Language Support (NLS). *See*
  Country support
NLS. *See* Country support
Numeric coprocessor, 25, 29

OS/2 application, 120, 122
OS/2 application programming inter-
  face. *See* Application programm-
  ing interface
Offset, 24, 30, 36, 43
On-line help. *See* Help
Open architecture, 221
OS/2 application environment. *See*
  Application environment
OS2INIT.CMD, 258, 267

PAUSEONERROR, 259
Performance, 45, 48, 199–200, 260, 263,
  264, 265
Physical keyboard. *See* Keyboard
Physical video buffer, 139, 140, 145–47
Pipe, 17, 62, 70, 122, 130
  creation, 71, 105
  example, 99, 112
  handle, 130, 131–34
Pointer
  far, 93, 98, 117
  near, 93
Polled I/O, 12, 20, 58
Pop-up, 140, 144–45, 149
Presentation Manager, 7, 140, 270
Printer, 127, 162
Printer device driver. *See under* Device
  driver
Priority, 15, 16, 28, 64, 68
  class, 69
    idle, 69
    regular, 69, 263, 264
    time critical, 69
  level 69, 264
PRIORITY, 264
Privilege, 15, 24, 34, 36, 37, 38, 39, 40
  I/O privilege (IOPL), 11, 38, 39, 40,
    46, 164–65, 262
Process, 16, 17, 46, 59, 62, 63, 64
  abnormal termination, 67
  child, 65, 66, 67, 110, 126, 128
  creation, 66, 110

example, 98
ID, 66
parent, 65, 66, 67, 112, 126
Processor. *See* Microprocessor
Program module, 217, 223
Program selection phase, 258, 267
Program Selector, 11, 60, 61, 62, 258, 267
Program termination. *See* Terminate program
Protect mode, 11, 13, 14, 15, 26, 33, 34, 37, 40, 262
Protect mode application environment. *See* Application environment
Protection. *See* Privilege
PROTECTONLY, 262
PROTSHELL, 263

Queue, 17, 62, 71, 72, 73

Random access memory (RAM). *See* Memory
Read only memory (ROM). *See* Memory
Read/write pointer. *See* File system, I/O pointer
Real mode, 6, 11, 15, 26, 32, 37, 40, 262
Real time, 8, 11, 17
Redirection, 66, 126
Removable media, 122
Request packet. *See under* Device driver
RMSIZE, 265
Round-robin scheduling, 68, 69
RUN, 263, 267
Run time dynamic linking. *See* Dynamic link

Screen. *See* Display
Screen device driver. *See under* Device driver
Sector, 170, 260
Segment, 14, 30, 43, 51
    descriptor, 34, 35, 36, 37, 38, 45
    discard, 14, 45, 50, 51
    huge, 50, 53, 54
    load on demand, 19, 47, 48, 219, 227
    motion, 14, 45, 48, 265

name-shared, 46, 50, 52
pre-load, 19, 47, 48, 219, 227
register, 30, 52
Selector, 24, 34, 35, 43, 46, 50, 51, 52, 53, 54
Semaphore, 17, 70, 76–79
    clear, 78, 79, 96
    exclusive, 77, 78
    RAM, 76, 78, 93, 133, 134, 196, 198
        example, 93
    request, 77, 78, 96
    set, 79, 95
    System, 62, 76, 77, 78, 198
Session, 59, 60, 61, 62, 63, 139, 148, 149, 154, 162, 258
    background. *See* Background session
    foreground. *See* Foreground session
Session manager, 60, 61, 147
SHELL, 266
Signal, 19, 70, 74, 75
    SIGBREAK, 74
    SIGINTR, 74
    SIGPFA, 74
    SIGPFB, 74
    SIGTERM, 67, 74
    SIGPFC, 74
Speaker output, 232
Spin loop. *See* Polled I/O
Stack, 24, 31, 64
Standard AUXILIARY, 130
Standard Device, 122, 129–30, 131–34
Standard Edition, 269, 271
Standard ERROR, 129
Standard INPUT, 129
Standard OUTPUT, 129
Standard PRINTER, 130
START, 267
STARTUP.CMD, 258, 266–67
Subsystem, 120, 121, 139–59, 173
    KBD, 121, 148–53
    MOU, 121, 153–59
    VIO, 121, 139–48
SWAPPATH, 265
Swapping, 14, 15, 45, 47, 48, 49, 115, 265
Synchronous execution, 58, 66
System Application Architecture (SAA), 18

System configuration, 257, 259–66
  BREAK, 266
  BUFFERS, 260
  CODEPAGE, 261
  CONFIG.SYS, 257, 259–66
  COUNTRY, 261
  country support, 261
  DEVICE, 127, 261
  device support, 261
  DEVINFO, 262
  DISKCACHE, 47, 260
  DOS environment, 265–66
  FCBS, 266
  file system, 260
  interactive, 259
  IOPL, 165, 262
  LIBPATH, 263
  MAXWAIT, 69, 263
  MEMMAN, 265
  memory management, 265
  multitasking, 263–64
  noninteractive, 259
  OS/2 application environment,
    262–63
  PAUSEONERROR, 259
  PRIORITY, 264
  protection scope, 262
  PROTECTONLY, 47, 262
  PROTSHELL, 263
  RMSIZE, 47, 265
  RUN, 263, 267
  SHELL, 266
  SWAPPATH, 48, 265
  THREADS, 264
  TIMESLICE, 68, 264
System initialization, 257–59
System installation. *See* Installation
  program

Task, 4, 6, 58. *See also* Multitasking
Terminate program, 92
Terminate-And-Stay-Resident program,
  120, 164
Thread, 16, 17, 59, 63
  coupling, 93, 98
  creation, 67, 68, 97
  example, 93, 112
  ID, 64, 68

  termination, 67, 93, 94, 99, 114
  yielding, 112
THREADS, 264
Tightly coupled, 63, 93, 98
Time critical. *See* Priority
Timer services, 79, 80
Timer tick, 80
Timeslice, 68
TIMESLICE, 264
Toolkit, 83, 84, 89
Tools, 83
TSR program. *See* Terminate-And-Stay-
  Resident program

Video
  functions, example, 89, 92
  output, 91, 112, 140–48
  see also Display; VIO subsystem
Video buffer. *See* Logical video buffer;
  Physical video buffer
VIO subsystem, 121, 139–48
VioDeRegister, 148
VioEndPopUp, 144
VioGetAnsi, 143
VioGetBuf, 145
VioGetConfig, 143
VioGetCp, 143
VioGetCurPos, 142
VioGetCurType, 142, 231
VioGetFont, 143
VioGetMode, 143
VioGetPhysBuf, 146
VioGetState, 144
VioModeUndo, 146
VioModeWait, 146
VioPopUp, 144
VioReadCellStr, 141
VioReadCharStr, 141
VioRegister, 148
VioSavRedrawUndo, 146
VioSavRedrawWait, 147
VioScrLock, 147
VioScrollDn, 143
VioScrollLf, 143
VioScrollRt, 143
VioScrollUp, 100, 113, 143
VioScrUnLock, 147
VioSetAnsi, 144

VioSetCp, 144
VioSetCurPos, 104, 113, 142, 231
VioSetCurType, 142
VioSetFont, 144
VioSetMode, 144
VioSetState, 144
VioShowBuf, 145
VioWrtCellStr, 141
VioWrtCharStr, 102, 113, 141

VioWrtCharStrAtt, 102, 113, 141
VioWrtNAttr, 142
VioWrtNCell, 142
VioWrtNChar, 142
VioWrtTTY, 91, 142
Volume management, 122

Windowing 7, 140, 270